SCRATCH THE SURFACE

A Tapestry of Israel & Palestine

Best Wishes
Julie Jones

JULIE JONES

Copyright © Julie Jones 2022

The moral right of Julie Jones to be identified as the author of this work has been asserted in accordance with the Copyright, Designs and Patents Act 1988.

All rights reserved. No part of this book may be reproduced or used in any manner whatsoever, including information storage and retrieval systems, or transmitted in any form or by any means, electronic, mechanical, photocopying, recording or otherwise, without the express written permission of the copyright owner, except in the case of brief quotations embodied in critical reviews and certain other non-commercial use permitted by copyright law. For permission requests, contact the author at scratchingthesurface30@gmail.com

This memoir is creative non-fiction. Conversations are recorded from memory, first-hand interviews and journals written over the last 30 years. In order to maintain anonymity, some names have been changed. Every effort has been made to acquire permissions to use text from other sources and the author has endeavoured to write without prejudice.

Telegram & parliamentary question documents reproduced with the kind permision of the The National Archives London.

First edition printed in the United Kingdom 2022.

ISBN (Paperback): 9781739129903
Imprint: Independently published
Typesetting & cover design: Matthew J Bird

A CIP catalogue record of this book is available from the British Library.

For further information about this book, please contact the author at www.juliejonesauthor.com

In memory of
Mam, Dad
&
Hanitai

Contents

Chapter		Page
1	What's it all about?	7
2	Our first day	14
3	An Evening in Jaffa	22
4	The Golan Heights	32
5	Suicide Bombing	45
6	An Ugly war	66
7	The 6-Day-War	91
8	The Manchester connection	100
9	Museums	117
10	Ammunition Hill	127
11	The King David Hotel	133
12	Stern Connections	139
13	Tel Aviv talks to me	156
14	The Road to Manshiyah	169
15	Rehovot	181
16	Ramle Cemetery	200
17	On the Gaza border	207
18	The Negev	232

Chapter		Page
19	Latrun	249
20	The West Bank	258
21	Ramallah Palestine	272
22	Hebron	284
23	Going Home	296
24	As you were – Carry on!	314
25	The Last Chapter	317
References		333
Acknowledgements		334
About the Author		336

Chapter 1

What's it all about?

In the Holy Land of Israel and Palestine, where ancient and modern sit side by side, the doctrines of Judaism, Christianity, and Islam were established many generations ago. Since then, great Empires, including 30 years of British mandatory rule in old Colonial Palestine, have become a distant memory and often ranked as insignificant.

The ever-changing Middle East, while peppered with a tapestry of Peoples, takes modern life a day at a time, never knowing what new government, off-shoot faction, or local skirmish may affect it. While Israel sits on the outskirts of the vast Arab world trying to combine western practices with ancient traditions, the Palestinian People struggle for equality and both sides hope the world will understand their particular circumstances.

Rich cultural, religious, and political divisions have led to current disputes, and continued tension simmering below the surface eventually channels its way to the past.

Many factors may suggest a common trait of slow healing on both sides, but the wounds are deep and constantly opened with new skirmishes. Mostly, I found that people are desperate for a long-term safe haven, but the challenges of old emotional fault lines across the land, greatly affect progress towards a lasting peace.

It may be true that my observations are oversimplified because I have not experienced the same feelings as those who live with Israel's daily dilemmas. Nevertheless, I have tried to understand the inherent turmoil in the hearts and minds of those I have met.

*****

In 1948, the founding of the State of Israel enabled the return of the Jewish People who had nurtured a yearning for a homeland during 2000 years of Diaspora. This triumph for new-wave Zionists followed a vote for partition of former British Palestine, by the League of Nations. Partition resulted in war and an ever-varying and controversial landscape that has occupied world opinion ever since.

Some see Israel's victory in the War of Independence in 1948/49, after the British left, as a Biblical prophecy. Others view it as early Israeli aggression at a great cost to the Palestinian People; a continual debate during the latter part of the twentieth century and likely to run well into this one.

Today, Israel shares borders with Egypt in the South, Jordan, and Syria to the East, and Lebanon in the north. Inside this small State, Palestine exists on shared land in the Occupied Territories on the West Bank of the Jordan River, or the cordoned Gaza Strip on the South-West Mediterranean coast.

In August 1993, on my very first morning in Tel Aviv-Jaffa, I was mesmerised by the view as I looked out from the observatory of the Meir Shalom Tower. This rooftop gave us an unexpected, peaceful, and thought-provoking space and relief from the chaos in the streets some 27 floors below.

Looking west over the Mediterranean, with the rest of the mysterious Levant sprawled out on the other 3 compass points, I will never forget the contentment I felt. I had arrived at last and I wonder now whether I could sense that this would be a turning point in my life.

Colin, my son, then 11 years old, seeing tears stream down my face, laughed and handed me a tissue from his rucksack as we began our journey as naive explorers.

Tel Aviv never felt alien to me, and while I had come to find out the truth about British Mandatory Rule, I hadn't expected that I would become another prospective tender for the land, if only on a part-time basis. Each time I return for my much-needed fix, it feels just as familiar as it did on that first day.

My late Father was right when he told me:

"I can't explain what it's like, but you'll understand when you get there!"

That was the indescribable thing that often rendered us both inarticulate when trying to portray the Holy Land, Israel, or Palestine, as he always referred to it, due to his time there in 1947. Mandatory Rule and the ever-changing landscape became our common bond during the last few years of his life. Not as a small gem to be fought over and clenched tightly by an aggressive fist, but something bigger that requires one's whole being to embrace.

My journey has given me experiences I want to share in a world where the reputations of 2 Peoples have often been stereotyped or represented inaccurately by multi-national media or biased concerned parties across the globe. Not intended as propaganda, for I am neither a left-wing campus academic on a mission nor a Zionist who ignores the faults of those in power. I'm just a passing historian with an awareness born from 30 years of study.

I don't know the best way to achieve peace, many greats have failed before me, and sadly, the more I learn, the more I despair at the barriers within the challenge. In some ways, I was happier when I was less informed and when I didn't know the reasons for tit-for-tat reprisals.

My experiences may still be shadowed by naiveté, but I have at least combated the images of Zionist dreamers who tried to convince me that when the State was founded; a miracle happened here.

I have discovered unfavourable truths on all sides, including the need to reproach some of my own Nation's methods under British Imperialism. It is impossible to look carefully at Israel's modern history without questioning British policy and events in the years immediately before its declaration.

This is a new country with teething troubles. Yes, 75 years in the concept of the age of the Bible Land, is a newborn State. It is inhabited by those with many opinions, who assert varying ideas on how it should be run, fashioned, and promoted. An addiction for Israel is not for a fair-weather fan, as since her birth, she has not enjoyed an agreeable climate. The region has faced one storm or another on various frontiers with Israel on standby to retaliate, often disproportionately, in the eyes of the world.

Who could not despair for displaced Palestinians who may carry a symbolic key to a family home which is either no longer there, inhabited by another, or still under high-court negotiation? I now know that when they moved out at the onset of war in 1948, as the State's independence was declared, they intended to return when the dust settled.

The War of Independence in May 1948, or the 'Catastrophe' depending on which culture you belong to or the opinion you hold, is a major factor in the current land issues between Arabs and Jews in Israel and Palestine.

Stories of refugees are not something new around the world, but in the Holy Land, there is an abundance of those who feel they have a say in the matter. The methods used by the State to ensure its survival are questioned by sociology experts, well-intentioned humanitarians, historians, or the ill-informed. There are vocal fronts that stereotype all Israelis as aggressive and others who associate Palestinians with constant Jihad.

The occupation occupies the thoughts or takes over the lives of everyone at some time, to different degrees. But generally, I find the majority would rather live in peace with their neighbours.

My mantra in observing this dysfunctional neighbourhood is not to judge a man until I have walked a mile in his shoes. Something my parents taught me in their even-handed perspectives, even about my Father's connection to British Mandatory Rule.

In the study of history, there has to be a counter-narrative, many versions giving alternative points of view. Imagine if one version of history was accepted by everyone. I would still believe, from childhood lessons, that the British Empire was conquered by offering scones and tea to the natives and that Imperialism was beneficial to all under British Rule. I would also remain content that any conflict following Britain's demobilisation happened because we were no longer there to keep the peace. The main myth disposed of, however, is that Israel was a land without a People for a People without a land.

Sometimes wandering upon the land of the Bible, I have looked back to 1967 and the childhood images I drew in primary school. At the age of 6, I believed that Israel was where Jesus sat under palm trees telling stories, and flat-roofed mud houses were comfortable dwellings for people in technicolour dream coats. How wonderful my church school made it seem. In reality, at this time, the 6-Day-War was changing the dynamics of the landscape forever.

When I first started digging into the past 30 years ago, Palestine and the British presence seemed like a forgotten war. Important information was still destined to be under lock and key in the United Kingdom until 50 or 70 years after the event and it felt like nobody wanted me to know about it.

I was fortunate enough to be able to ask the Israelis and Palestinians for their versions. Helpful people ensured things fell into my lap and opened doors to places I never knew existed. Hearing first-hand about what happened to shape the way both sides think has helped me to understand the situation.

Among these intense societies, tolerant integration sometimes presents itself but doesn't run deep enough to block out the undertow of difference. A friendly conversation can often turn into angry exchanges as old wrongs are exposed. This makes it difficult for the peacemakers who would like both to understand each other's similar issues of living within heavily fortified divisions.

It takes brave people to forgive and an open mind to listen to the perspective of the other side. More than this, however, it takes those who are willing to take a risk and move forward without the personal baggage of a century. I hope my journey gives some insight as I share with you how looking into British Mandatory Rule, I stumbled upon an ever-changing region.

Chapter 2

Our first day

On reflection, my son Colin (11) and I (32) in 1993, were quite brave to embark on a trip to Israel together. We had no idea what it would be like, but friends in the Jewish community told me we would be ok and recommended we go ahead with our fact-finding mission. Having enjoyed our first trip so much, we were lucky enough to go back again in August 1995.

The scheduled flights from Manchester to Tel Aviv always meant we started our holiday on a Tuesday morning, when we liked to walk up King George Street to the popular Carmel market, just off Allenby Street. This is the best place for quirky art and crafts. We did this before we headed for the observatory in the Meir Shalom Tower, but first, we would take some refreshments at Amnon's kiosk on Rambam Allenby.

He was the first stranger we ever spoke to in Tel Aviv in 1993. He recommended places to visit, gave us directions around the city and drilled into us, where to avoid and how much water to drink every day.

He recognised us immediately as we approached and was pleased to see us, immediately giving Colin an ice cream from his new glass-topped freezer. He was talking about it with such pride and as he patted it, I felt sure the new arrival should have been blessed by the Rabbi.

Amnon was a Moroccan Jew, whose family moved to Israel in the 1950's and lived in the tented Beersheba community for ten years. He had moved to Tel Aviv as a teenager and had managed to make a decent living, to the point of being on the verge of buying his first house.

He told us that he pined for his family and the desert, but was grateful for the gift of a city community to keep him busy. This was evident as we watched him conduct 3 conversations at once. He talked to his customer in Hebrew; while intermittently chatting to us in English and signing across the street to a passer-by, made some agreement that he would meet him for a coffee later. Providing his unreliable assistant managed to turn up at 3 o'clock.

A workaholic, who made his way with a few tables in the street, profits from lotto cards and a glass-fronted fridge for soft drinks which he sold to passing tourists. Behind the counter were rows and rows of cigarettes and he had a public telephone on a stand by the entrance which anyone could use for a shekel. Not forgetting the new arrival, also outside, but on a pallet, so he could put it inside the narrow kiosk with a pump truck when the shutters come down about 11 o'clock each evening.

After touching base with Amnon, we carried on our journey towards Rambam Street, passing an Arab cafe thrown together inside a huge black tent. The ladies, dressed in long black dresses, moulded thin bread on fabric cushions, and they and the Persian rugs on the ground, were dusted with a thin layer of white flour.

Here, where the craft market meets the everyday reality of locals shopping, the atmosphere changes to extremely busy, with the noise and smells of a souk. There is an abundance of colourful fresh fruit, generous spreads of nuts, spices, and other goodies capturing the imagination with pungent aromas of the Middle East.

We bought some grapes to snack upon. The stall owner had fashioned his scales from a short plank of wood, 2 washing-up bowls and a genuine metal cast weight. I'm not sure he was monitored by the weights and measures department, but I'm sure it must have been a kilo because the word 'kilo' had been painted on the weight. Nevertheless, the grapes were cheap and nobody seemed to mind.

Seeing 'Manchester United' written on Colin's baseball cap prompted the grape seller to inquire about our home and we engaged in talk of football for a few minutes while munching on unwashed grapes.

In those days there were more elders who remembered the founding of the State and more Yiddish could be heard, coming from the Jews who had made their way from Eastern Europe. Some elderly shoppers seemed to have troubled expressions and a generally tired condition and it was here that I first saw members of the senior population with tattooed numbers of their lower arms. Realising their connection to concentration camps was quite daunting.

A grey-haired old lady, walking in front of us, seemed to be struggling with her string bag and before I could help, it broke and her oranges ran away from her down the sloping alley. She was about 5 feet tall and her flowered cross-over apron almost reached her feet. She sighed so heavily with a pained expression, suggesting that she had never got used to the heat, but we were soon onto it and gathered them up for her. We suggested that she put them in her other, more reliable cloth bag and opening it up, dropped them in. Neither of us knew what the other was saying, but at last, she smiled and wrapped her arm around Colin's shoulder to show him her appreciation.

Life in the market was much faster than the elders could cope with. The city had changed every day since its birth in 1908 and you could still somehow sense Israel's lack of common identity.

At this time, I was surprised to hear Russian voices in the market as another wave of Eastern European immigrants had taken up the Law of Return and left the changing Europe of the early 1990s. They, together with the now established Ethiopian wave of the same decade, were poorly paid workers, living in cramped conditions on the cheaper side of town. The food side of the Carmel market is always good if you are looking for a bargain, but some newcomers were now selling other types of street food from rickety barrows.

Amnon had kindly explained recent changes in new nationals and with this, I was learning that the old claims against Zionist racism might not be so black and white. Grey areas were becoming apparent and the open door policy was now accommodating younger generations from all over the world rather than those out of the ashes of the Holocaust.

We were distracted again and again and our progress was slow as we continued towards the Meir Shalom Tower, famous in Tel Aviv since its completion in 1965 when it could rival any skyscraper in the Middle East.

There were mixed views in the city; people loved it or hated it as its modernity was squeezed in like a rectangular peg in a round hole. I think it must have been quite a shock to the low-level arrangement as it climbed higher and higher, dwarfing the shoulder to shoulder, Bauhaus dwellings of the early 1900s. In 1993, it was the tallest building near the coast. The El AL building on Ben Yehuda was no rival with its sixties egg box design and the tower of apartments near Dizengoff circle was a round and brick coloured building, with half as many floors. We loved the open terrace at the top of the Shalom Tower's 27th floor, and this was where we hung out.

It had been special to us ever since our very first day in Israel 2 years before and not only as a red-letter day for seeing the huge landscape of the Holy Land for the first time. It was where we laughed, ate croissants; drank coffee and cola; took photographs, learned the grid of the city streets and the lay of the land, almost as far as Jerusalem.

That morning, we were taught by a soldier on reconnaissance, about all the towns that stretched north towards the Lebanese border. She was looking through a sophisticated telescope, but while teaching us geography, gave very limited information on what she was observing and her notes were all written in Hebrew, so peeking was no use.

She apologised to Colin, saying she couldn't let him look through her telescope, but recommended he paid a shekel to use the public one on the northern corner of the building, and with this, he was happy enough.

She asked not to be in our photographs, but obliged us by taking one of us. Pity really; she was one of the smartest I had seen with her dark hair tied back and in desert, lightweights had her beret tucked in her epaulette.

When we looked a long way South, beyond the old bus station, past the city limits and towards the Negev desert, we imagined the way Moses came with the tribes. It was the way Lawrence of Arabia came with Arab hordes, and the way my Dad came on an open-truck in 1947 on his journey from Egypt.

My Dad had great admiration for Lawrence of Arabia and Moses, probably in that order. While he had some spiritual connection with the Old and New Testaments after a Methodist upbringing, he had an affinity with wanderers and saw the Bible as a useful geographical and historical record of conflict. He could skilfully connect eras and areas in the Levant as he did in the United Kingdom.

Below us, on Allenby Street, we could see the Dome of the Great Synagogue and I reminded Colin that I had never been there.

2 years earlier, we had hoped to go but I was very disappointed after asking directions from an old man sitting on a low stone wall outside a house with a big garden, somewhere behind Allenby Street.

He shocked us with his harsh reply:

"We don't want the British in our Synagogue!" he said seriously.

I stepped back off the kerb, shocked at meeting a man with old scores to settle.

"Well, he doesn't like us," Colin exclaimed as we walked away. "What shall we do?"

"Well," I said, as calmly as I could muster:

"We'd better go and have ice cream instead. Someone will show us the way on another day."

For a minute, I felt out of my depth as a newcomer. A woman of 32 in a strange land with an enthusiastic young boy, realising I had a lot to learn if I thought the whole of Israel would be glad to see us.

Nevertheless, 2 years later, Colin was certain he could navigate a path to the Synagogue. And he did. We were more confident and established by then.

We were welcomed at the enormous wooden doors of the Great Synagogue by a young man who told us to wander about inside as much as we wanted and leaving us, he went off to a kitchen at the end of a long corridor.

"Is it hats on or hats off in a synagogue?" Colin asked, knowing that it was hats off in a church. I explained that he should keep it on.

The comforting smell of freshly baked bread filled the air and we stood in the doorway of a room that was decked out for a huge banquet. The floor was swathed in rich Turkish-style carpets and the tables were adorned with white table cloths, crystal glasses, white china and neatly folded napkins in Israeli blue. The doors of the ark were fronted with a type of steel shards and I remember feeling disappointed that it wasn't particularly traditional.

We admired the stained glass windows behind the ladies gallery and around the edge of the ceiling dome. Then we took some photos that never turned out. In those days, they had to be developed and you took your chances with strange lighting, and didn't see them until a week after returning home.

Colin said he was a bit hungry, after smelling the bread, and we chatted about going along to a cafe we knew on Allenby Street. We relished the idea of the best apple strudel served with cream, making the flaky pastry soggy and scrumptious. We thanked the man in the synagogue kitchen before bidding him goodbye and he waved with a nonchalant, "Okay."

While eating the strudel, a man came into the cafe dressed like a French onion seller. He was wearing a striped t-shirt and black beret and he serenaded us for a few minutes. Nobody batted an eyelid and he left after a few verses. As we paid the bill, the owner asked Colin if he had ever tried some of the other cakes they baked and kindly gave him little pieces in a brown paper bag to eat later.

Strolling back to the hotel, we came across a crowd, debating loudly on the tree-lined Ben-Gurion Boulevard. It was one of those situations where everyone knows best. A tree had fallen over and crushed 2 cars that were parked there, and there was a lot of dialogue we didn't understand. We watched them for a minute, seeing a lot of head scratching, beard stroking and wavy animation. We stepped over a trunk and carried on. We had walked a long way and were very hot and tired by mid-afternoon. After reaching the hotel room and taking the obligatory glass of water, Amnon's medicine, we both fell asleep.

Chapter 3

An Evening in Jaffa

The telephone rang at 6 o'clock; it was Shai with whom we had kept in touch since we met in the same hotel on our first trip to Tel Aviv. He invited us to join him with a group of friends who were going to a festival in Jaffa that evening.

Shai taught me about the country in the early days and his outlook had helped to change my views on Zionism. He is not the stereotypical Israeli painted by some of the media and I was amazed at his attitude towards his neighbours. He certainly wasn't negative or filled with hatred.

On the evening we met in 1993, he had told me about the secret talks going on in Norway that were to become known as the Oslo Accords. The signing of the peace deal between Yitzhak Rabin and Yasser Arafat, with President Bill Clinton on the White House lawn in September, a month later. This long-term plan for a 2 State solution gave him more faith in the future, rather than the cynicism I encountered in many.

Shai and Amir collected us just after 7 o'clock and on the 10 minute journey, Amir honked the car horn as well as any Israeli, and Colin commented on the impatient drivers along the way.

Shai made fun of his, over politeness, in a British Officer accent; mimicry inherited from mandate days and we were exchanging Anglo-Israeli banter within minutes. Upon hearing from Colin that I had bought a new straw hat that morning, Shai took the opportunity to say,

"That's great; you can save it for Ascot."

In Jaffa, we saw a juggler on a unicycle, said to be the best in the Middle East, belly dancers, jingling and flaunting their navels, while a Mexican trio sang songs from South America beneath the palm trees of a typically biblical setting.

Everyone joined in when some of the crowd began singing traditional folk songs and, of course, as Israelis do, they danced in big a circle.

After the entertainment had finished, we decided to wander towards Jaffa Port. From a hillside above, there was a perfect viewing point by St Peter's Church to look across at the lights of a more modern Tel Aviv. Brightly lit hotels along the shoreline and the sparkling ribbons of traffic entering and leaving the new urban sprawl were a contrast to the stone walls and amber tranquillity of the old town of Jaffa.

Walking down some steep stone steps from the main square, we reached the ancient harbour. We passed through a lush green park established on an embankment above the sea wall. Colin and I had been there before, on a Sunday afternoon in 1993, but we hadn't stayed long as I had felt unnerved by the ancient narrow alleys, not unlike the architecture in the Old City of Jerusalem.

Colin and Amir went off to check out some huge yucca plants and date palms and Shai and I were a little way behind on the steps when the same sickly feeling returned and I stopped in my tracks.

Noticing I had dropped back, he turned around and looked at me.

"Why are you frightened?" he asked.

"I don't know! I feel cautious about who might be lurking."

"Come on!" he said, and with his hand to steady me on the narrow stone steps, I felt safer with locals to guard us.

As we reached the road to the port beneath the Al-Bahr mosque and the old disused lighthouse, Shai muttered in Hebrew to his friend and Amir came over to reassure me.

"This is one of the best areas in the world where Arabs and Jews have worked together to make this a nice place for everyone, especially tourists. 10 years ago, there were whores, junkies; hundreds of cats, but now it is respectable."

I was sure that they were right about it being safe, but there was something in this ancient passageway with which I seemed to have an issue.

The 4 of us were soon leaning on the old sea wall and we watched the wave's crash onto the rocks below and the silhouettes of fishermen, sailing away in the dark for a catch that would supply local restaurants.

The cool sea spray reached our faces occasionally as, together, Shai and Amir told us the story of the harbour dragon that would only be kind if he was fed a virgin every day.

SCRATCHING THE SURFACE

During the Ottoman Empire, a Sheik lived on the cliffs above and offered his daughter Andromeda, who was deeply loved from afar, by a peasant called Perseus. Perseus dressed in drag and tied himself to the rock where offerings were usually left and when the dragon approached, he stabbed him in the neck. The dragon turned to stone in the water and Amir pointed out the line of rocks in the bay where he still lay.

"You can still see the spikes on his back today!" He told us.

Of course, the Sheik blessed Perseus with the hand of his daughter and great riches and they all lived happily ever after.

We found Jaffa to be different from Tel Aviv and we learned that elders there included some Arabs who had never ventured into the centre of the new Jewish city a few miles away. Some were sheltered from the reality of its size; still hoping it was a temporary suburb that had been added to the outskirts, following the arrival of Jewish immigrants in 1948.Hope, for some, was still springing eternal, as they waited for their neighbours to come home from refugee camps and various bolt holes around the Middle East.

Shai suggested we eat something and said we could walk around the harbour, and make our way to Yeffet Street where, at the Aboulafia bakery, we would find goodies. The Aboulafia family has been well respected for many years. They are an Arab family that didn't flee from Jaffa, but carried on to feed both the Arabs that were left and the new population of Jews from around the world.

Amir told us: "Out of respect, they do not bake during Passover week, when Jews only eat unleavened bread."

This seemed to be a deciding factor that Mr Aboulafia was a decent chap, and though I was nervous about going into an Arab area, part of me wanted to ask the Aboulafias about their take on the situation.

As we reached the port side, we came upon the old ramshackle harbour warehouses with their battered wooden panels and corroded corrugated rooves.

"These are the sheds Granddad told us about!" Colin realised.

"Oh yes, they are!" I nodded.

"Tell them what he said!" he prompted.

I was a bit unsure about bringing up the activities of the British as he ran ahead towards one of the broken windows and looked through its neglected rusty bars into the darkness inside. We followed him and Shai asked,

"What did he say?"

"The British used some of this storage space." I said,

I didn't want to spoil the evening by saying that sometimes there was ammunition stored in the area or that the captured terrorists were jailed just up the hill in some old police prison.

Colin ran off to look at a nearby boat whose lights were shining on the water. He shouted the lads over to see where the little black fish seemed to be searching for scraps around its hull.

I stood for a few minutes, looking out to sea and my thoughts wandered to what it might have been like in the forties. I had seen the black and white photographs of soldiers on the beach, stumping out cigarettes on sandbags and watching for illegal ships on the horizon. I imagined those shoddy vessels; some that didn't make it foundering in the bay; others were often boarded or shot at by British troops.

"Shai placed a comforting hand on my shoulder and said, "It's ok; it's finished now."

Amir talked a little about how scary it was for the British in this area.

"Some of the places were closed off to the British and they weren't allowed to go out alone; it was very dangerous. I wouldn't like to do it!"

He stood and thought for a minute.

"Once," he continued, "I was hit in the face in Jambalaya when an Arab threw a big stone. It wasn't just any little stone, it broke my cheekbone, but we could see what they were doing. It was a big crowd in the street; it wasn't closed-in like these narrow places."

I knew little then, especially nothing about the wide road, where we had earlier attended a festival, or that it had been blasted through the town by the British. They claimed, in the forties, that it was to improve transportation and enable safe patrols; but anyone who had served then, knew of the chaos caused. British explosions destroyed houses and their action was the start of the displacement of Arabs, Christians and Jews in Jaffa.

Soon, it was obvious to me; my companions didn't have hang-ups about the British Mandate. They had plenty to occupy their minds with memories of their own military service and the events that were happening daily.

As we walked along, the conversation lightened and they shared their hopes of visiting Paris or London, absorbing information about the United Kingdom. Both were surprised to hear that the English didn't really consider themselves European. Many Israelis have more of a European connection than we do.

"But you live in Europe?" they insisted, but to me, it was more of an easy passage to the world than shared cultural similarities.

Nevertheless, they looked to a time when they hoped to travel around the Middle East as we do in Europe, and I admired their positivity.

Shai's parents were born in Haifa, but his grandparents were from Poland.

His name, Shai, means gift, but it is also the name of the first Israeli intelligent service that the Hagana underground army began under British Rule. He told us that his Grandfather had a sister to whom he was close. He had written to the family in the thirties, and begged them to get out of Poland. However, after the war, he never heard from her again.

Amir's Great Grandmother lived in Germany until the mid-thirties. The family had a grocers shop and one day, her parents were taken away and the shelves were cleared of goods.

His maternal Grandmother was a little girl then and she hid on a small shelf just under the counter until the raiders had gone. She came out and ran away down the street, but he didn't know the story of her journey to Israel.

"There is just us now! That's all I know," he said and I presumed the rest of his wider family had been lost in the Holocaust.

There were hundreds of people in front of the Aboulafia bakery on Yeffet Street, as it seemed many festival attendees had the same idea as we did.

Waiting in the chaos, I saw a dilapidated police station, but didn't understand the current set-up, so I asked Shai, in a roundabout way, who was running law and order. There was a flag pole attached to the ancient Ottoman, stone frontage. The Israeli flag was tattered and looked like it had been shot at on a few occasions.

"Are we in that police station?" I said without thinking, but he quickly leaped in with:

"No, we are now!"

We both laughed, he knowing I meant the Israelis, had turned the question into a reflection on British Occupation.

"I meant the Israelis!"

He knew, what I meant, with his wry smile. I was naive enough, in those days, to question whether there was a Palestinian Police Force in Jaffa. I had a lot to learn.

He explained that the police station was attached to the old Turkish prison, the Kisle, which was a British police station in Old Palestine. This was the first encounter with a building I would grow to love via an unexpected connection.

We had talked enough of heavy things, so didn't investigate further. It was almost midnight and time to talk confectionary. In the hustle as we reached the front of a 'sort of queue', Colin stuck with what he knew. He went for a chocolate croissant and a doughnut. Shai had some kind of pizza, while Amir chose a pastry with a fried egg in the middle. In my Bavarian cheese pita, topped with sesame seeds, some burned black leaves dropped out and those saved left an ashy substance on my teeth. I resisted some twisted bark that you dip in salt and Amir said it was probably for the best.

We made our way back to the car that we had left down a back street among the remnants of the market day debris.

Scrambling over empty cardboard boxes and passing cats who were feasting on raw chicken pieces in plastic trays, we saw a young man pick up a feral kitten and show it to his friend. It was amazing how one side of the high street was far less glamorous than the other.

Colin walked around parked cars like a traffic warden and commented on those that seemed to be abandoned rather than parked, telling the others why the street was blocked.

Laughing, they told him that they don't always go for the, orderly and tidy he expected at home.

Shai said quietly, "He spots things that are a mess. I'm impressed with how he always looks for a litter bin!"

It seemed a bit futile when the low walls where people had eaten were littered with bottles, cans and takeaway packaging, but I am glad he didn't follow suit.

We'd had a lovely evening and after waiting for a while until the traffic had cleared from the side street, we made our way back to Tel Aviv.

As we passed the junction of Allenby Street and King George, Colin told Shai that he had seen some women of ill repute standing in an alleyway.

"Never!" Shai insisted, "they are just not very conservative dressers."

We believed him then. Well, I did. Nevertheless, in later years, I learned more about areas of Allenby Street and I think Colin might have been right.

Chapter 4

The Golan Heights

On 20th August 1995, Colin and I travelled to the Golan Heights on a single-decker bus with a group of tourists.

It was a long day, with 2 hours at either end of the tour filled with picking up and dropping off others at their hotels.

Our guide greeted attendees in their language, but advised the general narrative of the tour, would be staged in English and French.

The commentary began as we headed towards Hertzlia, just north of Tel Aviv and we were told that the town was named after Theodore Herzl.

Herzl held the first Zionist conference in Basle, Switzerland in 1908, commencing his mission to fulfil the dream for the Jews to have a homeland of their own.

Laughter ensued when, speaking in English and then French, the guide was confused by the left and her right, stating:

"On the right-hand side, you will see a statue of Theodore Herzl!

Theodore was on the left, so everyone on the bus turned their heads to look upon a 10 feet high, air-filled Ronald McDonald. We missed Theodore, but Ronald gave us a cheery wave, his arms flapping in the wind. Poor girl, she didn't know what all the chuckling was about.

Further on we saw a succession of tank ranges around the Orde Wingate institute and as we passed some metal gates, we were told:

"He was a British Officer who helped Israelis between the Wars!"

Disappointing, I thought. If I had written the dialogue, I would have provided more information on Wingate. I had long since decided that if he had not been sent away from Palestine for going against the British grain with his inappropriate support for the Jewish Brigade, he may have become a high-ranking officer in the Israeli army. He was killed after being posted to the Far East, but on reflection, he must have been respected enough by the founders to have a training institute named in his honour.

This, of course, was my perspective I would see how guides appropriately colour their dialogue.

I was excited about being let out into the open to enjoy the spectacular scenery I had heard about in the north. Apart from visiting Jerusalem, we had not, hitherto, escaped Tel Aviv's city limits to revel in the varying landscapes that Israel has to offer.

Turning east towards the hills, we saw a beautiful scattering of 'Arab style' houses. The guide described them as Arab houses, but wasn't clear about who lived in them then. Some looked quite extravagant, but she switched her explanation immediately, saying that Israeli Arabs were not Palestinians. What are they then? I asked myself.

She continued, "They are happy here and would rather live with the Israelis than with the Arabs!"

"Would they?" I thought and wondered again whether the tour was slanted towards Zionist propaganda.

I loved the journey on the road through the old swamps around Hadera, now covered with hundreds of eucalyptus trees. We were encouraged to imagine how Israel looked when the early settlers arrived and showed how, under British Mandatory Rule, the Australian troops planted the trees around us because they had wide-spreading roots that efficiently drew up water from the soil. Looking at the vast expanse of the forest today with the occasional piece of swamp land still visible, I wondered how they knew where to start, with a better understanding of the difficulties in making the land bloom in both wetlands and dry deserts.

Here, I thought, must be one of the places early Zionist settlers of the 20th century encountered the difficulties of poor drainage and disease, often dying of malaria or being beaten by the challenge and having to return home to Eastern Europe. While admiring a small plantation of young carob trees, recently planted to replace those that were dwindling, I heard:

"They were a favourite of the Turks during the Ottoman Empire when they used to eat the fruit of the tree. The Turks would only plant this type of tree and made trouble for those who planted others." She explained how the trees had been neglected and withered in recent times.

Stopping on the outskirts of Hadera for a comfort break in a roadside cafe, we looked out over a knee-high stone wall separating us from the traffic. From these heights, we gazed into the distance and for a minute, we thought we were looking at the snow covering a hillside some miles away. We were advised that they were the white buildings of Nazareth in the heat haze and that the town was twenty times bigger than at the time of Jesus.

It was interesting to discover just how close the towns of Christ's teaching were, but of course, it would have taken more time to walk between them. There was no Egged bus for him. Here we were taught how to spot an olive tree in case we were ever hungry in the wilderness.

"Olive trees are a sign of peace in Israel," she said. "Their leaves have a silver shimmer in the sunlight."

In the shop adjacent to the small coffee bar, we found all kinds of eucalyptus products and bought some sweets for the journey. Not the best for a day trip, since they cleared the airwaves, caused much sneezing and we didn't particularly enjoy them.

We travelled on to Megiddo, a place where ancient battles had been plenty. According to the book of Revelations, the last battle will happen here at the end of the world; at Armageddon." Excavation here has revealed many layers of history, but unfortunately, we don't have time to cover this place in one day.

We seemed to climb for a long time and my mind wandered into the scenes from a favourite film, Exodus, an adaptation of the Exodus book by Leon Uris. In the film, parts of the Jezreel valley had been cultivated by Barak Ben Canaan, where Jews and Arabs lived side by side and helped each other before the War of Independence. Around the foot of Mount Tabor, the Arab villages I could see were akin to Abu Yesha, where Ari Ben Canaan (Paul Newman) and Taha (John Derek) had played together as boys. Looking across the vast plains of Esdealon in the Jezreel Valley, where Deborah gathered her armies to fight against the Canaanites in ancient times, I couldn't believe I was there to see the beautiful, Biblical landscape.

Safed was pointed out to us on a hillside, a place loved by artists, but employed in Orthodox practices and Kabbalist mystics that scare me to death. Here, where the Druze and Orthodox Jews were living, the invading Arab forces tried to cut the new Israeli State in half as the British were leaving in 1948.

As we approached Rosh Pina, a military presence became obvious. We had seen a few tanks parked by the roadside earlier, but now the hilltops sported radar beacons.

In recent peace talks, I had heard that this area was problematic. Israel was still providing a military presence in Lebanon; the arguments continued whether the Golan Heights should be returned to Syria; ongoing since they were taken in the 6-Day-War of 1967.

I felt privileged, yet saddened, to witness the movements of another important era in the region. We had looked upon battlegrounds from thousands of years ago and could see current conflict simmering constantly.

The guide took great pride in telling us of the general kibbutz struggle before the war:

"Before 1967 when we took back this land, you could be shot by someone in the Syrian strongholds for farming here; we lived in bunkers a lot of the time. The valleys, as you can see, are lush with vegetation and this wasn't possible before."

We saw a smattering of populated hamlets, but many of the houses had boarded windows.

"You can see that it is dangerous to live here and many have moved away."

Occasionally, some party would be building in the middle of nowhere because the land was cheap and if the land was deemed fertile, there was an opportunity for someone to grow something and make a living.

"We build," she said, "then they will have to think twice about moving us on!"

Although I wasn't exactly sure who she was talking about at that stage, it was a philosophy of - if we do a good job with the land, they will have to let us stay.

In hindsight, the more contended territory adopted the more problems the authorities have in moving communities or using the land as a bargaining chip for peace.

Writing in 2022, about 1995, I see it was a very different time, and due to current hostilities in Syria, the border with Syria is no longer unpopulated. The vast openness of no man's land I saw then is now a very busy area. It accommodates refugee camps, field hospitals, and an Israeli military presence that watch the activities of Syrians, Russians, and a complicated mix of factions. Some of the Syrian-trained commandos, it is alleged, are now being sent to Ukraine, where, in February 2022, Russia's invasion began. Russian forces have been advising on and fighting in the Syrian conflict over the last few years and Syria is one of her biggest allies.

Kyriat Shamona was our furthest point for the day. A somewhat, war-torn area 12 miles from the Syrian border,

The buildings were modern, but modest, with no properties displaying much affluence. The army watched over it and upon the high ground, were ram-shackle communication towers.

A gaily painted tank sat on the grounds of a kindergarten, and we were advised that the area could be subject to random missile attacks projected by the mobile units of Palestine's Liberation Organisation (PLO) who had taken up residence in Lebanon.

Syria's various factions had recently dominated areas in neighbouring Lebanon and we were warned of possible spasmodic gunfire or the odd stray shell, but reassured that F16 fighters were in the area and would soon retaliate. While Israel's response may have been considered disproportionate, our guide was proud to say that we and the local population would be protected. She even suggested that staying with the locals would be a cheap holiday and a better way to feel the pulse of the situation.

After gazing in wonder at the fertile planes of the Hula Valley and Mount Hermon, we arrived in Banias for some free time. Banias is an Arab corruption of the word Panias, derived from the Greek God Pan. (God of the forest and shepherds). A Temple stood here in Caesarea-Philippi before a Christian Church was built around 400 AD during the Christianisation of the former pagan world of the Roman Empire. It is widely believed that Jesus, while teaching here, renamed his disciple Simon, Peter the Rock and appointed him the keeper of the keys to the gates of heaven. (Mathew: 16:18)

We walked along a wooden bridge, suspended on ropes. The trail led to a lush green area on the banks of a tributary. This flows at great speed towards the Jordan River, during the rainy season.

We joined an Afro-Caribbean group paddling in calmer water that reached knee-high. A kindly gentleman, with a broad grin, was offering water to people passing by, making make-shift cups from huge green leaves that grew on the riverbank. Studying the peculiar hairy surfaced leaf that the gentleman proffered, I turned upon hearing an excitable group behind me. They were praising and blessing Colin for his assistance in helping their elderly Mother down some steep steps and we chatted as we proceeded towards the Banias waterfall together. The flowing water refreshed the air as it crashed down some 30 feet as, industriously, it pushed the flow toward the Sea of Galilee.

Back on the coach, the climbing road meandered through the Galilean hills to 800km above sea level and the guide explained that we might not feel like we were so high. The Galilee is so-called because the undulating flat tops of the hills resemble waves. We felt were up in the clouds, however, as our ears began to pop. Colin felt this more, I think, as he suffered from sinus trouble.

There was nothing else to do but get him to suck more eucalyptus sweets and he couldn't decide the worst of 2 evils, earache or the taste.

We saw some Bedouins goat herding on the roadside, their makeshift tents strewn between the trees. To me, they looked like desperate people, but over the years I have watched as the government tries to get them settled in a town.

The Bedouins need to wander and don't see their lives as desperate, just traditional. The men sat smoking, the children ran about together while the women washed clothes in old oil drums. Tomorrow, I thought, they may move house and choose different trees as tent props.

The landscape was continually changing and it now looked as if it had been carved out of bright orange rock resembling cinder toffee that glistened like sugar in the bright sunlight. Then suddenly, enveloped in an eerie fog, I could just make out man-made canals, 2 feet wide, resembling a concrete bobsleigh run. This course went in different directions down to the Sea of Galilee, now shrouded in the mist.

When the terrain levelled out, the fog lifted and we were among vast grey fields. Closer inspection revealed harsh shards and crumbled stones of basalt rock as we were told that King David had a black staircase made from this in the second temple in Jerusalem.

"Nothing will grow on this volcanic debris", said the guide, but you will see various soil experiments on the route in the form of random planting."

We stopped and got off the coach for a few minutes to survey the border of Syria and Lebanon. Here, propaganda in favour of the Israelis continued:

"The bad land is in Syria and the lush green, with a line of trees to show where it ends, is Israel."

It was true, farmland and orchards stopped at the buffer zone; miles of nothing else spread out in front of us on the other side of the border.

You could see that the nurturing of land was more obvious on the Israeli side and the arid fields did look neglected on the Syrian side, providing appropriate props for justified occupation. The only form of life seemed to be the United Nations based in a barren no man's land, their camp flanked by white flags.

Looking out further on towards to town of Quinetra, I learned that following the war of 1967 Henry Kissinger decided to embark on a peace mission between Israel and Syria. The idea, according to our narrator, was to have a mixed town on the border where they could all work together. Journalists came from all around the world, excited by the prospect of harmony, only to witness another argument.

Syria had occupied it before the war and it now lay in the new Israeli zone, but both sides said they would give it a go.

Entering the town, all viewed absolute war-torn mayhem and evidence of filth and negligence. The Syrians said the other side should clear it up as they had made the mess. The Israelis said it was a pigsty long before we ever turned up.

Needless to say, the joint venture never got underway and Quinetra was left.

The sky was blue and empty of clouds and military aviation and it felt like the hottest place on earth. A sandy road meandered up the hillside, leading to the more sophisticated radar equipment. Some in the style of big golf balls, high aerials, and windmills ensured they could hear someone sneeze in Beirut, which is said to be just 10 minutes drive away by car.

Back on the bus, grateful for the air conditioning, we drank some more water and hung our sweat-saturated baseball caps on the hooks available. I removed some hard flint shards that were embedded in the melting rubber on the soles of my sandals and felt less than presentable.

The guide continued her narrative:

"You can see if we didn't occupy the Golan Heights, how easy it would be to fire on us from the hills."

Listening to this biased monologue did get a little monotonous, when, "Before 1967" started many sentences.

"The fields were empty; no fruit; no houses; no children!"

We passed an old barracks; mainly brick and breeze block in design with flaking whitewash and patched concrete hard standings for vehicles to park. If this was accommodation, it was little more than a shed, throwbacks from past conflicts, but the area still sufficed to house fuel tanks.

"Please don't take photos of the vehicles!" We were told, but I sneakily captured a blurred vision of a Merkava tank, to show my Dad the converted model of a centurion with its engine at the front. Land rovers and tanks were adorned with partially obscured Hebrew letters and their bodywork and tracks were dusted with troublesome sand.

Before we started back to Tel Aviv, we were taken to a cafe at Katzrin and advised that the owners depended upon tourism for their living. Walking across a huge lawn, we headed for a wooden shack where we were made to feel at home sitting down along wooden picnic tables. Told to help ourselves to bread from the open loaf on the countertop, we ate this with chicken schnitzel and fried potatoes, washed down with a bottle of cola. The cafe itself was clean and the hundreds of ants wandering on the window panes were at least on the outside. We walked across a private canteen in search of the toilets and saw the walls covered in photographs of military personnel, including regimental football teams who had been competing in a tournament. Just outside the bathroom was an ancient circumcision chair and I wondered whether the community gathered there for celebrations.

Outside, there was no relief from the heat and I perched on a plastic chair that had been placed under a parasol in the garden.

A huge chocolate Labrador dog lay panting on the lawn beside a hosepipe and Colin decided he might benefit from a baptism. Switching on the nearby tap, he filled its bowl and the dog jumped up, and wagged his tail, momentarily sticking his head under the water flow. We believed it was a game he liked to play, but we thought we might be chastised for wasting the water. We switched it off after a short while and as the dog drank, we followed our fellow tourists back to the coach with 2 bottles of our water bought from the cafe.

We took a similar route on the return journey, only stopping one more time to look at a Yom Kippur War memorial and to wander in the old Syrian trenches that had offered them ideal firing posts during the Yom Kippur war of 1973. The oil drums and barbed wire surrounding them had become rusty and the memorial itself was harsh metal shards and, to me, displayed anger rather than peace. The view of the Hula valley was again outstanding as we were subjected to a little more propaganda. Nevertheless, on discussing the story with Shai and Amir later, I learned that this area was too far south to suit her half-truths and I wondered whether she had been all together qualified to host the event.

We had enjoyed ourselves, taken in so much information, and been shown many sad realities. I was sure my holiday would not offer another such eventful day, but, within 12 hours, I would be proven wrong.

Chapter 5

Suicide Bombing

Ramat Eshkol Bus Bombing 21st August 1995

We were tired out after our Sunday visit to the Golan Heights and went to bed early, having had a bite to eat on Dizengoff Street.

I awoke in the very early hours of Monday morning and the events of the previous day seemed clearer. The day had left me in need of space to absorb all the information we had taken in. I got out of bed in the darkness and as I drew back the curtain, the streetlights allowed me to see that it was twenty past three.

Colin was asleep; with his bed covers strewn everywhere and I covered him with a sheet as the air conditioning had made the room chilly. Switching it off, I opened the veranda door to let in some heat. I didn't disturb him, but made some tea by the light from the bathroom and took it onto the veranda.

In Dizengoff Square, 4 floors below, a man hosed the area around the front of his shop and swept the water into the drains.

The morning was quiet apart from the sound of his broom and the odd car passing on the road underneath the sleeping fountain.

The trees rustled in the breeze and occasionally a bat would fly by before disappearing into the foliage. We can't go on another trip today, I thought, restlessly eager not to waste any time on my short trip, but I was physically and mentally tired.

I leaned on the wall, mug of tea in hand, and watching the street cleaner pour the contents of his bucket into the roots of a nearby palm tree, I noticed that the sun must be coming up. We faced west, but the sky was awakening and the silhouette of the box-shaped buildings and their multiple antennas began to achieve that amber colour of the Middle East.

I reflected upon the path that had led me to this place and though I was disconcerted after becoming more mindful of Israel's lot, I felt as if it already had a hold on me.

I had no answers to their problems, but looking upon a new day, I was aware that unknown things would continue to occupy my curiosity and that this was a fixation I would not be giving up in a hurry.

Life here, it seemed, had always been complicated, and seeing it firsthand wasn't going to make any difference or make things much clearer. No long-term solutions, just marginal improvement here and there, a piece at a time, but always someone ready to knock progress as it achieved the next rung on the peace ladder. Compromise didn't seem popular in the general scheme of trying to make things more harmonious. After an hour of thinking and watching, I went back to sleep, only to wake at half past seven with a revived thirst for more.

Colin got out of bed asking the usual questions:

"What time is it?" and "What shall I put on?"

The latter question was answered with the usual,

"We'll discuss your wardrobe when you've showered."

Ready for breakfast, I finished off in the bathroom and Colin having switched on the television, was immediately alarmed by the airing of a local news report. On the screen was the wreckage of a single decked, Egged bus surrounded by emergency services.

Unable to understand the language, I called reception and asked:

"Where was the bomb Yohav?"

"Jerusalem, half an hour ago," came the reply. I thanked him and hung up.

Telling Colin that it was in the capital, I asked him to go and brush his teeth. I didn't know what sort of coverage would be shown, but guessed that there might still be bodies on the bus and wanted to protect him from any horrific scenes. I was relieved that he had left the room, seeing the Orthodox Burial Societies who had already started picking up limbs and putting them into black bin liners.

As he returned, I switched off the television and said,

"Come on, let's go and eat!"

The radio in the hotel kitchen played in Hebrew throughout breakfast, so I was only party to the gasps of horror and expressions of dismay on the faces of the staff.

The English speakers were sheltered from the updates and we didn't refer to it as we ate.

Colin asked if he could go and watch the American breakfast channel he had become accustomed to in the past few days and assured me that he would stick to Star Trek, rather than looking for gory news reports. He was accustomed to the workings of his favourite channel and had learned a song from an advertisement about a Matzo man.

During my second cup of coffee in the hotel foyer, the young receptionist, whose name I never knew, stood watching the tragic scenes in Jerusalem on the television. He leaned on the counter and he began to translate, advising me on the morning's events. The media had not yet revealed the name of the street; just so far, 105 people were injured and 6, including the suicide bomber, had died.

Ruth, the hotel Manager came to join us, explaining that it was the eve of the opening of talks on the redeployment of troops from the occupied territories and we all assumed that any plans would again have to be postponed for now. The disruption had been achieved again with this morning's intentioned spanner in the works.

About 11 o'clock, I passed Ruth again on the way to the bank and she explained that I should be prepared for anger in the streets.

She was explaining to other guests that the buses would be running and the country would try to continue as normal. She seemed hell-bent on promoting the resumption of normality as soon as possible to ensure tourism wasn't affected.

The street felt heavy with both the situation and the weather. There was no air and my clothes were sticking to me within a minute of leaving the air-conditioning. In the bank, there was a small queue for foreign exchange and I had to wait with a group of serious-faced people who were also listening to the same local radio station that seemed to be playing quietly in every establishment.

As the cashier said, "Yes!" and I reached the bandit screen, an elderly lady interrupted us by waving some tickets under my nose.

She had dark, weather-beaten skin in contrast to her bright flowered dress and a white headscarf. On her feet were gleaming white training shoes, like clubs at the end of each short thin leg, and they looked extremely out of place in this well-groomed business environment. The cashier shouted some abuse at her and she shouted some back before shuffling slowly out of the revolving door.

"Yes!" she said again, to me, but I was curious and was learning to take abrupt manners with a pinch of salt.

"Who was that and what was she doing?" I asked.

"Wait!" she ordered and sped off behind a partition, bringing another lady with her who explained.

"Hello. My friend wanted me to tell you. The woman is collecting for the synagogue, she comes in every week and every week we throw her out, but she will not harm you."

I was amazed at the effort they had made to make me feel comfortable with her. I had to laugh, especially when the cashier said thoughtfully:

"Synagogue? Synagogue? A strange word for, Bet a Knesset, in Hebrew?"

I thanked them for taking the time to explain, with no regard for the disgruntled band queuing behind me. Having changed my traveller's checks for shekels, she wished me a nice time as I left.

On the way back across the square, I stopped to buy some monkey nuts, as Colin is very partial to them. I could feel their heat through the brown paper bag after they had spent the morning in the sun.

An elderly man we had recently befriended waved to me as I passed and I realised he was rising to his feet and beckoning me to the table where he sat. His face was sad as he shook my hand and said,

"Shalom!" he gestured that I sit down.

He had moved away from the usual party of about a dozen other elders, who were engrossed in debate. Another 2 were playing chess on a park bench. I was a little puzzled and felt out of place, but the tall, silver-haired man, who was probably in his seventies asked me quite severely:

"Well! What do you think of Israel this morning then?"

I didn't know what to say, seeing his face set in resigned disappointment as he paused. Who knows where the thoughts of this gentleman took him, standing in front of me with his hands in the pockets of his lightweight trousers. He continued:

"Have you seen the news this morning?" I nodded,

"You don't want to be here in the middle of all this today, look at the men over there, arguing at what to do next – and they have no say."

We both looked across at the group, and I wondered why anyone would care about my opinion. He continued in broken English.

"For 60 years we've never rested. 60 years ago I came here, for so many of those years we have had mornings like this. Arabs killing Jews, Jews killing Arabs and none are saints you know? Do you know where the answers will come from?"

"No," I said, "Days like this are new to me Sir."

"Yes, you and young people here all believe in peaceful solutions because they've not seen the many things that fail."

He continued looking around and appeared totally disillusioned with it all.

"I'm not sure the Knesset has all the answers about peace," I said, hoping I wasn't talking nonsense, "but Mr Rabin has seen as much as you have. How do you think he brings himself to sit and talk to people? Even he can't be a hundred percent confident?"

"No, probably not, so what's he playing at?"

I shook my head, not because I didn't know what Yitzhak Rabin was doing, but felt that whatever I said the gentleman would have heard it all before and as a humble visitor, I wasn't qualified. I had great admiration for Rabin's efforts, if he thought there was a chance of peace, how could I not hope along with him and many others?

The elder continued, in frustration.

"We built this country, no not this one, another one, where people knew the value of it. Do you understand?"

"Yes." I said, "You had to fight for a homeland."

"Yes," but your generation, they don't see this as the land of milk and honey because they never walk the streets in fear.

Some say that the negotiations are helpful, but ask them, who would go home with you if you got them a ticket. England is the land of milk and honey!"

"Do you all feel the same?" I asked, gesturing a hand towards his friends.

"Yes, we know the peace talks will go on and so will the terrorists and the anger. And you see him?" he pointed to a man sitting on the wall by the fountain, "He said to leave it to God."

He shook his head as if he couldn't believe how resigned and irresponsible such a comment was.

"Do you believe in God?" he asked.

"I suppose so," I answered.

"Well, you ask him what he thinks the answer is."

"Have you not asked him?" I asked

"Many times," he paused, "but today, I'm not speaking to him."

He paused again, still surveying the scene like a security guard and I thought it was probably time to leave him to his thoughts, but he surprised me by continuing:

"Do you feel like you want to go home? How do you feel about today?"

"I don't know," I replied, "I've had a lot to take in. Yesterday I was on the Golan Heights; I didn't sleep very well and now this. I can only describe it as a type of stomach ache. I'm ok, not panicking. I wanted to see Israel as it really is, but I don't how I would feel if I couldn't walk away?"

"I'm sorry," he said, suddenly calmer. "Will you write to the Knesset and tell them that the terror frightens the tourists and they are spoiling your vacation with silly ideas?"

"As I said, I came to Tel Aviv to see how it is."

"Well as long as you have learned that this Holy Land must be without God!"

This was very sad, bordering on depression, and so I tried to change the mood.

"I don't pretend to know what you have been through, but do you think Israel is better to continue as a closed Zionist State and then in 20 generations, still she cannot negotiate with her neighbours? The economy will just get worse and worse. I think Yitzhak Rabin is brave, to try and look forward."

He half-smiled but sighed. I think his space from the heated debate had done him good.

"Maybe, but maybe I wanted to leave it as it is for now."

I nodded, he was weary with it all and he triggered passages I had read previously. Conversations I had had about veterans who are at the end of their tether.

I explained this to him and told him about a man earlier that week. The man was originally from Czechoslovakia and told me about David Ben-Gurion, Israel's first Prime Minister. When he got tired of politics, after many years of trying to solve the problems of the State, he retired and went to end his days on a kibbutz.

He was still committed to the State and insisted on working hard, but enjoyed a quieter existence. There's nothing wrong with being tired of fighting.

He nodded thoughtfully.

I carried on. "The other thing I have read is: how frightened Rabin was before the pre-emptive strike on the Egyptians in 1967. Not everyone agreed then, did they? Do you not think a Zionist should have some faith in the man?"

I'm not sure I made any sense, but he actually managed a smile then and offered his hand again saying:

"Thank you for talking, it has been very nice!"

"No, thank you, the pleasure is mine."

I meant this sincerely, always honoured to speak to an experienced person. I bid him Shalom and a few days later I met him with his friends again and took a group photograph for Colin to take home to show his Granddad Israel's equivalent of the British Legion, I thought. His friend told me that the man's name was Weiss, pronouncing a W as a V. It seemed to be a joke and I'm not sure it was his real name.

"We call him this because he has Weiss hair!"

They were all laughing again, as sitting around chessboards in the square they had settled again, for a while.

I sometimes wonder about Weiss, whether when he was building the country, as he called it, was he in the Hagana, Irgun, or with Stern, perhaps? Where was he in 1947? In the year 2000, I took the photograph back to the square thinking he might be there, but a lady told me he was gone now. He had taken his history and philosophy with him.

Back in reception, I told Ruth about my rendezvous with the man. We talked about the younger generation, many of whom wanted to leave Israel. The consensus was that everyone, like all young people, wanted to travel, but she emphasised that they would all return at a moment's notice in the event of a crisis. The value of 'Homeland' is drummed into them from an early age and though the younger generation didn't wear the history of the Jewish people on their sleeves, they had great respect for the founders. Ruth considered herself lucky, to be a hotel Manager and said her living was acceptable for the times and the state of the nation. However, she did resent paying so much tax to subsidise the defence budget and I sensed she was fed up with being a reservist. She saw giving up a month every year as a duty rather than something she loved to do. She turned her attention to the television.

"Look at that," she said, "here is the anger in Israel I told you about."

An angry mob, outside the government buildings in Jerusalem, were carrying placards, waving their fists and shouting in Hebrew.

"Don't ask me what the answer is," she said sadly shaking her head at the scene, "but this won't do any good."

Colin had come down with a slight sniffle, as I had suspected the previous day, and didn't feel like going out. The climate and the eucalyptus were clearing his head. He was pottering around the hotel, eating fruit and drinking juice, from the dining room, so I thought he too must be a bit out of sorts after the long journey the previous day.

We heard via the media that the suicide bomber had boarded the bus in Tel Aviv, which brought it closer to home and I wondered whether this was a factor to do with him wanting to stay indoors. He said not, but I couldn't blame him if he was thinking about it. The bomber might have passed the hotel in transit to Jerusalem.

We stayed in the hotel, rang England for a second time to put my parent's minds at rest, and chatted with the hotel staff members, who treated us as friends, making sure we understood everything that was going on. They lightened the mood by telling jokes and translating them for us, we could all laugh together. They asked us about our lives and one especially wanted to know more about how the UK was split and governed, not understanding that the UK wasn't absolutely English. A couple of young lads from the local Indian restaurant came in for a coffee as business was very quiet that afternoon. They decided to take the opportunity to design a new menu and Colin enjoyed helping them with design ideas; we were quite a happy industrious bunch armed with bottles of water and not interested in food until the day became cooler.

About 3 o'clock, a carpenter came to fix the front door as it was scraping on the metal well that held the doormat. He wore jeans and a navy blue vest with his red shoulder-length hair tied back which seemed to be a popular fashion for men. When Yasser Arafat appeared on the television screen to speak on behalf of the Palestinians, he downed tools immediately to listen to him.

Speaking in Arabic, with Hebrew subtitles, I was lost, but everyone listened until he had finished his short broadcast. The carpenter was stony-faced and angry which inspired me to ask:

"You don't approve of what he said?" I questioned, "What did he say?"

"That's right," he answered, "The man's a liar and said what he always says: 'We condemn these terrorist attacks and it will not affect the peace talks."

"Do you think he tells us one thing, then goes back to Ramallah and says something else?" I asked.

"What do you think?" he asked. "Why did you say that?"

"Well, he makes these speeches and plays to the media. Recently I saw a documentary where he spoke to a crowd of Arabs who seemed to worship him. The translator said that he referred to the little ones standing by him as his 'blessed children of the stones', seeing as the kids throw stones at soldiers; just my thinking."

"Exactly, no one knows what he says to his people, but we never see them being punished for what they do."

"In England, I see in the media that the road map to peace is portrayed as a wonderful thing, but today no one seems to think it is a good idea. It's such a big journey."

He agreed that the journey was massive and I thanked him for his translation.

Soon after, the job was finished and he packed up his tools, but before he left, he took the time to speak again.

"A news report just said that the border soldiers have gone on 24-hour patrol and the West Bank and Gaza are closed."

He explained how the curfew would make the Arabs angry and the soldiers should expect hostilities on the borders and around the Jewish settlements they protect. He recommended that if I was interested, I should watch the news later as there would be cameramen in these areas. Having given me the military update, he informed me that the scattered pieces of the suicide bomber had been put back together to reveal that it was a woman. Also, an angry mob had gathered outside Yitzhak Rabin's house in northern Tel Aviv, so security forces had seen it fit to ship him out of Jerusalem for the night for his own safety. The protest was against the ongoing dialogue for the Palestinians to achieve self-rule in the Occupied Territories where the Arabs had been on the receiving end of aggression from Israeli Settlers. The negotiations had been disrupted on more than one occasion with failure to meet deadlines and chants from some Jewish extremists of: "Death to the Arabs - Death to Rabin!" Mr Rabin, however, still maintained that the Peace Process would go on as Hamas and Islamic Jihad terrorism wasn't truly representative of the Palestinian people.

I was grateful and indebted to everyone who had seen my genuine interest and not only wanted to keep me fed on information, but accepted that I had an opinion too. I don't feel the reports were propaganda; maybe some of the reports were one-sided, of course, but the day had certainly shown me a close-knit community with an immediate connection to events. Their concerns lay with the families of the victims and the people they knew who were serving in the army.

The afternoon passed and we ventured into the evening, more people seemed to be walking about in the square again. Seeing normality resuming, Colin regained his appetite and asked if we could go to McDonalds'.

In the street, the sweet smell of the crepe stand dominated aromas and we agreed we might try one at some time, but not today. The shops were open as usual and the intense atmosphere seemed to have lightened compared to the morning, but I didn't know whether the air of uncertainty was just mine; I wasn't used to all this.

We walked past the dirtiest fruit shop in the Middle East and held our breath, as we always did, to protect ourselves from the rancid smell. We were thinking about food as we approached the crossing when the bus at the head of the traffic queue suddenly backfired as it gained momentum. I almost jumped out of my skin, and everyone around us stopped in their tracks and waited for a second until they had assessed the noise.

I realised, I wasn't the only one running on adrenaline. Colin guided me across the road to the entrance of Dizengoff Mall and I wondered, when does the child become the bodyguard while out walking with his Mother?

The security guard scanned our bodies with a metal detector before another looked into my handbag. The shopping precinct spans the street by glass bridges and inside the McDonalds Bridge is the restaurant itself, where we always sit and look down at the busy street below. There is a succession of bus stops underneath and I asked Colin if he would prefer to sit inside the precinct away from the buses. Having thought for a minute, he asked,

"Do you usually get 2 bombs in one day?"

"Not usually," I told him, "but really, who can say how they think?"

"When was the last one?"

"About 6 weeks ago. They may not want to undermine the sacrifice of the suicide bomber by making another martyr in one day. But don't rely on my opinion son!"

"Oh, I'm not bothered." He said heading off for the stairs. "Let's sit on the bridge; everyone else seems to be just getting on with it." I admired his resilience.

I found we were quite relaxed while eating our meal. I sat thinking that life was cheap on the parallel of the fanatics, and wondered whether they mind how many they lost. I wondered whether families were proud of their martyrdom in Islam.

Though on reflection, was it macabre to sit eating burgers and fries with my 13-year-old, who was asking how much explosive you would need to blow up a glass bridge? He was philosophical, just as the kids here have to be every day. This is the life for lads of his age here, I thought, only 5 years away from national service. My thoughts also touched briefly on the sad lives of the Palestinian boys at the same age. Surely and hopefully, they didn't all believe that fighting was the only way.

Colin looked through the window into the street to where a young lady was playing a fiddle and remarked, positively, that things seemed to be getting back to normal.

SCRATCHING THE SURFACE

He had jumped on the bandwagon of carrying on regardless and on reflection, showing a spirit I didn't contemplate much at the time. We both accepted that days like these were expected in Israel, at the moment, and sailed along with them in the same boat.

A young couple was sitting at a nearby table, probably in their late teens; holding hands as they gazed at each other over their meals. Both were dressed in khaki uniforms and my attention was drawn to their belongings. Placed under the girl's chair was a yellow rose preserved in a cellophane tube. In stark contrast, under his lay an automatic rifle of some kind. This seemed normal for life in a war zone, and I felt saddened by the hopelessness of it all. I pointed it out to Colin, but his thoughts had turned to apple pie in the bakery on King George Street.

"Can we get some for afters?" he said, with all the enthusiasm of a kid on a beach holiday. And why not?

So we took the back door out of the mall onto King George Street, the young duty soldier opened the door for us and we stepped into the usual noisy bustle of people. We soon returned by the same door with the idea of sitting by the broken fountain in the mall to eat our dessert. The soldier disappointed us by letting us back in without a search. To me he had failed in basics, I had a brown paper bag containing pastries, so he knew where I had been, but I could have been anyone. I remembered the pep talk we had received at the airport. Security had told us that we would be treated as suspicious, not because we were, but because the Arabs would use us. The lady had pointed a warning finger at us, saying we were vulnerable targets for the transportation of explosives and we should expect hassle at any checkpoint.

I didn't dwell on it and we decided to return to the hotel, visiting a small shop for bottled water on the way. Colin was interested to know whether Israelis drink orange cordial. In the shop, we found an older soldier, this time with unsurpassed observation skills and only too keen to point out my mistake. He was sitting on a bar stool eating a sandwich, his khaki uniform neatly pressed, with the immaculate red boots of a paratrooper and a rifle slung over his shoulder. He turned to see us enter and Colin immediately opened the upright drinks fridge, saying he could only find coke and water in there.

"Excuse me." The soldier said politely: "The button of your shirt is undone."

I looked down to see the reveal of my underwear. Without much of a reaction, I said,

"Oh, thanks for that!"

Colin, however, was dying of embarrassment and letting the fridge door slam on its spring said,

"Oh, Mother!" which amused both the soldier and the shopkeeper.

"Oh it's no big deal son," I said, fastening my blouse, "Have you found what you are looking for?"

He joined us, lugging 3, litre bottles of water, and stated, somewhat protectively, to the grinning soldier,

"If you are so smart, can you tell me the Hebrew word for orange squash?"

"Squash?" he asked. "Mitzapuzim?"

"No, not orange juice," he answered, "Orange that you add water to - to make it weaker!"

They had a bit of a debate, the soldier asking why you would want to do that when you have thousands of oranges and can just drink freshly squeezed juice everywhere. The shop owner joined in the conversation, telling them that they sell squash in America and sometimes he had seen it in the supermarket, but he didn't have it.

He suggested that Colin added water to the juice if he found it too strong and I agreed that this would be a healthier option than the artificial stuff.

We paid for our goods and on leaving the shop; the soldier asked cheekily.

"Can I help you with anything else?"

"You just keep your eyes on the border!" I told him.

Colin shook his head and said, "Come on." impatiently.

It was dusk when we arrived back on our balcony, the sun setting on this day over the hard white, angular rooftops. In Dizengoff Square, people were gathered around the fountain while children fed pigeons pieces of pizza and pita bread.

Suddenly, the short burst from an ambulance siren broke into the noise and all fell silent and turned towards the road. The traffic stopped and a convoy of Magan David Adom, (Red Star of David Ambulances) crawled past. I didn't know what was happening and then the activity returned to normal. Shortly afterward, a report was given on the English television station, explaining that the bodies and stray limbs taken from the bus wreckage had just passed through Tel Aviv.

I heard that the University forensic team will be busy throughout the night, trying to match the pieces before the next day, funeral services.

I remembered how my day had started with the burial society picking up the pieces in the street and placing them in a bin bag.

A miserable, yet eventful day and I had encountered a small portion of the Israel experience of 1995.

A new perspective for me was the divided dialogue between the people living inside Israel. I had seen the passionate feelings of the peacemakers; the resigned expressions on the faces of the old founders; noticeable aggression apparent in some conversations. For them all - today had been just another day.

24th September 1995

I wrote the following in my diary on 24th September 1995, just a month after returning from Israel. Notes; taken from television news reports about peace talks in accordance with the Oslo Accords.

Jewish New Years' Eve 5755 / 5756

They talked for 80 hours this week, Shimon Peres and Yasser Arafat included. The document outlining the new agreement is said to be 400 pages long and they are saying that Peres has sold the Israelis short in offers to extend Palestinian self-rule.

A radical Palestinian group has denounced the agreement as a disaster and there have been clashes with troops in the

West Bank and the city of Nablus and troops have shot dead a teenager who was brandishing a rifle. Hebron is on high alert; both settlers and the Palestinians who live there expect to see more bloodshed.

The new West Bank Accord between Israel and the PLO states that troops will withdraw from 7 Palestinian cities and 450 Arab villages over the next 6 months.

An elected 82-member Palestinian council will regulate most aspects of life in the West Bank and Gaza.

There will be a temporary international presence in Hebron where Israelis will retain the power to protect 400 settlers who live among 100,000 Arabs.

Israeli troops will stay in control of the roads that are used by settlers in the West Bank.

Thousands of Palestinian prisoners will be released, in 3 stages, once the plans in the Accord become official.

The Palestinians will revoke those articles of the Palestinian covenant calling for the destruction of the State of Israel.

Talks on the future of Jerusalem, Jewish settlements, and Palestinian refugees will start in May 1996.

Chapter 6

1947 An Ugly War

I have heard some say, that the person you think you are doesn't exist through the eyes of others. Everyone we know has a particular impression in mind when hearing our names. Independent images, either consciously or subconsciously, are either based on experiences we have shared, or another's opinion creating a pre-conditioned bias.

This was the case during my early thirties when I began learning about British Mandate days in Palestine. Not about individuals, but the reputations of certain organisations. I had an inherited view of each underground faction and having heard talk of the 'ugly, forgotten war' I naively stereotyped members who had been involved with each organisation.

Hagana 1947
"It wouldn't have been the Hagana that blew up an ambulance!" I heard men say. "Hagana, as a faction, would have insisted on a moral war - many were officers and gentlemen. They respected the British and everything the Jewish Brigades had learned from them while they were fighting Hitler together."

But then, did they use that knowledge against us? Did they turn on us when it came to the crunch?

My understanding was that the Hagana were those who fought Hitler, with our allies, as if there was no 1939 white paper restricting Jewish immigrants from entering Palestine. Ridding the world of Nazi practices was a priority, but they were still keeping an eye on the situation and helping with illegal immigration. Nevertheless, things gradually changed in the early 1940s as news filtered through about the atrocities the Jewish People were facing in Europe. The wool was often pulled over the eyes of the British to save those who had escaped genocide. Still, in my mind, Hagana were the nice ones.

Irgun 1947
I had learned that the Irgun wanted to blow up the British and saw Hagana's methods as a soft touch. British soldiers were told:
"They were hard men, Communists, Bolshevik revolutionaries, who would stop at nothing. They saw honour in meeting their death, and sang the songs of partisans while trying to see off the British." The disillusioned saw them as men coming in on illegal boats to blow up their mates.

LEHI 1947
Even in Israel, I was told by elders: "LEHI - The Stern Gang, definitely wouldn't think twice about killing someone. They expected to die themselves."
Some said "No scruples; they mustn't have had if they were created as an offshoot of the Irgun because they didn't believe their hard-line methods were tough enough". They would stop at nothing.

LEHI was the worst. What sort of men were these I wondered. I just know I was told to:

"Keep away from them!"

The British in Palestine had given them a wide berth unless they were hunting them down in force and some old Israelis I had spoken to were still despairing at their inexhaustible violence.

70 years later, as I talk to elders in Israel, who have spent a lifetime dealing with one crisis after another, I find that some memories of the time when the State was founded have become a bit hazy. Other times, those in the winter of their lives sit in the sun chatting together, and while putting the world to right, the old times get dredged up and everyone has a story.

Ultimately, the members of each faction had to fight together in consequent wars and some old scores have been written off for the sake of comradeship and the nation's focus on survival.

In the 1990s, in Dizengoff Square, I heard old men say:

"They did what they thought they had to do!" While others are embarrassed by the lengths hard-liners went to as they gradually became known as terrorists, not only in British circles but among the locals.

Perspectives in hindsight often change, as time passes or first-hand knowledge becomes more available. I see different stories emerging and, having discussed events with those who were there, my first impressions fade into that earlier untutored era.

SCRATCHING THE SURFACE

My late Father, while serving in Palestine, was the victim of an improvised explosive device that blew up a vehicle in his convoy. He was shipped home to endure his injuries and a post-trauma that never totally left him.

Soldiers only really talk about the awful stuff to fellow comrades and in post-war Britain, it was customary to, 'get on with it', and not dwell on personal tours through one conflict or another. What a soldier saw wasn't generally shared with a daughter, and with my Mother on guard, telling us to leave it alone, we weren't allowed to pursue the matter.

Nevertheless, being close to the consequences and gradually gleaning information on the drawn-out Palestine affair, I have to question:

"At what price did we save sixpence; clinging on to the remnants of Empire? Why didn't we know when it was time to go home?"

Marching into Jerusalem in 1917, the British had been welcomed as triumphant against the Ottoman Empire. 30 years later, personnel from all services experienced unconventional warfare from a band of terrorist factions, trying to secure a homeland for world Jewry.

Many worked within the British administration to prepare for the coming of the new State. But, at the same time, some were spying for the underground, stealing ammunition or cobbling together crude devices, under the noses of the British.

My Father occasionally told us muted stories. There was a day at Jaffa police station when a Jew, dressed as an Arab and walking with a camel, was arrested after a routine search revealed he was carrying ammunition in his panniers.

"I was sent into the courtyard to look after the camel," he told me, "but I didn't know what camels eat so I gave it a bucket of water."

In Jaffa, while wandering around the walls of the old Turkish prison, once used as a British police station, I have often pictured the day when the oblivious creature, also caught up in chaos, had a drink with a 19-year-old lad from Oldham.

*****

In 2012 an Israeli soldier sat with me in the former Headquarters of Hagana in Tel Aviv when I was privileged to read the diary of an unnamed Palestine policeman, stationed in the area in 1947.

The young recruit had not chosen front-line duties, but instead, was spending her national service as an administrator. She had found contentment working in the archives of one of several military museums.

Her khaki attire clashed with the turquoise butterfly on her diamante phone cover and she kindly asked again and again if I was being disturbed by the music coming through her pink headphones. Across the desk from me was a student whose baby slept in a pushchair beside her and when he awoke, she breastfed him to keep him quiet while we read.

SCRATCHING THE SURFACE

The Policeman's report painted a miserable, yet vivid, picture of the situation and conditions endured by those carrying out duties in 1947 and I sat for hours, immersed in the era.

I was on the same foreign ground; had felt the unbearable temperature outside and the special amber light of the Middle East streamed through the windows. This helped me to visualise the events the Policeman shared, and knowledge of familiar streets provided appropriate props for my imagination.

As the customary honking of car horns on Rothschild Boulevard continues today, I learn that it was the British who taught Israelis how to clear the way. They barged their way through in enormous staghounds. A very noisy armoured car with a siren, but withdrawn because they were using too much petrol.

This business area wasn't as densely populated in 1947, and impatient Israelis have replaced the claxons of wireless reconnaissance vehicles trying to detect stray signals from the underground's radios.

Today, when I take a break and go to my favourite cafe for hot chocolate, I will be flanked by men and women of commerce, and armed paratroopers chilling after a training day. They are taught in the same old Hagana institute that teaches me.

At the end of World War II, the Hagana and their elite brothers, the Palmach, were disappointed that the British had reneged on conditional promises made for a second time. Speaking broadly, the first understanding with the British

Government was in November 1917, when a letter was sent from British Foreign Secretary, Arthur Balfour, to Lord Rothschild, the then leader of the British Jewish Community.

It stated that His Majesty's Government viewed with favour, a national homeland for the Jewish People in Palestine and asked that this information be shared with the Zionist Federation. The British were promoting the prospect of a Jewish Homeland in Palestine once Ottoman Rule had gone. At the same time, Arab independence was being promised in related territories if they assisted in seeing off Turkish Rule.

Secondly, Jewish Brigades, Hagana included, expected a better return in real estate for their contribution to fighting Hitler's regimes beside the British. In 1946, when Holocaust survivors were liberated from death and labour camps, but not welcomed in their old towns in Europe, Foreign Minister, Ernest Bevin's quotas did not allow them to immediately find the refuge expected in Palestine.

I focus mainly on 1947 because of the family connection to this year, not to point out that this time was the worst time for those serving in Palestine.

The 30 years of British Rule in Palestine was eventful throughout the whole campaign, though it changed dramatically in the amount of service personnel and reputation throughout the years.

In July 1920 a new Palestine Police Force consisted of less than 20 officers supporting 55 policemen. There were about 12,000 men on the ground whose duties were described as: Fulfilling ordinary duties of a constabulary, such as preservation of law and order and the prevention and detection of crime, act as their numbers will allow as escorts for the protection of tax collectors, serve summonses issued by judicial authorities, to distribute Government notices and escort Government treasury throughout the country.

At this time, Vladimir Jabotinsky, a member of the Zionist Executive was in favour of a Jewish Defence Arm and arranged a demonstration in Jerusalem promoting this. Clashes between Arabs and Jews ensued and the undermanned force was soon outnumbered with the military assisting to restore law and order. This was a taste of things to come as Arab gangs established themselves in the hills and fired upon roadblocks after luring the British on remote winding roads.

Edward Horne said that in those days, "Defending themselves with valour unto the last man!" Often foot soldiers and those with only the protection of a model T Ford were vulnerable, to say the least.

In 1929, bringing about a local calm among the Arabs would soon be replaced by the need to deal with new Jewish factions fighting against immigration policies. Some of whom would not stop until they saw the back of British rule.

Clashes between Jews and Arabs increased in the mid-30s as the Jewish numbers grew again with fascism spreading across Europe. Various states of emergency led to the increase in British forces to assist Civil Policemen in keeping the peace and by 1947 there was a complement of 100,000 soldiers and Palestine Policemen.

It would be impossible to chronicle all mandate activities in one chapter on the Mandate, but my informative Policeman has give me inside information about the period leading up to demobilisation in 1947 and early 1948.

Other information is with the kind assistance of Joseph Kister and his book, The History of the Irgun.

1947

January 1947 saw the evacuation of women and children related to Mandate personnel, with another topping up of troops. 3 terrorists were ordered to be executed for the possession of arms and others were arrested and detained after the flogging of a kidnapped army officer.

The Irgun said: "If flogging is good enough for us, why are the British surprised that we undertake the same practice?"

Tel Aviv was declared out of bounds for those, not on duty, maintained until the end of the Mandate, following threats of kidnapping, heard through illegal radio stations.

On 15th February, the question of Palestine was to be put before the United Nations General Assembly as, the Policy on the British Mandate for Palestine, did not allow for partition or the making of 2 States.

The situation in the region was made more complicated when clashes between the Hagana, Irgun and LEHI occurred, as a result of disagreements on measures that should be taken towards both the British and the Arabs.

SCRATCHING THE SURFACE

On 1st March an explosion demolished the officers club in Jerusalem killing 20 people and injuring another 30. Martial law was declared in areas of Tel Aviv and Jerusalem in retaliation to increased terrorist activity by Irgun and LEHI forces. The Jewish Agency sympathised with the effect this action had on the general public, but said the whole population was being punished for the actions of a few dissident gunmen.

16th April saw 4 terrorists hanged in Acre prison, but not without the first senior British Officer refusing to order the executions; he was relieved of his duty.

The summer of 1947 was an ugly period, when the Anglo-American Commission recommended that 100,000 refugees should be allowed to enter Palestine, on condition that the local community agreed to disband all illegal armies.

Even the more passive Hagana saw this proposal as a threat to the whole of Jewish existence. They also believed that once the British were gone, the Jewish population would be left in the hands of the Arab League and ramped up their efforts to assist in getting more displaced Jews into Palestine.

I read in the Policeman's diary:
"Hearts hit rock bottom and Jewish illegal immigration increased through the efforts of leaky, vessels used in desperation, though not adequate or seaworthy. For the lucky few impelled forward by the memories of the horror they had left behind in Europe, British politics could not overcome their will to live.

The Arabs stood smugly by while the British enforced policy on the Jews."

With curfews imposed on the civilian population and efforts to control the situation with periods of martial law, military and service personnel carried arms at all times for personal protection. Wireless cars patrolled residential areas, in an attempt to track down illegal radio stations and plain-clothed CID officers visited cafes disguised as locals to seek out well-known terrorists. The Policeman said:

"This often proved futile because, apart from the Jews always knowing, 'their own', the sunburned Tommy was given away by a red complexion and the natives saw him coming. The back doors of cafes were usually found wide open, as, in a tight-knit community, everyone remained alert. Generally, Jews in the community hid those who were on wanted posters or transported ammunition under the guise of their regular merchandise. Intelligence was random, as were arrests, showing that the whole administration was in dilemma. British measures encouraged a recruitment exercise, provoking the Jewish community into more actions of terror.

During the most extensive investigation in the whole of the Mandate, a 4-day curfew in Tel Aviv and Jaffa, every male in the city was interviewed. The lack of the Hebrew language proved to be a huge handicap during interrogation. Some regular soldiers, often as young as 21 years old were not interrogation experts, and working on instincts wasn't the best way to reassure justice. The wrong look in the eye didn't mean they were guilty and some suspects waited in custody for as long as 3 months awaiting experts.

The attitude of the weary, angry, often anti-Semitic soldier was sometimes: cringingly embarrassing and the conditions of the post and the weight of the duty began to tell on the strongest constitution.

Often the soldiers had expected spineless people and were disappointed that they weren't easier to handle".

The difference between the behaviour of the Jews who had been rounded up in Europe throughout the thirties and World War II was phenomenal. The British were dealing with a band of survivors and some might say that the reason they were so successful was because the British were not the 'Fascists' some propaganda in Palestine would have them believe: The Policeman despaired:

"We were a spent force in Palestine with mixed feelings toward a 'stubborn people, to quote officers who were hopelessly trying to control the situation.

Get along there Shu Ismak. (What's your name?) An insulting remark usually intended for an Arab, but aimed, this time, at an educated Austrian Jew, whose cutting response was:

"Are you the product of that British tradition that always assists the underdog?" A better briefing and enlightenment of the situation may have spared the soldiers' blushes."

Great men from Europe being insulted by the average lad who had taken the King's shilling for an excellent career opportunity, dodging bullets, pushing women, and rounding up the homeless in a God-forsaken country we could ill afford.

On 4th May 1947, the famous Acre prison break freed 41 of the underground. There was heavy fighting in the area and subsequently increased terrorist activity. Intelligence was vague and in desperation, the British rounded up hundreds of male Jews and found themselves engulfed in suspects. Some were held under arrest for days until an interpreter became available.

In retaliation to nightly curfews and the British refusing to increase immigration quotas, the Irgun went into action causing unrestrained chaos. Military vehicles exploded as service personnel went about their daily routines. Bridges were set on fire to hinder troop movement and there was extensive mining of rail freight and passenger trains, especially those carrying troops.

In June 1947, a booby-trapped, Irgun tunnel leading straight into the British Headquarters at Citrus House, Tel Aviv, killed the Hagana soldier who discovered it.

The sophisticated 15-yard tunnel was found by a member of the Hagana who alerted the authorities just before the device exploded. The turnout for his funeral was phenomenal and army intelligence officials acknowledged that the man had prevented the deaths of those who could have been working in the building at a busier time of day.

Confined to barracks again, unless on duty and foot patrols had to be accompanied by armoured car support in Tel Aviv.

Everyone became tunnel conscious as they were given the additional duties of looking for them.

A different fear shrouded the British. It was bad enough looking out for themselves and other comrades, or checking vehicles and buildings above ground. Now the threat of terrorist activity going on beneath their feet gave a resigned feeling of hopelessness. There seemed to be no sense of safety, especially when clearing up the mess after drive-by rebels shot through the flimsy walls of canvas guardrooms.

The diary said:

"18th June 1947 – in command of a TA police station, 5 soldiers were kidnapped and a mysterious parcel wrapped in newspaper was found there. We used a razor blade to remove the paper, as carefully as possible and found a piece of iron piping that had been used to club the missing soldiers. They had disappeared and no amount of searching turned them up.

Later 2 soldiers were released, but no one knew where the other 3 were, then a packing case appeared on a side street and they were in it.

Soldiers were called to assist the 3 who had been rescued, but on the way, a Brigadier in a local hotel came out to address the random, in-the-air firing, traditionally used to disperse traffic getting in the way of a convoy.

He later sought the Commanding Officer responsible for the hullabaloo, saying had been disturbed. Nevertheless, having been told that his troops were on the way to retrieve 3 of their buddies, whom they thought were lying dead in the street, he reluctantly dropped the matter."

Bitterness was at a peak, especially towards the end of July '47 with the conclusion of the Sergeants affair. 2 kidnapped soldiers were found hanged in an orange grove following the execution of terrorist leaders at Acre Jail. The bodies had been booby-trapped and cutting them down was fraught with danger. No further political prisoners were hanged after this act of vengeance.

In 1997, just after my Father passed away, I appealed to Royal British Legion members through their monthly magazine, to see if anyone would like to share with me, their time in Palestine.

I received a letter from a gentleman and I am ever grateful for his account. Out of respect for him and at the request of his local branch of the British Legion, the gentleman remains anonymous, but contained some excellent information from someone who served.

I was one of the first to arrive in the Netanya orange grove where two Sergeants had been tortured and hung. Their warped minds still wouldn't let them rest in peace as they booby-trapped them, causing more mayhem.

Yes, there are bitter memories, but we weren't all snowy-white as we had some bad people on our side. One who I guarded was a Captain whose, methods of asking questions were very un-text book 'shall we say. I have often listened to groups of individuals telling stories about the Holy Land and mentioning his name. I just smiled to myself and nod as if I'd never heard of him and said nothing. Suffice to say, the Irgun and Stern did their utmost to get rid of him, even in this country – a bomb blew his house and brother sky high.

SCRATCHING THE SURFACE

*****

Rex Farran (26) was killed in May 1948 after opening a parcel addressed to Mr R Farran at the family home in Wolverhampton. The intended recipient Major Roy Farran was on holiday in Scotland; their heartbroken Father, Stephen Farran, would later reveal:

"I was there when my son died. My boy asked that there should be no revenge, and that is how we all feel."

A day after the attack, branded a "wicked outrage" by the home secretary, Chuter Ede - an anonymous phone call was made to the Banque de l'Union Parisienne offices in Paris. Described as being as chilling as it was remorseless, it revealed the identity of Rex's killers.

Claiming to be from the underground terror group, the Stern Gang, the caller dictated an official statement that the purpose of the incident had been twofold: "to punish Farran for the murder of a Jewish youth and a reply to the sending of British reinforcements to Palestine."

It also warned: "Farran will pay the price" and was signed: "The war against the British occupation – Stern Gang."

The parcel bomb was delivered around a year after the disappearance of 16-year-old Alexander Rubowitz in May 1947.

Witnesses saw him being bundled into a car by a man carrying a pistol. He was apprehended putting up posters celebrating, Fighters for the Freedom of Israel, more widely known as the Stern Gang.

Major Farran was accused of being involved in the disappearance and suspected murder of the youth but, when it came to trial, the case was dismissed. The Stern Gang, then threatened they would, "follow him to the end of the world".

Officers from Scotland Yard, headed up by Superintendent Tom Barrett, an expert on Jewish terrorism, searched the bomb-shattered family home. The investigation, which also discovered fragments of the remains of poignant lines from Shakespeare's plays Henry IV and Henry V, including references to rebels and rebellion, concluded the bomb was probably made in Paris and then posted on to London.

Barrett said: "We have a definite idea who we are after now, but ideas don't get your man".

The trail to the killers went cold and a jury later returned a verdict that Rex had been. "Feloniously killed by some person or persons unknown."

In a statement, the Wolverhampton Jewish Community said:

"We cannot, too strongly, disassociate ourselves from the acts of terrorists who have learned their methods in Hitler's Europe."

The murder remains unresolved - the crime file is still open.

(Information courtesy of Justin Halifax – Birmingham Live 7th October 2015)

Other service personnel faced additional ordeals dealing with illegal immigrants and the distressing business of boarding random crafts. Those on board were moving passengers from several boats onto one vessel before they reached Palestine's waters. The empty boats were saved for another trip.

Therefore, the packed crafts that went on to Haifa were carrying thousands of survivors from Europe.

The boarding parties were met with the unexpected task of herding frail women and children and grappling with angry men and women who, though under-nourished, had reserved some fight and a will to survive.

As the Policeman said:

"Hitler was out to destroy a People but succeeded in creating a Nation. No human being could have watched the struggling refugee in the arms of a soldier without feeling pity for the people who had suffered tortured lives and had bitterness of heart - only wanting a promised land."

Hagana forces sabotaged the launches of Navy patrols moored in ports on Cyprus. When arrested, they were placed with other human cargo and sent to displacement camps on the island. While in captivity, behind barbed wire, incarcerated Hagana forces taught refugees to fight.

By the time the War of Independence began in May 1948, they had trained 11,000 soldiers, who were immediately ready for the new Israel Defence Force. Around 650,000 personnel were trained in illegal armies in the run-up to Independence, a fifth were said to be illegal immigrants. This had a profound effect on the outcome of the war and the founding of the State of Israel. According to the Policeman:

"August brought back Arabs versus Jews and 4 Jews were killed in a cafe in Tel Aviv in a spate of Jews killing Arabs and Arabs killing Jews. Arab tribesmen made goodwill visits to the newly built Jewish colonies to encourage harmony; everyone was stretched to the limit. Bodies found strewn in alleyways were obviously killed by Arabs or oriental Jews

with a knife wound to the lower back into the kidneys or the lower part of the neck behind the collarbone".

At the end of August, conflict was evident in the border area between Jaffa and Tel Aviv. Some Jews had been brightened by the announcement that partition would probably happen, but the Arabs were totally against it. Others, on either side, at this stage, believed that the British would never leave and continued their own private guerrilla warfare against their own particular opposition.

During periods of martial law, the British were hoping to prove that they still had some control. The government tried to show they were still in a position of authority and were able to ruin economic life. Banks and schools were closed and telephone communications were cut off. The only haulage allowed on rail and road were those to transport food and other essentials. Newspaper reports and broadcasts from Pathe news in cinemas showed the miserable conditions at the hands of terrorist factions.

The general public at home was becoming more and more sickened by the violence endured by troops in Palestine. Military personnel, mainly on National Service, were dying daily while trying to maintain impossible policies. Lengthy debates were heard in Parliament, eventually resulting in the decision to bring the British out of Palestine and handing the future of Palestine to the United Nations, Britain announced in November 1947, that they would be gone by May 1948.

During the final months of the Mandate, there was no credible authority left on any side. Arab, Jew, and British soldiers, all lived every moment under a cloud of suspicion and mistrust for each other.

Reading on, I could not mistake the pity the Policeman had for the troops.

How difficult it must have been for them to shake off the things they had witnessed on the streets after the terrorist activity had destroyed their vehicles and their comrades.

"There was no palliative to outrage feelings, no policy; no right; no wrong; can wipe out the memories of a comrade's burnt body. No sedative. No excuse. We were seen as strangers in a hostile land."

The British were made welcome when they arrived in Palestine in 1917. They were greeted by applauding crowds in Jerusalem, full of optimism, and the population was grateful that Ottoman Rule was finished.

Few took the trouble to turn out as British Mandatory Rule ended quietly in May 1948. Evidence of this era gives a clear indication that the British had lost direction and shows an increasingly difficult end to 30 years. The mosaics of People left were disillusioned after broken promises from the governing body. Arabs and the Jews say they believed the land would be theirs when the British went home. An extremely vague overview would be to say that both parties believed they had earned a contract for the Holy Land after fighting beside the British. Later, however, they felt that the British had dealt with each situation on the day, without vision and their behaviour had been calculated.

Mandate Palestine was eventually handed over to the United Nations in February 1947 and the partition plan was announced in November 1947. Civil war erupted as the Arabs refused to accept the proposal for partition, at a time when British authorities were reducing the number of service personnel.

Mandate management had failed at a huge cost and decisions made at this time in history would have a resounding effect on the future of the Middle East. The British cannot be void of all blame for events that have happened since 1948, and consequently, the current situation.

The Soldiers posted abroad did their best under impossible circumstances, and accounts of their assistance to the public can only be praised as mentioned in reports and despatches written by proud officers. They carried out their duties in an honourable fashion against all odds.

The blood bath of the War of Independence or Nakba (catastrophe) was already underway before the British departed as the position of reduced occupation became untenable. The battle didn't commence as a peace-keeping force, 'left them to it', as old-fashioned teachers would have us believe. It was already ongoing, and I often contemplate the delay in bringing the British out of Palestine. Was it necessary to leave limited personnel to miserable challenges under a collapsing Empire?

SCRATCHING THE SURFACE

1. Parliamentary Question on preventative measures against terrorism, 7th May 1947. *Supplied by The National Archives London*

PALESTINE
Terrorism (Preventive Measures)

23 and 25. **General Sir George Jeffreys** asked the Secretary of State for the Colonies (1) whether, in view of the continuance of terrorist outrages in Palestine, more vigorous and sustained operations against terrorists will now be undertaken, including the placing and keeping under martial law of all Jewish towns and settlements;

(2) whether, in order to impress upon the Jewish population of Palestine the necessity for its full co-operation in the suppression of terrorism, collective fines will in future be levied and prominent citizens taken as hostages in localities in which outrages are perpetrated.

Mr. Creech Jones: The maintenance of good order in Palestine depends very largely on the co-operation of the people with the administration and the discharge of the normal requirements of citizenship. In present circumstances, the administration is obliged to carry a difficult and onerous responsibility. It is for the High Commissioner to consider, in consultation with the military authorities, and in the light of events, whether the situation calls for the introduction of military administration in any particular area. The authorities are tackling this problem of terrorism with the greatest resolution and with the most appropriate methods within the capacity of the available resources.

Collective fines have not, so far, been levied on any groups deemed collectively responsible for terrorism. As I mentioned in reply to a question on 30th April by the hon. Member for Orpington (Sir W. Smithers), the question of possible steps to recover the cost of damage done in terrorist outrages is now under consideration, and I cannot, at this stage, add to my reply of 30th April to the hon. Member for Orpington.

Sir G. Jeffreys: Is the right hon. Gentleman aware that these are two separate Questions, and that his answer gave very little information? Is the right hon. Gentleman further aware that the intermittent operation of martial law which has so far been exercised in Palestine, is far from being effective, that the strain on the troops is very serious indeed, and is being given expression to by the troops, and will the right hon. Gentleman go into this matter much more fully than he has done at present and give a free hand to the local commander to knock out terrorism?

Mr. Creech Jones: All I can say is that the High Commissioner is charged with the responsibility of order in Palestine; he is working in the fullest co-operation with the military authorities; there are no hindrances put in the way of either the High Commissioner or the military authorities by London, and so their decisions are made in the light of the local situation.

Mr. Oliver Stanley: Will the right hon. Gentleman tell the House whether any new action will be taken as a result of the incident at Acre gaol, which has brought British prestige very low?

Mr. Creech Jones: I shall be replying later to a Question concerning that outrage. I have caused very special inquiries to be made, and will be considering what further action can be taken.

Mr. Edelman: Will my right hon. Friend bear in mind that the system of hostages advocated by the hon. and gallant Member for Petersfield (Sir G. Jeffreys) was used without success by the Nazis during the war, and will he also bear in mind that vicarious punishment is completely foreign to the traditions of British justice?

Mr. Janner: When my right hon. Friend is considering these matters, will he please bear in mind that the towns and villages referred to played a very active part, with the Allies, in the course of the war, and will he see that the innocent in Palestine who are doing their share in attempting to stop terrorism will not be prejudiced by such measures as may be taken to put down the terrorists?

Mr. Creech Jones: Obviously, all these points will be taken into consideration, but I am not in a position to make a statement with regard to collective fines.

7 MAY 1947

2. Parliamentary Question on Acre gaol attack, May 1947.
Supplied by The National Archives London

TERRORIST ATTACK ON ACRE GAOL.

2.35 p.m.

VISCOUNT SWINTON: My Lords, I beg to ask His Majesty's Government the following question, of which I have given them private notice—namely, whether they have any statement to make on the terrorist attack on Acre Gaol in Palestine, and the escape of the prisoners.

THE FIRST LORD OF THE ADMIRALTY (VISCOUNT HALL): My Lords, at half past four in the afternoon of May 4, a party of armed Jews, some of whom were wearing British military uniforms, arrived in British military transport in the market place at Acre. Simultaneously with their arrival explosions occurred in the town and firing broke out in various localities. Four main explosions occurred in the vicinity of the old Turkish baths which abut on the prison and as a result one wall surrounding the exercise ground was breached. This attack took place at the time when the prisoners were at exercise and numbers of Arab and Jewish prisoners escaped through the breach in the wall. At the same time grenades were thrown by the attackers into the criminal lunatic section of the prison, wounding several inmates, and automatic small arms' fire was directed at the prison from various points.

The attackers were engaged by police and troops both in Acre town itself and in the vicinity. Immediately after the attack military and police patrols were organized, and one of these, a party of paratroops, having been fired on by a number of Jews, returned fire and inflicted five casualties, one of which was fatal. This was a Jew dressed as a Captain in the Royal Engineers. Troops also intercepted two vehicles carrying Jews north of the town. After a brief engagement twelve Jews were captured, two of whom were dead and three wounded. One of the dead Jews was dressed in the uniform of a Captain in the Royal Army Service Corps. Another dead Jew dressed in British military uniform was found in an Army truck abandoned on the outskirts of the city.

After the attack, roads in the vicinity of Acre town were found to be mined. Six soldiers travelling in a military truck were wounded by one of these mines. Other casualties during the attack on police and prison personnel were limited to one officer slightly injured and a British constable seriously wounded in the leg. In the action immediately following the attack, fourteen Jewish prisoners were recaptured, of whom four were dead and six injured. Of the Arab prisoners, twelve were recaptured, of whom one was killed and two injured. Extensive operations have continued for the recapture of the escaped prisoners and further details are still coming in. My latest report on May 6 stated that twenty-nine Jews and 214 Arabs were still at liberty. The fullest investigations into the circumstances of this occurrence are being made.

VISCOUNT SWINTON: My Lords, I am obliged to the noble Viscount for that full statement. Arising out of it, may I ask him two further questions? First of all, of the twenty-nine Jews who are still at liberty, could he say how many of them are convicted terrorists who were in the prison? Secondly, as it is obvious that the object of this unfortunately successful attack was to release terrorists who had been sentenced to long terms of imprisonment and who were incarcerated in Acre prison would it not be a much wiser policy that terrorists who are convicted should be incarcerated in some part of the British territory outside Palestine, instead of being kept in a prison on which it is almost certain that terrorist gangs will make an attack?

VISCOUNT HALL: My Lords, in reply to the first question put by the noble Viscount, twenty-one of the twenty-nine prisoners referred to were members of the Irgun Zvai Leumi. Of those twenty-one, sixteen were serving sentences of fifteen years for carrying and discharging firearms, imposed in April, 1946, following an attack on the railway. Eight of the twenty-nine were members of the Stern Group. Of those eight, five were serving

SCRATCHING THE SURFACE

3. Parliamentary Question on Acre gaol attack, May 1947.
Supplied by The National Archives London

[Viscount Hall.]
life sentences imposed in June for carrying and discharging firearms. With regard to the second question, it is true to say that certain of the terrorists have been incarcerated in Eritrea, but—as is well known—difficulties have arisen in connexion with that territory. Some of the prisoners have been transferred to Kenya. The difficulty is to get territories to which one can send the terrorists. An attempt is being made to deal with this matter. It is being considered.

VISCOUNT SWINTON: I am much obliged to the noble Viscount, but surely, though there may be difficulties, those are difficulties which we have often encountered before, and overcome. We have, for instance, put many persons of different kinds in the Seychelles. After all, the lives of British troops are at stake. Here we have a reinforcement of some of the most dangerous of these terrorist gangs; those people have now escaped and have gone back to reinforce the terrorists. Surely this is a much more important and urgent matter than the difficulty of finding somewhere within the wide confines of the British Commonwealth to place those people? May I venture to remind the Government that during the war, when we expected invasion, we found no difficulty in sending the most dangerous Nazi prisoners outside this country, and it was a very good thing that we did so.

VISCOUNT HALL: One could deal with problems of this kind very much more easily during the period of the war than one can now. It would be almost impossible to put any number of these terrorists on a small island like the Seychelles.

LORD HARLECH: Why?

VISCOUNT HALL: There is the question of defence and, indeed, the question of protecting the remainder of the population. The noble Viscount can be assured that this matter has been and still is being considered.

LORD HARLECH: Might I ask this question following on the noble Viscount's reply? Having been at the Colonial Office, and having sent dangerous people to the Seychelles and St. Helena, I should have thought it would be legally possible and much better, to send dangerous terrorists of this kind to some place where they can be approached from outside only by the sea.

VISCOUNT SWINTON: Yes.

LORD HARLECH: The Irgun Zvai Leumi and the Stern Gang have not got ships; and ships would be detected from those places. As those terrorists are absolute desperadoes and fanatical people, the only hope is to get them far away from places where their co-fanatics can repeat the Acre incident, whether in Kenya, Eritrea or elsewhere. There are the West Indian islands. After all, we are entitled to remove them to anywhere within the British Commonwealth, and I hope that this matter will be seriously considered.

THE EARL OF CORK AND ORRERY: My Lords, in the answer given to the noble Viscount, the Acting Leader of the Opposition, by the noble Viscount on behalf of His Majesty's Government, it was stated that immediately after the explosions patrols of the military and police were formed to search the surrounding areas. But, with a prison situated as this one was, full of hostile prisoners, where it was of the greatest importance to the terrorists that those prisoners should get out, was there no system of patrol in existence beforehand? It would appear almost incredible that preparations for their escape could have been made if military and police patrols had been searching the area. I should like to ask the noble Viscount whether he can assure the House that the military authorities have not been prevented from taking the precautions they would have liked because of any question of appeasement of the population, or any nonsense of that sort.

VISCOUNT HALL: I can assure the noble Earl that there is no interference at all with the military authorities. The military authorities and the civil authorities have been working in the closest co-operation on this matter.

4. Parliamentary Question on terrorist convictions, 12th May 1947
Supplied by The National Archives London

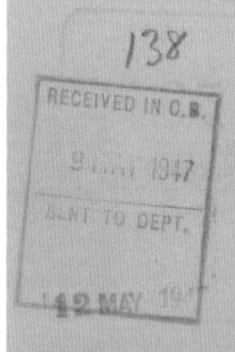

24. **Sir G. Jeffreys** asked the Secretary of State for the Colonies how many convictions of terrorism have been recorded in Palestine in the 12 months ended 30th April, 1947; how many death sentences have been passed; and in how many cases the death sentence has been carried out.

Mr. Creech Jones: Ninety-seven Jewish terrorists were sentenced by military courts to terms of imprisonment, and 28 to sentences of death. There were no convictions by civil courts. Of the Jewish terrorists sentenced to death, two committed suicide while awaiting execution, and four were executed.

Sir G. Jeffreys: Was not this leniency very misplaced, and cannot the persistence of outrage and murder be attributed, to some extent, to the leniency with which offenders and murderers have been dealt?

Mr. Creech Jones: That is a matter of opinion.

Mr. Stanley: Could the right hon. Gentleman say how many of the 97 terrorists sentenced to imprisonment have since escaped?

Mr. Creech Jones: I am not in a position to say, but I am trying to get that information.

Mr. S. Silverman: Does not my right hon. Friend agree that all these lamentable events will never be fully eradicated, and law and order will never be restored in Palestine until His Majesty's Government announce and introduce a constructive political policy, and that it is impossible for the Government to impose order merely by force without any policy of any kind?

Chapter 7

The 6-Day-War

This chapter goes off the beaten path, in a more academic fashion than I would usually write, for events in the Middle East in 1967 must be addressed. The 6-Day-War is paramount to understanding the history of Israel; it has an important connection to the issues of today. Ever conscious that this chapter is more pro-Israel, academic, and removed from my particular journey, it is an important building block to understanding the situation.

I am not qualified to say whether there is such a thing as a just war within religious teaching, though the government of Israel has been accused of using ancient biblical concepts in response to divine command regarding the land.

Though there is said to be no concept of a 'just war' and although war is preferably avoided, there are times when it is said to be necessary to fight. In Jewish Religious Law, wars are either obligatory or optional.

In ancient times obligatory wars were undertaken in response to a divine command, as when God commanded Joshua, after the death of Moses, to lead the Israelites across the river Jordan into the Promised Land:

An optional war is embarked upon when diplomacy fails - a principle that has held fast since approval was required by the Sanhedrin in Roman times.

While some commentators may suggest that the Israeli Government may use these ancient concepts as a pretext for an attack on her neighbours, it is the continuity of such traditions that has ensured the survival of the Jewish people in the face of fearful adversity for almost 6000 years. Nevertheless, unfounded contentment in assimilation, throughout Diaspora, has often found them on the back foot.

To the Israelis, the fighting which accompanied and followed the creation of the Jewish State in 1948 was a continuation of that struggle. As the British moved out, following the United Nations' acceptance of partition, Arab armies crossed the borders of the new State from every direction to 'push the Jews into the sea. Despite the many problems of new Israelis speaking different languages, with little technology and few weapons, Israel managed to defend herself successfully. It was a do-or-die situation a short time after the end of World War II.

The underground armies who had prepared for Arab attack, as quietly as possible under British Rule, had revived the Hebrew language and saved the newly founded nation with little support from the rest of the world. This unorthodox fight for survival, which on reflection looks somewhat uncontrolled in many areas, meant a catastrophe for the fleeing Arab population and marked a prominent era resulting in decades of conflict between the new State of Israel and her neighbours.

SCRATCHING THE SURFACE

Whilst the Palestinians who fled for safety believed they would return to their homes after the war of 1948/9, the truce, persuaded by international intervention, left what was defined as Israel's natural defensive borders. These lines varied from the original plans intended by the United Nations partition. This new map remained and the Arabs who had fled in 1948, on what they believed to be a temporary basis were left beyond Israel's revised borders. Broadly speaking, dispersed in refugee camps or started new lives in the surrounding areas of the Middle East. Some had stayed and held their ground, but complex issues created at the creation of the State have been ongoing ever since.

Less than 25 years later, on 5th June 1967, the security of these borders was to be tested by what has now become known as the 6-Day-War. While for Israel this was a conflict seen as justified on the grounds of self-defence, and another chapter in the Jewish struggle for survival, to the Arabs it was a war of aggression provoked by an expansionist Israel.

From the Israeli standpoint, the war was the outcome of the escalating harassment on her borders. Skirmishes were nothing new, but in early 1967, the Syrian bombardment of the Golan Heights and Galilean villages had already provoked some Israeli retaliation.

Israeli farmers were working in armoured tractors with permanent artillery guards in case snipers in Syria's elevated strong holds shot at them in the fields. Civilians had begun to spend a considerable part of their day in air raid shelters as border clashes became more ferocious in early May. The early exchange of artillery fire resulted in both sides resorting to aerial attacks well before June 1967, and both Israeli and Syrian planes had been lost.

On 16th May, when Israel had paraded through Jerusalem on Independence Day, the Egyptians deduced that the lack of military hardware on show meant that troops were deployed elsewhere in readiness for invasion.

Almost immediately, Egyptian forces moved into the Sinai desert in the south, threw out the peacekeeping United Nations force, and by the 22nd of May had closed the Straits of Tiran to Israeli shipping. Israeli intelligence reported that Jordan and Saudi Arabia were also moving troops toward Israel's borders.

By this time, Egypt's President Nasser had come to see himself as the leader of an Arab coalition, intending to rid the Middle East of the Jews and their British allies. This was just the start of his long-term ambitions to further his Pan-Arab objectives. His only ally in the west was Russia whom he saw as a contributor to furthering the Arab cause, by supplying both arms and support. In a speech following the closure of the Straits of Tiran on 29th May, he told National Assembly members:

"We do not fight Israel in this situation; we confront Israel and the West. Those, who created Israel and back Israel, which ignore us as Arabs, before and since 1948. Brothers, the revolt, upheaval, and commotion which we now see taking place in every Arab country is not only because we have returned to the Gulf of Aqaba or rid ourselves of the UNEF(United Nations Emergency Force), but because we have restored Arab honour and renewed Arab hopes."

He emphasised to his audience that Israel had boasted of its continued support from Britain and the United States and warned:

"They have confined the issue to the Straits of Tiran, to UNEF, and the rights of passage, but we demand the rights of the Palestinian people. If the West is partial to Israel, then we must recognise friend from foe and knowing our foes, treat them accordingly and without fear".

He expressed his confidence in Russian support, referring to her as a friend who had stood by them:

"They have sent us wheat, arms, and now a message from the Soviet Premier Kosygin that he would intervene to help the Arabs restore their pre-Suez crisis status".

Nasser maintained that his main aim was world peace and he referred to colonialism in Aden with the words,

"Brothers, we have not forgotten you, present matters have taken our minds from Aden."

To Israel, he confirmed that:

"Whoever starts with Syria finishes with Egypt."

Aggression was opportune for Nasser, whose leadership in the Arab world had been flagging, and whose social revolution at home had failed. A defence of his Arab brothers faced with a supposed Israeli invasion was one way of restoring his fortunes, and swept along by the emotional support for his tactics, he broadcasted a further message on Cairo radio. His main aim was to 'purify the land' by ridding it of its Jewish population. He declared fearful propaganda to Israel and her world followers that the Arab people wanted to fight and were calling for the total destruction of the State of Israel.

In hindsight, it seems unlikely that either side wanted these hostilities to develop into a full-scale war. Neither side was fully prepared and desperate for a lead from the United States or the United Nations. As time went on, this seemed increasingly unlikely as the world watched and waited.

America was bogged down with her troubles in Vietnam and the United Nations who had left Sinai and Gaza without protest had no stomach for direct involvement; Despite Nasser's earlier beliefs, neither had the Soviet Union. They had backed the Arab cause in diplomacy and propaganda but failed to provide Nasser with military support.

Meantime, in Israeli eyes, the Arab threat was intensified by Jordan's support for Nasser. For King Hussein, the choice was between isolation, should Nasser emerge supreme, and focusing on the continuity of the Hashemite kingdom. In desperation, he linked his fortunes with Egypt as the Egyptian and Iraqi armies shared their own agendas in Jordan. On 30th May the King flew to Cairo for a 3-hour meeting with President Nasser. After which, he signed a joint defence agreement allowing an Egyptian General to become commander of the Jordanian forces.

Throughout May 1967, the Israeli government debated its response as fear of war mingled with anticipation. Local parks in the Tel Aviv area were designated to accommodate 10,000 bodies and hotels were emptied of guests in case they should be needed as first aid stations.

Israel's government wavered and Prime Minister Levi Eshkol continued to hope for peace by negotiation. Debates continued in the Knesset (Israel's Parliament). Some thought a pre-emptive attack would be the best thing to do, while others thought such an action would be putting the country into mortal jeopardy. Mobilising the army may encourage the wrath of a coalition of Arab states. Considering and faced with heavy odds held on again in the hope of direction and foreign support.

The Arab states were almost equally uncertain of the next move. For the Arabs, the very founding of the State of Israel had been an act of aggression enforced by world sanctions. This bitter pill, together with the fact that since 1948, thousands of Palestinians had been wandering in their own miserable Diaspora, kept the harsh reality of past conflict simmering very close to the surface.

Nonetheless, there was no accord throughout the Arab States that the time had come to strike a fatal blow and it was the Israeli Government that brought matters to a head. Ignoring Ben-Gurion's warning and fearing Arab attack; the Israeli government eventually opted for a pre-emptive strike on 5th June.

It took just 3 hours of Israeli bombardment of her neighbours' airfields to decide the outcome of the war. Arab air power was decimated and the army, knowing that the future of the State was now in its hands, went to complete the ground offensive. The miracle of the ground offensive was that 3 Israeli brigades were able to overcome 6 Arab Legions in just 10 hours and destroy the 7th on the following day.

A war of defence then became a war of expansion. Moshe Dayan decided on the 4th day, to follow the defeat of the Egyptians in Sinai and on the West Bank with an attack on the Golan Heights. Such a decision was in line with Rabin's overall plan.

Within 6 days Israel had captured the entire Sinai peninsula, the Gaza strip, Judea and Samaria, and the Golan Heights, with a loss of 777 soldiers, far fewer than anticipated, but a heavy blow for a tight-knit community of 3 million. On this occasion, however, unlike her decision in 1956 following the Suez Crisis, she did not withdraw to the 1949 borders drawn up after the War of Independence. Promises of international intervention had proved meaningless in the past and were unlikely to prove feasible in the future. Secure boundaries were seen as necessary, not only to safeguard civilians from the terrorist attacks they had endured in the years since independence but, to ensure Israel's very survival.

To the Arabs who now moved out of the conquered territories in panic and fear of the new regime, it would appear to them that the true Jewish intention was to take back, piece by piece, the land that is a Biblical Greater Israel.

The unification of Jerusalem would always be a major bone of contention and while Moshe Dayan spoke of unifying the City of Jerusalem with peaceful respect for all religious groups, the Muslims who remained anticipated both a menacing military presence and an uncompromising, Israeli occupation.

Whatever the political, ethical, or strategic realities in Israel itself, the war was seen throughout the Jewish world as one of defence and survival. The new boundaries were generally accepted as the only assurance of Israel's continuance; the war itself was a response to a threat of extinction. The victory over hostile invaders had been the creator of safe boundaries, so great that it would have a long-term impact on the identity of Jews throughout the world.

Chapter 8

The Manchester connection

"I have crossed Europe seeking the history of my people and all the way I have met with stories of death. Here in Manchester, I have found friends and a more settled history."

An Israeli visitor I spoke to at Manchester Jewish Museum in 2002.

In June 1967, as a 6-year-old child living in North Manchester, I was not privy to the activities of the Jewish community some 5 miles away. As far as I knew, my family had little contact with this area of the city.

I recall one day when my Mother commented on our neighbour; a young Jewish woman who had married a Catholic man. She believed it very unfair that only one of her 7 siblings ever visited to see how she was doing in early married life. In a close-knit family, she had no concept of brothers and sisters disowning each other because of their choice of husband.

"The Jews usually keep themselves to themselves," she said, "but they don't ask for anything, they normally look after their own."

My connection to the Jewish way of things was non-existent. Even though, I was lectured daily, in my Church of England primary school, about the life and teachings of the most famous Rabbi of them all. Odd that it was some years later that I found out Jesus Christ was Jewish. Either, I hadn't been listening properly or the vicar who taught us had managed to gloss over that fact.

In the first week of June 1967, England was getting back on its feet some, 20 years, after World War II ended. The youth of the day were dancing to the Monkees, America's equivalent of the Beatles, who were number one in the hit parade. Those less inclined to jig, sat at home watching Z Cars or Voyage to the Bottom of the Sea. Children were playing football in the street, reliving England's victory over Germany in the World Cup Final, the previous year.

The free-spirited were preaching a philosophy of peace and acceptance of alternative cultures. The countryside was scattered with flowers, thrown from the baskets of hot air balloons. Britain was experiencing spectacular progress in science by launching the QE2, debating the future of the hovercraft, and producing Concorde.

I have vague, childhood memories of 1967 when I wore my yellow Whitsuntide outfit, purchased from a Manchester warehouse just off Oldham Street. My Great Aunt Sarah-Anne gave me a shilling to place in my matching PVC handbag. My best friend, Elizabeth, was going through a jeans phase and had chosen something a little less Mary Quant.

3 miles down the road, but a world apart, the lives of the Jewish community were suddenly disrupted. News of the impending war between Israel and a massive Arab league led by Egypt's Nasser reached Manchester. Many of those already involved in the Zionist movement and sympathetic to its cause: "Saw it coming," according to Sir Sidney Hamburger, who in June 1967 was a leader in the Zionist Community.

Others, after 20 years of the State's existence, had come to take it for granted as a permanent refuge that could be relied upon to reinforce identity and an escape route from anti-Semitism. Some, proud of Israel's creation and survival, derived more confidence from its existence than they were perhaps aware. It had become a homeland for the Jewish People after the trauma of the Holocaust, but, only a small proportion of those who lived in Manchester considered moving there permanently.

The organised Zionist movements in Manchester coordinated by the Zionist Central Council (ZCC) were in no doubt about the centrality of Israel to the Jewish People in Diaspora. It was more than a place of safety in a potentially anti-Semitic world. It was a source of Jewish pride and dignity; a symbol of Jewish determination to rise above the imagery of atrocities so marked in previous decades. Zionist organisations were well aware of Israel's vulnerability and had been seeking to persuade the community of Manchester that it was obliged to, at least, offer moral and financial support.

When Sidney Hamburger, a life-long Zionist became chairman of the ZCC in 1963, he saw it as an opportunity to promote Zionist feeling and to coordinate the forces of many affiliates. He recognised that if optimum support for the State of Israel was to be achieved, the only option was strict neutrality within the concentric circles that rippled out from hard-core Orthodoxy to the less observant. Only united action, he believed, would provide the funds necessary to support Israel's internal needs and oversee their defence.

"Israel", he told the community, "was occupied with a huge and expensive task of housing, providing services and educating immigrants, while needing to be ever prepared for hostile Arab attacks and blockades. Israel required moral support and favourable propaganda from communities like Manchester and throughout the Jewish world. The Zionist community had to be at the centre of fundraising initiatives."

Earlier, in 1963, a new group, Achdut (Unity), had been formed. Members were encouraged to knock on doors and to rekindle enthusiasm for fundraising. Their mission, in the United Kingdom, was to have a better understanding of Israel and to fashion a spirit of solidarity for Israel's cause.

This general Zionist renaissance began to boost funds as more of the community started to feel a sense of duty towards Israel. Much of this resurgence was against a background of an unashamed Arab threat. Egypt's Nasser had been escalating hostility long before he eventually closed the Straits of Tiran to Israel's shipping on 22nd May 1967.

Manchester Jewry was gradually being alerted to the build-up towards war, and as a gentleman from a Synagogue in South Manchester told me:

"Oh yes, I can tell you that by the time the 6-Day-War came along, the Reform community had also, for a long time, been much more supportive and become more overtly Zionist in its outlook."

On 23rd May, the Manchester Evening News brought home the total urgency of the situation when their article reported: "Egypt claims that Russia is behind Nasser in the closure of the Straits of Tiran. World leaders call on Israel to exercise restraint".

Jewish fear was increased by Arab threats from various rostrums, claiming that the Middle East would be purified. The family links that now existed between Israel and Manchester brought home the severity of the situation. In the words of the then Achdut chairman Norman Feingold:

"We said right now; this is personal! This is family!"

On the 23rd of May, the ZCC launched the Joint Palestine Appeal (JPA) emergency fund with a target of £1 million. Posters around the city pleaded with the community to identify and claim ownership of Israel; asking for all-out support.

An article in the Jewish Telegraph on 2nd June, just days before the official outbreak of the war, reported on the amount already collected. Manchester Jewry had raised £82,000; compared to London's larger community's £1,850,000. The Chairman of the Manchester branch of the Joint Palestine Appeal, J M Hyman, in the same article; urged people to: 'give until it hurts'. The leaflet, whose printing was aided by the Jewish Telegraph, pleaded: THE NEWS IS GRAVE! Identify yourself with Israel – NOW! If you have given – GIVE MORE! If you have not given – GIVE NOW! This is the least you can do!

The community rose to the challenge with exceptional generosity and an unusual show of unity. religious and political rifts were healed in the interest of pulling together between the right and left. Rarity saw the most religiously liberal sitting alongside the Ultra-Orthodox to work for a single goal.

Weddings and Bar Mitzvahs were postponed and the money intended for celebrations was donated to the JPA. The Jewish Ladies Guild adopted the motto 'Every Little Helps', as members worked tirelessly to arrange coffee mornings, baked cakes, and sold crafts on stalls labelled, Little Israel. They encouraged benefit concerts and collections in local schools, while revenue intended for local development was diverted to funds for Israel. Some organisations emptied bank accounts and gave the money to the appeal, as their committees agreed to save again in better times.

Norman Feingold, a legendary fundraiser in Manchester, told me how he used all his force and character to persuade the well-to-do to part with their money.

"I took the 'Biggy Givers' into a room and spoke to them privately. If they'd been giving £500 to the new State before, it was time to give £2,000 or £3,000 for its survival."

Norman told of the consciousness of fringe members who to a great extent, had previously shaken off their Zionist responsibilities, but now returned to help.

"They came out of the woodwork and queued to give. People who had forgotten they were Jews came along with family treasures. The Jewish people are on a big piece of elastic and when there's a crisis, it doesn't matter how far you've stretched it – one tug and you're right back in the middle."

On the evening of 5th June 1967, various newspaper headlines notified the world that Israel was in 'All out War'. Fear was amplified when fake news reports followed, alleging that the Syrian Air Force had bombed the city of Haifa's oil refinery, saying they had overwhelmed Israel. Egypt claimed that they had destroyed the Israeli Air Force. Faisal of Saudi Arabia was quoted on BBC radio as saying: *"My country and its people stand by our Arab Brothers."*

In 1967, there wasn't the up-to-the-minute media coverage we have today, and it took a few days until a reliable update was received. Based on the erratic reports and with defeat likely, the immediate mood among the Jewish People of Manchester was pessimistic.

On the morning of the 5th of June when Sidney Hamburger returned from the synagogue, his wife greeted him with the news:

"The war's begun." He told me. *"I was absolutely, distraught because we were completely isolated. I didn't think honestly, that we stood a cat in hell's chance of winning. There were no escape routes, don't forget, so we had the option of fighting or drowning."*

Israel faced the possibility of extinction. The warnings given by the Arab League, to purify the Middle East of Jewish blood and finish the job that Hitler had started triggered feelings of despondency. The new State nurtured with pride, taken for granted for almost 2 decades, lay central to Jewish identity but faced annihilation by a crushing force. The sense of determination to back Israel's defence that had been growing in the days before the war, now reached a crescendo as panic reigned.

Bet Habonim became the epicentre of the biggest public appeal ever seen within the Jewish community of Manchester. It was an appeal for volunteers as much as funds. Civilians had volunteered to go and cover posts on kibbutzim, in factories, hospitals and schools, to free reservists for the field.

Amazingly, after a few days and against all odds, a rapid turnaround came out of the blue, as news broke through from the Middle East. Fear of defeat rapidly gave way to hope of victory.

On the evening of 7th June, the Manchester Guardian reported that Israel's infantry was gaining ground against Egypt and pushing back their allies in the Sinai desert and the West Bank. On the same day the Manchester Evening News reported the taking of Jerusalem in a dramatic account:

"They encircled the city and waited a while to allow the hopelessness of the Arab situation to sink in. The troops marched in through walls built by Suleiman the Magnificent in the 16th Century and jubilation swept through the country as the news came back that the troops were once again standing by the Western Wall. It's only a matter of time now until they claim Hebron and Bethlehem.

A Manchester man told of his relief as he sat by his wife's bedside with a radio to his ear, as she gave birth to their son. He had been waiting for news that the paratroopers had reached the Western Wall, a poignant day in history for him and the future of Israel as the Jordanian foothold, left in place since 1949, seemed to have been displaced.

It was some time before Manchester Jewry was able to persuade itself that Israel had survived. Sir Sidney Hamburger told me:

"We didn't know what to believe, we just hoped the propaganda was true this time. Fortunately, we didn't have to wait more than a few days before the truth started coming

through and news of the victory triggered a fresh surge of fundraising."

Sir Sidney took his appointment diary from the shelf and showed me the entries for the 7th of June 1967. It read:

11 a.m. JIA meeting
12.30 p.m. An emergency meeting; talking to students.
8 p.m. A meeting in Southport
10 p.m. A fundraising appeal in Whitefield

The Manchester Evening News told how a young Catholic nurse had walked into the Manchester Reform Synagogue and requested immediate transit to Israel.

At Heathrow airport, 400 volunteers, from all faiths, were gathered awaiting British Overseas Airways Corporation (BAOC), to designate more of their new VC10s for the journey, They held certificates, provided by local doctors, stating they were fit to go. Medical and pharmaceutical supplies, that had been donated and stored at the Co-operative Insurance Building, were loaded onto the aircraft.

In conversation with the late Sir Sidney Hamburger, honoured by his hospitality and the kindness of his Manchester office team, I asked him who should get a mention if we noted anyone's contribution in Israel's hour of need.

He replied unassumingly and unselfishly,

"Oh, Norman; definitely Norman."

He was referring to Norman Feingold, a founder member of Achdut in 1963. Norman believed that other groups working in support of the State of Israel were not forceful enough. He felt the amounts raised by other Israel charities were far from adequate.

Then, a man in his early thirties, Norman was largely responsible for funds raised during the 6-Day-War and was, in his own words, during my interview with him at Manchester University in February 2000, a player.

"I was a Zionist player in Manchester, rather than a member of the audience. I'll boast. Manchester Jewry was a reservoir of aid and resource for Israel and the people today still marvel at how their cup runneth over with the love for their people."

Norman explained the methods his collectors used:

"When collecting from door to door, we looked for a Mezuzah (parchment scroll in a decorative case) on the door post. If the Jews had moved out, I never left without asking for a contribution to the State of Israel. We were seldom turned away."

The true historical significance of the support, financial, moral and voluntary, given to Israel before and during the 6-Day-War was to suggest solidarity in a normally diverse Jewish Community.

The threat to Jewish identity appeared once again, and divisions in party politics and religious observance are said to have been closed. While this may have been a temporary thing in the interests of a common good, it suggests that once the external threat is apparent, divisions are bridged by a spirit for continuity.

Zionist campaigners were quick to point out to me, that this marked the changing image of Israel. She would no longer be a fragile nation, just going through the motions in the shadows of the Holocaust. The victory showed the beginnings of a minor improved power requiring effective and sustained propaganda. In the years to come, world forces, especially those promoting the cause of the Palestinian People, would brand Israel as an aggressor.

The impact of the war on Manchester's internal community was both deep and permanent. It led immediately to a new level of pride in being Jewish, which almost reversed the defensive postures of Anglo-Jewry in earlier years. Since the mid-19th century, it had been the strategy of communal leaders to keep a low profile when anti-Semitism emerged in societies where they lived. Their acceptance was seen to depend on an image of Englishness, patriotism, civic pride and respect for the law. This could be described as survival by camouflage; retaining a Jewish and religious identity, but in other ways culturally dressing for the part expected of them by the mainstream.

Jewish leaders within Anglo-Jewry had hitherto been mindful of the consequences of being seen to place the creation of a Jewish State above their loyalty to Britain. They were ever conscious of the old image of Jews playing into the entrenched stereotype; of Jews as outsiders, conspirators, and potential traitors to the realm.

Many immigrants of the early 20th century were favourably inclined to Zionism, but were blighted by conditional Anglicisation by those who were respected leaders and businessmen.

Norman Feingold described the spirit of Eastern European generations, whom he was proud to follow:

"Every Friday night, many of our Grandmothers, as they lit the Sabbath candles, put a penny in a cup, and it was only a little cup for they had no wealth. Or a little tin box holding what would belong to the future state of Israel. It was for the Yishuv - they were called the Yishuv, the settlement of the Jews in the land of Israel before the declaration of the State.

Within a generation of being in England, however, they were persuaded into opting for a degree of assimilation.

One improvement to exemplify the rise in self-regard was the universal wearing of the Yarmulke (scull-cap-Yiddish) by young men; the reverse of earlier low-profile attitudes. According to Norman Feingold:

"They used to wear a hat as a less conspicuous head covering, but now they walked tall with pride and with a kippah (scull-cap–Hebrew) on their heads. It toughened us and unified us; the effect was wonderful. It was a very exciting time for Jewish identity."

Sir Sidney Hamburger, representing the Orthodox community explained that they saw the war as bringing about renewed religious commitment. Sir Sidney believed that attitudes of integration and assimilation in earlier years had run the risk of eroding Jewish belief and practice. He believed that the victory of 1967 was the work of God, working in the opposite direction and intensified Jewish observance.

He told me:

"Our parents and grandparents had emigrated from the Continent and come to live in this country because of the cultural and religious freedom that they had. The danger was that we were turning our back on our religion and our history and things like that. I always remember something we used to say and that was that our parents were turning us into 'English gentlemen of the Jewish faith' and the trouble was that we were often forgetting the latter part of that aim and objective.

I certainly think that we had captured our pride in our nationhood. You see we'd always said that Jews couldn't fight; Jews couldn't become miners or couldn't become engineers. We'd heard this all the time in the 1920s and the 1930s, that we were the businessmen. We were the financiers or whatever. When the wars came in 48 and 67 and we proved that, for our very life, we had to become fighters, well killers; there was a different sort of side to the picture of the Jews.

Yes- there was a very great belief in the hand of God in the 1967 victory. I know the secularists say, 'Oh what a lot of bloody nonsense', you know – it was the army, it was the air force, it was the planning of the paratroopers. I take none of that away from them, but to have been able to withstand the attack of the united Arab world, with the minimal number of casualties - although, we did suffer the loss of hundreds of lives. The very fact that we weren't exterminated made many people feel that God had been there working on behalf of the Jewish people."

My Jewish friends differ in their religious observation, prosperity and the journeys their families have made over the last 2 centuries. However, I believe new generations are more confident about choosing their religious direction. In the 21st century, there is still an undertow of difference that requires increased security to protect those who are met with anti-Semitism. The world, the Middle East and Europe are all constantly changing and this has a bearing on the security and perspectives of Manchester Jewry. Some have only a far-flung association with the State of Israel, but wherever their loyalties rest, the ill-informed often conveniently decide they are all representatives of Zionism.

The other transformation that followed was the image of Israel. Perceptions of the Jewish State as a vulnerable fledgling requiring protection and sustenance had already been dented by the events surrounding the Suez Crisis of 1956, but after 1967 they became untenable. Israel had now defended herself by military victory; she had acquired territories and here, began the occupation.

She had made enemies, not only of the Arabs who were defeated and dispossessed, but of those nations who sought to consolidate a Middle Eastern presence by supporting the Arab cause. The Arabs had powerful allies for another reason; oil. Whatever Israel's gain, the Arab states continued to control the supply of oil to the West. However much Britain, for example, continued its support for Israel, there were politicians, both in and out of the government, who saw the need at least to placate the Arab world.

There was pressure from the West in June 1967 for Israel to retreat from her new colonies. Meantime, the far left of British politics soon emerged as a platform for those who now saw Israel as an aggressor; an imperial power, and as exercising colonial rule over the beleaguered Palestinians.

In British Universities, including the University of Manchester, anti-Israel propaganda gradually emerged from both Arab student groups and student left-wing formations, with the 2 occasionally acting together. Non-Jewish opinion gradually changed, moving away from being sympathetic to Israel's cause during the war. Over the years since, attitudes towards Israel have become more diverse and, occasionally, hostile.

Zionism in Manchester was forced into a defensive stance. While continuing material support for Israel it was now necessary to mount counter-propaganda to portray the State as a civilised nation still surrounded by enemies bent on her destruction. Israel had extended her boundaries, but the counter-argument needed to portray the State defensible, and not one intending to create a Greater Israel through expansionism.

Anti-Zionist propaganda from Israel's enemies, neutral intellectuals, or politicians, will always demand a reply. New generations had to follow Zionist leaders who had stirred unique solidarity and raised funds during the war and many organisations work tirelessly to do similar work today.

Manchester remains a city with proud Zionist representation with a curious mix of Jewish People, plagued by new forms of anti-Semitism that this continually changing world brings with each decade. While differing opinions may cause divisions, the legacy of confidence born of events in a week in June 1967, lives on.

Chapter 9

Museums

The museums have been great seats of learning for me over the years and I have always been welcomed in them since my first week in Israel in 1993. It was a Sunday morning, when I had come across the Israeli Colonel having coffee in the lounge of my hotel. He had just returned from Whitehall London and was staying there for a few weeks while working on a training programme at a nearby barracks.

Having taken the opportunity to absorb as much as I could get out of him, he let me know that he knew of a group of soldiers who were going to the Jabotinsky Institute, round the corner on King George Street that very morning. He suggested I go as they would be happy to let me join the tour.

I was hesitant, but Shai encouraged me to go and even said he'd ensure my son Colin, who was watching Star Trek, would be ok. Colin didn't want to go when I asked him, but the Colonel told me to:

"Leave the baby alone mummy! We'll feed him if he's hungry!"

Telling Colin I wouldn't be more than an hour, I nervously, took the five minute walk to King George Street.

My Dad had said, "If there's any trouble – stick with the Jews – they'll look after you." I thought about this as I approached 20 or more in khaki who were sitting on the steps of the institute, eating pastries and chocolate. They were not young recruits and I didn't have clue what was going on. Hardly camouflaged in a pale green summer dress, they parted for me to ascend the steps. I must have looked totally lost.

"You ok?" came the sound of an Israeli with an American accent.

I confessed that I had been told by another soldier that I might take a guided tour with them. "Sure!" he said. "Come on in!"

I was taken to a lady who greeted me and found a translator to accompany me as the guide would be speaking in Hebrew. The gentleman helped me to understand what was being said and there were cards written in English by any props that were used. The soldiers listened and I tagged on behind like a spare part.

Practices being taught in Israel today had long-since been established under Mandatory Rule. Films on how to search people, showed the tricks the Irgun had used in trying to get past checkpoints and could be used by the Palestinians today.

I saw hardback books with enough of the middle cut out in order to hide a hand-gun and learned how to check for wires on the body.

We were shown how the Irgun had put dynamite in fake milestones and how to keep an eye on the road surface ahead for unconventional improvised devices that might be just visible or have a trip wire.

The activated model of the King David Hotel complete with moving vehicles showed how the Irgun had got into the basement with ammunition hidden in milk churns. It was peculiar as the guide looked at me and told me that the British should have been more vigilant on the day, but they chose to ignore the warning. While the debate on events relating to the blowing up of British Head Quarters in Jerusalem has gone on and will continue, it was just another fact. No expressions changed on the faces of my fellow attendees, it was just a hard fact and nobody present made it personal. On the contrary, they were learning from lessons we should have learned and told that such a set up was an assault waiting to happen, with so many important departments in one place.

The walls of the museum were adorned with old front pages from the Palestine Post and we stopped at one in particular showing demolition in the centre of Jaffa. The British had said that the design of the town, with people living so close together made it more dangerous for patrols. They blew a wide road right through the middle of the town to avoid leaving themselves wide open to more indiscriminate attacks. Pictures showed bulldozers pushing the rubble of both Arab and Jewish houses aside to make way for tanks. This bore a stark resemblance to Israeli movements when they undertake similar practices in the name of security in the New Palestine of today.

I learned on that day, that it was the British who taught the Israelis to make safer borders by creating open spaces at a grave cost to those living in the neighbourhood. This was quite daunting, a baptism of fire for me, but it helped me with perspectives then, and in the future, when moral British critics cast their, unflawed stones, towards the Israelis. The kind lady invited me to go along any time to watch films in their archives that were in English, she said she wasn't good at English herself, but would always find someone to help.

I watched an old news real report in that little room which showed events relating to searches carried out by 17,000 military personal and British Policemen. On Saturday 29th June 1946, they uncovered arms caches and made mass arrests of leaders of the Yishuv and public figures in an operation that became known as Black Sabbath.

The first day with Hanitai at Palmach Museum

The Palmach, Hagana and other Jewish Brigades were among the organisations that had co-operative relationships with the British. The decision to create The Palmach, as a striking force was made in Hagana Head quarters in 1941.

A benchmark in history is particularly remembered in the late 1930s when Arabs riots broke out. Their mission was to display all-out resentment against the influx of Jews coming into Palestine, and the Palmach and Hagana joined British soldiers and Palestine Policemen to stabilise the situation.

Over time, the Palmach units developed and varied methods of combat became apparent. This Youth Movement, who had been training privately, protecting new Settlements, came out into the open to set upon the Arabs hiding in the Jerusalem Mountains to counteract ambushes. They later fought against Hitler's Vichy French contingencies in Northern Palestine, in Lebanon and, in Syria.

Entering the Palmach museum, as Hanitai and I did on the first day we met in 2009, we were greeted by a massive, floor to ceiling, memorial wall, graced by hundreds of black and white photographs of Palmachniks; some of famous politicians in their younger days. Here I saw, a young Yitzhak Rabin, with thick dark hair, clad in a basic uniform, looking wistfully into the desert.

The famous uniform of traditional khaki shorts and shirt with a woolly hat turned up at the rim was very apparent in the pictures of agricultural workers and soldiers. Among the kibbutz portraits were others doing target practice, with pieces of card, pinned to fence posts. There was obvious, around the camp-fire singing and those standing in large circles, either working on quick reactions together, or traditional dancing.

We viewed the history of the Palmach in pictures and heard first-hand narratives from founder members.

Hanitai shared in a heart-felt lesson, in his own particular guttural, yet melodious accent whose inflection always makes him sound quite amazed at the world.

"Here you see the soldiers have Sten guns. The Sten gun was used in the First World War and passed to the Palmach when they were fighting with the British against the Vichy French in Syria and Lebanon in 1941. The English let us down. Before they beat Rommel in the desert they were quite happy to call on the Jews of Palestine to go up north. The Nazis were working with the Vichy French and planned to take Palestine from the North. Once borders were secure, the English went back to their old policies; they didn't keep their promises. Some Jews joined their army, but others did not trust them and their words, so stayed with the underground."

He seemed saddened about the situation and had always regretted that the factions hell bent on hard line activities against the British, hadn't decided that negotiation would have been better. It was evident as he paused to find his words in impressive English, that his head was full of stories to share, but it was so complicated he didn't know where to start.

"The violence was awful; the Stern Gang and the Irgun had no respect for the English as the authority, but they had no respect for them as human beings. In the kibbutz, we tried to listen and even shared each other's woes, but the underground did their own thing, there was no control."

We were suddenly in the company of an American lady, whom we learned, was visiting from San Francisco and had obviously been listening and wanted to join in.

"If I can just say." she said, "their mentality didn't allow for respect for any authority, even in their own camp. They didn't want to talk; they just wanted to say that they saw off the British. They came from awful places, which made them very sad and angry and the situation here made them worse. I am not only talking about those who stayed in the underground when the Hagana were recruiting to help the British, but those who came as illegal immigrants had to fight to get into the country, they didn't want to rub shoulders with the British. They were revolutionaries; they came to blow up trains!"

The lady showed anger as she described an appalling situation, but I couldn't work out who angered her most, the British or those who took an aggressive stance to their policies.

"Listen!" Hanitai said quite gently.

"The Stern group, who had no respect, were only about 900 people, they were terrorists in their behaviour, but not everyone thought like they did. The Hagana and the Palmach tried to work with the British. Many people who came on the ships; well even they joined the Hagana. We all wanted some peace in a homeland. You can't really say who thought what, we were all different."

I understood and acknowledged that we couldn't say there was a stereotypical mindset in the LEHI, Irgun or Hagana. Fair enough, the strategies were set down in the guidelines of each party, but it was complicated and people took whatever course of action they thought best; they had to achieve long-term survival. Policies on the ground sometimes changed on a weekly basis, for everyone, including the British.

The Nation in the making between 1945 and 1948 consisted of a British Occupation and Jews of different nationalities and cultures trying to get into Palestine. Politically from left, right and centre, to join either those who were recent immigrants or those who had been there for decades.

A gentleman joined us then. He had brought his 14 year old granddaughter to Israel for the first time and they listened to our conversation on why you cannot possible say how a collective such as the new arrivals were thinking.

What was it like to suddenly find you were in a new ghetto, where would be leaders couldn't agree and newcomers also thought they knew best? Some looked down on their fellow refugees, their tent mates or even their detention camp mates, to include those that found themselves behind barbed wire on the Island of Cyprus.

The travelling hordes were physically and mentally punch drunk, with the hungry; those recovering from illness; the dying; the philosophers; the devastated; the angry revolutionaries; the stuck up; the rich and the poor. New arrivals, who had lived in closed religious communities, now found themselves among the cultured rich from Vienna who were used to finery and opera. There were those who wanted to live quietly, the Rumanian peasant or Russian farmer, whose initiatives would eventually lead to the staple diet of cream cheese in Israel. There were doctors and nurses who had far too much work to do in dealing with the undernourished, children and the exhausted elderly. The Orthodox Jews who would rather have waited for the Messiah to give them Jerusalem, but couldn't go back to Europe, had been transported by rescuers who had found them somewhere in a bewildered wilderness.

There may have been some Hasidim, dressed in black and white like their mentor, a 17th century noblemen, whose ancestors had kept the faith through 2000 years of Diaspora. They were developing alternative ideas for the foundation of the religious homeland to come. They would never have dreamed of a Zionist, post religious Israel, or indeed the fanatical ones whose families were humble then, but have Bible map expansionism in mind today. Among these, there was the ridiculed Berlin businessman, who believed he would always be respected by the Germans. His Father had been decorated for his service in World War I, and his family name was recorded on a memorial ward in a Berlin hospital, in honour of his Grandfather's work in science.

It was as impossible to typecast the State's founders as it is to stereotype Israelis today. If they had anything in common, it was the shock of displacement and the way they had been treated by Hitler's old world order or the new recovering world of the late 1940s.

They were in a new, hitherto, unrecognised country, taking stock of the life and the family they had lost. They were a generation who had experience a massive upheaval and to a huge degree, this had a bearing on their behaviour.

Discussions were plenty at the Palmach museum. I was already overwhelmed with information.

As World War II came to a gradual close, harmony diminished between the British and those who realised they weren't going to reap the benefits of promises made. The White Paper of 1939, restricting immigration, remained in place. It stood between everyone and their respective hopes.

This and other factors relating to unfavourable British Policies, including dismissal and treatment of immigrants aroused violence from the budding army in waiting. Dissident groups were vocal about who should have listened to who where British trust was concerned.

Increased bloodshed resulted in countless arrests and a massive undertaking to confiscate weapons.

"My Father told me: "We had to take the weapons back, they had turned on us and using them against us. They were blowing us up with our own ammo."

Previous chapters have portrayed events between 1945 and the founding of the State in May 1948, but the impending War of Independence was on the minds of those who predicted the Arab invasion, as it looked like the Empire and

Colonialism in the region was about to fall apart. The Palmach and Hagana had to prepare for this as Arab armies did the same, hoping to avoid the catastrophe of handing over their land and property to the Jewish people.

As the State was declared, following votes for Partition in May 1948, those celebrating in the streets were the first victims of the invasion. It happened within hours.

In the Palmach museum, I heard how future Prime Minister, Yitzhak Rabin commanded Palmach units on the road to Jerusalem and in the Mountains around the city. He described himself as devastated when his Brigade, made of 16 year old boys from the Settlement Youth Movement lost their lives. He felt responsible. Nevertheless, those left regrouped and were soon on the way to northern border clashes; some young men went inside Lebanon and Syria.

The museum depicts the spirit of the Palmach by the personal stories of individuals. They were a unique band, who used their own initiative, having been trained to use whatever they could get hold of and they managed with minimal resources.

Chapter 10

Ammunition Hill

We drove high above Jerusalem, stopping at a spectacular viewing point and looking across at what ought to have been a new Palestine; the big picture became clearer to me.

"Look at it, how can we give this away?" he said desperately and I felt the heart of someone who had spent his life fighting for it and longed for some understanding from the rest of the world. A world he was convinced of, hated everything his life's work stood for.

Standing quietly for a few moments, totally spellbound, there was a presence that was bigger than all of us. It took my breath away! The vast valley stretched out before us being shared, loosely speaking, by both sides.

Just below, on the terraced embankment, there were Arab shepherds tending their flocks. This was East Jerusalem, just a short drive from the Old City. I could hear the faint clanking of goat bells on the breeze as they made the best of the sparse pasture on the hillside. This Biblical setting among stone ruins left by both ancient and recent conflict was a stark contrast to the dual carriageway which ran down the hillside to the checkpoints and the monstrous concrete defence wall.

In peace, I was drawn in my mind with the desire to sit among the goat herders, to see what life was like for them. Perhaps go to greet the little Arab boy I could see there, though hopelessly regretting that we would have difficulty communicating if I ever had the time to stay. My language and culture were my whole life away from him, and I sadly wondered whether his mistrust would be his short lifetime away from me.

I was painfully aware of the mammoth task to find any type of mutual agreement and for me to be able to fully understand the situation. I could have stood there all day, just gazing; for in spite of the political situation, unrest, and civil war in the air, there was a sort of tranquillity, something I couldn't touch hovering over the magnificent landscape. Standing there, chilled and entranced by a spiritual, historic beauty I was intoxicated. All this was enveloped in amber light and a marginal heat haze over the Jordanian hills in the distance.

"It's such a beautiful mess," I said

And practically, bringing me back to earth, my Israeli commando, to whom it was all old hat, stated,

"We're safe at this point; this is ours we only have to worry about snipers."

"Well that's alright then," I said nonchalantly without altering my gaze, the military observation going over my head. I could see the border crossing and the guards, but with the view, I was halfway to paradise already.

"This is what the big fight is all about," I said, "and no wonder!"

Half an hour later, we stood in the shade of an Olive tree on Ammunition Hill and looked out towards the West Bank. It was one of the 182 trees that had been planted when the place was inaugurated as a memorial to those who died fighting Jordanian forces during the 6-Day-War. The Jordanians had held a foothold in the solid stone trenches all around us since the War of Independence in 1949. Occupying this compound with its fortified bunkers, built by the British in the 1930 and used as ammunition stores, was paramount in controlling this area outside Jerusalem, and in 1967, taking the area from Arab Forces, proved to be one of the most bloody battles of the war.

The amount of cold tea and coffee I drink when I am in Israel is much more than hot. We stop for a drink, look out at the views and lose ourselves in some history which often leads us back to the current situation. Lateral thinking is necessary when talking to the Israelis and Palestinians. One thing always leads back to another; tit-for-tat reprisals, ancestral hurting, or bitterness; who started it and who won't compromise.

I have yet to master the ability to portray the depth of feeling or the weight that hangs over the Middle East. How do you explain the difficult past written on people's faces or describe the pain of memory in someone's eyes?

Personal history is never boring here; everyone has an unusual story. Every street used to be something else, someone else may have lived there in a totally different world, in an Arab life or in an orange grove that no one seems to have a map of anymore.

The State comprises a mosaic of people from all over the world, whose ancestors experienced an unsettled existence and who are now conditioned to expect victimisation and continual threat.

We found ourselves discussing what had happened at the Camp David peace summit between Ehud Barak and Yasser Arafat, with President Clinton acting as a mediator in July 2000.

"I used to think that Arafat would have done everyone a favour if he had accepted the offer on the table." I said, "And hadn't walked out. I know now that he couldn't sell the Palestinians short or expect the hard-line factions within Palestine to settle for it."

He came back with the philosophy of many Israelis:

"There are those within Palestine who will not settle for anything less than pre1967 borders or even the total elimination of the State of Israel."

The reserves are programmed to be on standby and daily life is interrupted at least once a year in order to keep up-to-date with the demographics of a small strip of land. Israel, the size of Wales, is continually improving its armoury, its security systems, and technology in case they are called up to fight again at a moment's notice.

As I sat down on a Jerusalem stone wall and dangled my legs into the old trench, I noticed a Sherman Tank on the grounds on Ammunition Hill. Hanitai was chatting to a man by a bunker and I watched a group of paratroopers standing in a horse-shoe formation, listening to some briefing.

Hanitai came back after a few minutes and introduced me to a young girl in khaki, she was on National Service. She gave me a compact disc of some kind.

"This is for you!" she said. "It's the English version of what you are about to see in the film."

Hanitai had worked his magic, as usual, and we were about to join the paratroopers in a small theatre and see how two generations before, men in the same uniform had taken Ammunition Hill.

Before we went to see the film, I chatted to the soldier, who told me she was finding her time in the army quite hard. She had been placed among the elite and while her job was well within her remit, she felt inadequate beside them.

"Do they treat you badly?" I asked.

"No!" She said, "But these are intelligent people and they don't seem to have anything to say to me!"

I tried to encourage her by saying she might be surprised at their lack of confidence, as it was early days for all of them too. They were all in the first few weeks away from home, at 18 years old. I asked her to give it some time.

We had our photograph taken together and then exchanged a big hug. I look at the photo now and wonder how she went on.

After leaving Ammunition Hill, we drove around for a little while and Hanitai pointed out how the land lay in Jerusalem proper. We stood overlooking the Mount of Olives and he pointed out the separations inside the Old City.

Here, I told him about my regret at not seeing the Garden of Gethsemane until 2007, some 10 years after my Father's death. It had been a personal promise to go back on his behalf, but during a visit in 2003, a riot had prevented tourists from venturing into the area.

We cannot deny what happened there, for there is evidence enough that this is where Jesus of Nazareth was arrested. For those of Christian faith, it feels as if any celestial atmosphere is more likely to linger there than some half a mile away on the Via Dolorosa with its stations of the Cross.

Walking down the hill from Gethsemane, outside the Old City walls, and passing through the arch of Lion's Gate, it was quiet and you could hear the birds sing.

Dad was right, in comparison to this divine garden, searching for hallowed ground in the tourist hubs of the Old City, was like looking for peace in the centre of a busy souk. For a young British soldier, in 1947, it was a sanctuary, when there was a lot more to fear than the pick-pockets of today.

Chapter 11

The King David Hotel

The King David Hotel was the British Secretariat in Jerusalem during Mandatory Rule. Here, historical meetings took place and the stereotype higher ranks met for drinks, lunches and dinner parties and Jewish and Arab representatives, joined in to bargain for land. The Secretariat employed, both Jews and Arabs often working together in the Government Offices that occupied a large wing at one end. Some were loyal to the British; some were trying to uncover top secret information; many were manipulated to work for the underground under threat. I've been told it was possible, for the brave, to get a document out of the building, photo copy it and get it back into the filing cabinet within hours.

Across the street, the most lavish YMCA (Young Men's Christian Association) I have ever seen was another hub for socialising. Officers wandered through Jerusalem from their quarters, through the arches of Old City Gates, just a short walk from the King David Hotel every morning. Others drove in from further afield.

I had mentioned to Hanitai that I would like to stand on the steps of the Hotel. My Father told me that he had once seen Ben-Gurion and Moshe Dayan in the area in front of the main entrance.

An officer had come out to meet them and said, "Hello David!"

Dad was confused; he couldn't see anyone else – so why had he greeted a David?

I told him, "Ben-Gurion was called David."

Dad thought his name was Ben. I explained, that David was his first name and Ben, meant – son of. Even though, originally he was called David Green, but he decided to change his name when he arrived from Russia.

My Father told me, that after some 50 years, I had cleared up confusion that he'd thought about occasionally. I cynically thought that it went some way to confirming that the young British soldier had been ill informed.

One afternoon, on the day we were due to go to see the King David Hotel; Hanitai took me to an Arab cafe in Jerusalem, where I could sample the best mint tea. There seemed to be more mint than tea in the glass cup and I wasn't really used to it. It was bitter and seeing my expression upon sipping it. He said: "Put some sugar in it!" I did as he suggested.

"Shall we try some cake?" I asked, but he surprised me by saying,

"No, you can have cake later!"

"Oh right then!" I said. I was a bit bemused.

Nevertheless, I drank the stringy tea and he, his awful coffee, and we went outside and looked at some Ottoman architecture near a very old market.

We drove to the Hotel, just minutes away and parked outside. It always reminded me of a mill made of orange stone. Many windows of the same size on about 7 floors, 2 I think have been added during renovation.

We stood on the main steps and looked around the hedged garden and a grass fronted area. Hanitai left me and walked toward the guard on the door, but I didn't know what he was doing.

The guard opened the door and Hanitai, turned to me smiling and said, "Come on!"

"I'm not dressed for here." I said, looking down at my dusty cream trousers after being in the Jordanian trenches on Ammunition Hill.

He wasn't bothered about my attire, just beckoned me in and we went straight to the grand reception desk. The desk and its vast surround was make of a rich dark wood and above it, King David Hotel, was written in gold leaf.

The receptionist made a phone call and a smartly dressed man came out of a side office and introduced himself to me as the Manager. Hanitai had rung ahead earlier in the week and arranged it.

"Welcome, he said, you are my guests for tea!"

I couldn't believe it, as we were escorted to the old British wing, where there were old photographs of the hotel from the time the British were stationed here.

The floor was tiled in white, but they had taken signatures from the guest register and on each tile was a famous name, in black.

Walking along, we read them. Golda Meir, David Ben-Gurion, Madonna,

Winston Churchill, Bill Clinton, Menachem Begin and many others.

The Manager took us through two enormous wooden doors, along a corridor and into a meeting room. The huge light oak table was decked with note paper, pens, microphones and headphones. He told us:

"Don't tell anyone you have been in here until next week. Governor Schwarzenegger and President Clinton are in residence and they have been attending a meeting here today. They were participants in the 6th Saban Peace Conference."

I was amazed I had been let into the building.

We went back into the foyer and were asked to take a seat on huge couches surrounding marble occasional tables; each had a vase of freshly cut red roses placed in the centre. The design of the main lobby, where tea was served is said to be a mix of Colonial Elegance and the glorious style of Biblical David.

Sitting there quite amazed at my situation, with the son of a Hagana commander, who was a retired Lieutenant Colonel from the Israel Defence Force, and who played a part with armoured units in the Sinai Campaign and Yom Kippur War. It all felt very official as Hanitai spotted the Chief of Staff standing by the revolving door in the foyer. "He may have been party to the peace talks!" he said.

I people-watched, half hoping that they weren't watching me as before the trenches, I had been with Kojak the Camel on the Mount of Olives and, as lovely as he was, he did stink a bit. Nevertheless, we enjoyed beautifully dressed lemon cheese cake and drank tea, of course, just has the British would have done.

Discussions then would be with The United Nations, or the League of Nations, when votes for partition were being influenced one way and another. They were trying to sort it all out then and the peacemakers are still doing the same thing today. If only these walls could talk, I thought, they could tell me about who has had their own political agenda over the years.

We went out onto the terrace by the swimming pool, and seated, we overlooked the old walls on of Jerusalem and pin pointed Jaffa Gate about half a mile away.

The Hotel Manager appeared behind us and said, "Governor Schwarzenegger is leaving now, would you like to wave him off with me?"

We followed him to the door and took some photographs of him and his wife getting into the typical black bullet proof SUV that often appear in American cavalcades.

Wandering around the building, we discussed how it was in the forties as the Secretariat Office of British Mandatory Rule in Palestine and the Head Quarters for the Armed Forces of Palestine and Trans Jordan.

On 22nd July 1946, the Irgun disguised as delivery men and waiters planted a bomb in the basement nightclub, The Regent. Explosives weighing about 50 pounds were carried in milk churns and tied to the main stanchions supporting the floors. While it is widely accepted that the Hagana as the impending principal government knew about the plan, they did nothing about it. Some say that they asked the perpetrators in the Irgun to cancel the mission.

Varying versions I have heard through oral testimony leave me a bit confused about the facts. Generally, most elders in Israel say that the warning call to the switch board was not taken seriously and if the alarm had been raised, more people would have been saved.

The British often maintain that no warning was received by anyone official within the Departments of Secretariat. Chief Secretary of the Palestine Mandate, John Shaw denied emphatically that a warning had been received when Menachem Begin insisted the call had been made.

91 people of various nationalities and faiths were killed and over 70 were injured as the floors of the South West corner were literally blown into the street. There is a plaque fixed to the railings outside the hotel that reads:

King David Hotel

The hotel housed the British Mandate Secretariat as well as the Army Headquarters. In July 1946, Irgun fighters, at the order of the Hebrew Resistance Movement, planted explosives in the basement. Warning phone calls had been made urging the hotel's occupants to leave immediately. For reasons known only to the British the hotel was not evacuated, and after 25 minutes, the bombs exploded, and to the Irgun regret and dismay 91 persons were killed.

Following the clear up which took three days of searching through rubble and removing the debris, Operation Shark was launched. This involved mass house to house searches with many hands being drawn in to comb areas where ammunition and weaponry might have been hidden by the Irgun or any counterpart.

Chapter 12

Stern Connections

In 2012, I was craving Israel again; time to dig some more, and I contacted those I knew to let them know I would be making the trip. I hatched a plan with Hanitai to go on tour for a few days and rang various museums in Tel Aviv to organise some reading.

I had made arrangements, over the telephone, to meet with the head archivist, Amira, at the Jabotinsky Institute on King George Street. An old haunt of mine by then.

Here another of my old points of view would be challenged, bringing about one of the toughest conversations of my research time in Israel.

A smart, thin lady with dark shoulder-length hair invited me into her office and we exchanged pleasantries across the desk. We were pleased to meet each other in the flesh after our recent telephone conversations.

On explaining the paths I had taken to uncover the past, I told her I was, sort of on tour with the Hagana, getting used to the way the Irgun thought, but couldn't bring myself to go to the LEHI museum.

"Why not?" she asked, with some surprise.

"Because there's something scary and dark about the behavior of the Stern Gang and I think it might be upsetting."

"Oh! You should go". She urged pleasantly. "Stern was my uncle!"

With this, she gestured behind her to where a black and white picture of Avraham Stern hung on the wall. I immediately saw the resemblance and felt a bit shaken.

I later learned that she had felt the same after finding she was sitting with the daughter of a British victim. We were both a bit out of our comfort zones as we eventually discussed her uncle's shooting.

I remember her angry comment as she told me that Stern was killed in cold blood. This was a new concept for me, I had never questioned that he was shot as he tried to escape, I knew very little about it.

She was angry at Geoffrey Morton's behavior and almost spat his name as she told me that Stern had a son he had never seen and his son, Yair, never knew his Father.

"Your Father was allowed to see you grow up!"

"Yes with one eye!" I replied. "He didn't just get up and get on with it; he was in the hospital for weeks."

There was no point in arguing about it, and as I recall we seemed to get over the blip pretty quickly.

I didn't have any idea of the inquiries or questions asked over the years. The shooting had taken place at 8 Mizrachi Street when Stern was staying with a family friend. Tova Svorai was the wife of another LEHI member who was in hospital after being shot, also by Morton in a raid in Dizengoff Street, two weeks before.

I believe now, Amira's reaction was in response to my ambiguous knowledge about the way her uncle died and the results of inquiries she thought were unjust.

SCRATCHING THE SURFACE

Morton would later win several libel cases after suggestions that the facts of the killing were not entirely accurate. Former Prime Minister Menachem Begin, and former Irgun member, accused Morton of murder, in his book, The Revolt. Morton sued the English publisher.

The British reports of Avraham being shot as he headed towards a window were accepted for many years and this version still stands officially with a slight variation on whether he was escaping or heading for a device that might blow up the apartment after Morton evacuated the building for everyone's safety.

The wanted posters in the city and local newspapers, placed by CID, had put a £1000 reward on his head. He had 4 bullets in his body when placed on a slab and photographed by the British.

If the reader is interested in research already undertaken, I suggest they read an excellent book. The Reckoning by Patrick Bishop is a cleverly written analysis, not only of valuable statements made on the day but of LEHI activities related to his death.

I still have questions about whether he was tying his shoelaces when pulled up from the couch. Was he handcuffed when he got up from the couch and headed for the 4th-floor window? Did the CID members believe he was about to set off a device since Stern had said he would rather take his own life than die at the hands of the British?

The morning after 15th February 1942
The English edition of the Palestine Post read:
LEADER OF THE STERN GANG SHOT DEAD.

TEL AVIV Thursday – The notorious gang leader Avraham Stern was captured during a raid in the Florentine Quarter near the Tel Aviv-Jaffa border, shot dead after he made a bid for freedom.

*****

Amira made a huge effort for me, asking her assistants to find daily telegrams sent to the Ministry of Defence in Whitehall from my period of study in 1947. We looked at old photographs on her computer screen and she told me about the work the team was doing to digitize their archives. It was a huge undertaking and Amira ensured it was a job well done before she retired after 30 years at the Jabotinsky Institute.

That day in 2012, Magda, the lady I had met in 1993, on my first visit to the institute, made me a cup of tea and I settled down in a bright spacious room that reminded me of an old-fashioned drawing office. In the far corner, studying some old newspapers sat Joseph Kister who I had also met a few years before when he had a signed copy of his book for me. The History of the Irgun was given to me in a downstairs room where he had told me about some of his own time in battle during the 6-Day-War. He didn't recognise me, of course, but when Amira popped in to see if I was okay, she introduced me to him again.

I was left to my own devices, but occasionally, I would see one of the staff looking through the pane of glass in the wooden door and I felt like the one who had come to find out what had happened here. Surely I wasn't the first to follow up on their Father's story.

After a few hours of analysing incredible information from the documents I had been given, the closing time approached. Amira and I sat together for a few minutes. She told me that I could possibly read the same papers at Oxford University as their opposite departments had been working together to develop a comprehensive archive.

I explained that being in Tel Aviv felt more personal and gave me a better connection to the past. Seeing the old British props left on the dusty streets brought me closer to an almost inherited memory and gave me great satisfaction. I loved to be in the same Middle Eastern light and feel the often unbearable heat. In Tel Aviv, I was party to the similar, though probably less pungent smells and wanted to look out on a sea stretching out to the same past horizons the troops watched. Sitting in these rooms where decisions had changed history or may have been debated was a far better setting than a distant academic hall at home.

She asked if I wanted her to investigate the perpetrator responsible for my Father's injuries, telling me that she had once seen a photograph of an ambulance that had been blown up. The inquiry was met with a definite, "No!" at which she seemed surprised. I didn't want a name and neither would my Father, this much I knew.

"What's the point of that?" I said. "I don't want a name so I can inspire hatred now!"

As both, Dad and Hanitai said, "It was war, and in war, bad things happen and people make mistakes!" These things are better left. I don't want a person to hate or forgive, just to look at the situation and accept it as it was.

Possibly, comparing my feelings to hers, she asked if I would have felt differently if my Dad had died. Then, we laughed!

"If he had died, I wouldn't be here!" She too had realised that, but I understood what she meant.

We said goodbye and I have since learned that she never expected to see me again. She had her expectations, I suppose coloured by stories from her own family when they talked about the British.

She expected me to disappear and we parted with a peculiar sense of the unknown and a strange caution from both of us.

As days went by, I absorbed what had happened and with some disbelief at my new connection. I'd got over my in-bred guilt trip, realising I wasn't really collaborating with the enemy. I didn't want to keep a wide berth anymore. Not only from the point of keeping in touch with a primary source from whose oral testimony I could learn so much, but I thought it might be good to build a bridge.

*****

I decided to go to the LEHI museum, which has been placed in the very apartment where Avraham Stern was shot. Like many other museums, there is a grand memorial hall for the appropriate organisation.

It is a sanctuary with old Standards on battered flag poles, together with modern blue and white Israeli flags, strategically placed like guards of honour around many photographs of LEHI members. Here, there is a difference from other museums. It is intimate, quiet music plays as you sit on a chair in the ill-fated room.

This is where Avraham sat writing at a round table when there was a knock at the door. Tova, his family friend, and landlady almost managed to convince the officers that she was alone. It was the wet shaving brush placed on the dresser that convinced them otherwise. The small wardrobe where the very slight man hid behind clothes is still there and from there he must have listened to the conversation and heard footsteps clattering on the staircase. I don't remember how I felt about being there. A bit haunted maybe, an overspill from tales I had heard as all the faces looked at me from their illuminated cases. It was a huge prop from Mandatory Rule that I never dreamed I would see.

*****

When I came out of the museum apartment, in a poorer and working-class district of Florentine, it wasn't long before I came across a small synagogue in a terrace that overlooked a small swing park; it had been shoe-horned in between the old Bauhaus apartment blocks. Or was it there, long before them?

A few, elderly ladies were feeding stray cats with dry biscuits at a regulated cat feeding station and a feline pride seemed to come out of the walls, weaving in and out of pedestrians, trying to get the lion's share.

I turned around and looked back up to the window that Avraham Stern was alleged to be heading for when he was shot. I think it's blocked up as part of the museum apartment now, but I imagined the distress of his landlady in the custody of British Intelligence officers outside.

Was there an official black car, a detective wearing a long coat with a trilby hat; armed soldiers in khaki shorts with long socks and dusty boots; dotted about watching this way and that? Who else was in the area, peeping around the curtains or keeping out of the way? They too could have been wanted by the British

Memories of that day and subsequent reprisals would haunt British soldiers for years as their contempt was passed down to anyone at home who showed an interest in Mandatory Rule. I was told never to venture near anyone with any connection to LEHI. Now I had learned a little about a man whose ghost I had hitherto filled me with terror. I had found human beings, just as I had when I went to Ireland to try and see things from both sides.

"One man's freedom fighter is another man's terrorist." My Dad used to say.

Stern was a poet, like Patrick Pearse, as revolutionary as Michael Collins perhaps, but maybe only ever in theory. He was the brains behind what has always been referred to as a nasty business' or 'a dirty war'. The leader of this band of gangsters was a visionary poet, who shared his heart-felt prophecy to recruit those who would be happy to offer the ultimate sacrifice to achieve it.

Like Pearce in the Irish Republican war, he never personally fired a shot. It was his passionate followers, who in their hearts, believed there was no alternative but to get on with what they had to.

Elderly Israelis today may question the measures taken by a bad lot, while some say it was about survival and making things better for the downtrodden. The disapprovers cannot agree with the factions who caused havoc for the British when they were packing up to go home in 1948. Others talk about who was collaborating with them, who was for them, and who was against them. Who was party to and influencing their long-winded negotiations?

There was chaos, political mayhem as well as violence.

Many Jews thought the Arabs would end up with the lion's share of everything. There was no harmony on any level, no thoughts of co-existence, even then. The Arabs could see that these people from the West were communicating with the British; they had grand European ways in common.

The Arabs were fighting for their land, the Jews wanted a homeland, and the British wanted to go home.

When my Dad talked about the things the Jews did to the British, my Mother always asked, unashamedly. "And what about what we did?"

Yes, what about what we did? Nobody knows for definite, the finer details of what happened in that room. It was unquestionably a reprisal for what the Stern Gang had done to our chaps, and I know some would say. "Well, that's alright then!"

Avraham Stern first wrote poems in Russian, but after becoming involved in defence activities, his poetry seemed to have an undertow of self-sacrifice and a longing for Israel as a homeland for the Jewish People.

He published inspirational work in the secret flyers of the underground and composed a passionate dialogue for broadcast over the Voice of Zion underground radio of the 1930s. This was further encouraged by the Arab Rebellion between 1936 -1939 when the British were working to redefine policy on Jewish immigration quotas, which came into force on the Eve of World War II. At a time when the Jews of the European Diaspora, or further around the world, desperately needed sanctuary, the British white paper of 1939 announced a limit of 1200 Jews a month.

*****

Amira talks fondly of a complex character who, upon arriving in Israel, tried to combine his visionary dream to accomplish a Jewish homeland stretching further than partition would achieve, with his personal life.

At University, he was the quiet man thinking - or the life and soul of the party who danced and sang. He was a good-looking fellow who charmed the ladies, but, for a long time, didn't want to commit to a long-term relationship. His writings and his poetry are marked with the sadness of facing death or marching gloriously into battle. He has been likened to Patrick Pearse as a visionary dreamer with a hint of romance in the mythical story. Concerning fighting the British - Irgun and LEHI methods mirror those of the early Irish Republican Brotherhood.

Personal feelings about these historical eras can be delicate, with a need to look at many things including, personal connections, conditions in which the military found themselves, and a will to heal and move forward.

Amira looks at me somewhat puzzled when I tell her that I don't want to get to the bottom of who blew up my Father and has offered to find out who it was. But it was war and I feel confident that my Father wouldn't want to know himself as we had talked about the humanitarian aspect of war often and we always liked the parts where the guns stopped and each side chatted.

He liked the idea of decent people playing football in no man's land during Christmas 1917. Going to meet Germans, he shook hands with those whose River Rhine river bridges we had blown up. He talked to Germans at the Mohnesee Dam (The area of the famous Dam buster Raids) about what it was like for them when their towns flooded.

*****

When Amira and I met again in 2015, she talked to me about Avraham Stern's son, Yair. He was named after his Father's underground code name. Born in the same year, they had experienced many emotions together, especially about the manner of Avraham's death and dealing with the varying opinions of LEHI activity.

Gradually, Avraham Stern's reputation changed from that of a terrorist to an Israeli legend. Amira told me that Prime Minister, David Ben Gurion, had also had a change of heart about Stern's part in history. She explained about a day out with her family when she was about 12 or 13 years old. They visited a family friend, Joshua Cohen, a former leading member of LEHI, who had ended up as Ben Gurion's bodyguard in the kibbutz where he lived after he retired from politics.

He was alleged to be particularly anti-LEHI at the time of the State's founding. Amira explained to me that the former Prime Minister's wife, Paula, had asked Cohen who he was expecting as guests on that day. Her curiosity led to Ben Gurion meeting Yair, Stern's son in Kibbutz Sdr Boker. He was then an elderly gent who had heard many stories from Cohen, and told Yair Stern, the younger, that he understood a little more of the LEHI's perspective and had eventually gained some respect for his late Father. For some, Stern had posthumously been turned from terrorist to folklore hero within 20 years.

This shift was typically encountered by all the family as the years went on. Stern's wife Roni, who lived into her nineties, experienced this change personally. In the early years, living in the shadow of LEHI association, people would cross the street to avoid talking to the wife of a gangster.

Amira portrayed Avraham Stern, the gentleman. Her Aunt Roni had described to her how being wooed by a romantic poet who brought her flowers was wonderful. He truly loved her, yet wanted to protect her from his reputation and 6 or 7 years passed before they married in 1936. Stern was hungry for the cause, but not at the expense of feelings he had for his wife. However, he never wanted children as he predicted they would probably end up orphaned. His son, the young Yair, was born 6 months after his Father's death and told until he was about 6 years old that his Father was in America. We don't know why he wasn't told about his death earlier.

Amira showed me a note written in a young child's Hebrew hand and translated it for me as we sat in her Tel Aviv office; it was written to her Father, David.

"Dear Uncle, when will my Daddy come back from America?"

It was not until the State of Israel was announced that Yair found out his Father was not coming home. On the evening of the celebration, he asked why everyone was dancing.

He was told that there would be the State of Israel from now on, and his Father had died fighting for it.

Taking another book from her cabinet, she showed me Stern's beautifully neat handwriting, written in exacting, lower-case Hebrew script.

"This is as he always wrote during the thirties," she said, and then showed me a later note.

"Before he died in 1942, thinking the British may recognise his handwriting in messages he passed to other members of the organisation, he had changed it to larger geometric Hebrew letters."

Elders still debate on which organisation made the greatest contribution to the founding of the State of Israel, but for LEHI, whose reputation preceded them, their actions, good or bad, were often kept quiet. In 1948 the differences in opinion were voiced and often very loudly. I have come to believe that reflections over the years have become calmer.

"Some made mistakes, but that's what happens in war," Hanitai told me.

Much has happened in Israel since 1948; fewer veterans are around to wear this history on their sleeves. The War of Independence and the activity that led up to it at the end of British Mandatory Rule was a long time ago.

I always believed the Hagana worked well alongside the British, and on a scale of those to be very much feared, the Irgun and Stern Gang would stop at nothing to force the British out of Palestine.

On the political stage, David Ben Gurion, Israel's first Prime Minister, who had been a member of the Hagana, didn't seem to refer to the Stern Group as much as he did the Irgun in the early years of the State. Probably because, as things progressed, Menachem Begin, who had been an Irgun commander, became the leader of Ben Gurion's opposing political party. It was an ideal opportunity for Begin and his terrorist band to receive bad press in the newly founded Knesset.

*****

Breaking from history for lunch, Amira showed me the memorial on the corner of Dizengoff Street and King George Street, to commemorate the victims of a suicide bomber in 1996. I remembered the day well. I had heard on the news that the bomb had gone off and called my friend, Shai, at the Center Hotel on nearby Zamanoff Street.

He had finished his shift and left, but I couldn't contact him at home. His colleague made inquiries for me and I was relieved to hear that he was fine and had gone to visit his parents in Haifa. He rang me with an update the following morning, saying he had walked through an ugly protest. People were becoming more afraid to go out into busy areas, where suicide bombers may appear at any time. He was very saddened to hear the angry mob calling for, "Death to the Arabs!"

I reflected on how the situation had challenged the positivity I had met in him 3 years earlier during the Oslo Accords. The Peace Agreements were already falling apart.

We passed the long-standing bakery where Colin and I used to buy apple cakes and where the big tree fills the pavement with its expanding routes. A beggar was sitting on the ground, wearing shorts and an old coat. His legs were a mass of red blisters and he looked in poor health. We remarked on the sadness of the homeless situation around the world, as further on, more men lay on the floor with their heads resting on flattened cardboard boxes.

Over lunch, we talked about families and our work life. There was a lot of laughter between us. We talked politics; going round and round in circles as such conversations usually do.

We failed to resolve many problems but didn't feel guilty about it, since so many others have failed before. We agreed on many things and shared a general sensibility. Nevertheless, I had to disagree when Amira insisted, like others I had heard on that visit:

"The whole world hates us!" she said.

She talked about a new anti-Semitism that European Jews were experiencing. I couldn't disagree that Israel had been brought under a new analysis since the Gaza Strip had been cordoned off in 2009. This world obsession was stereotyping the average Israeli as an unreasonable expansionist and the Jews in Diaspora were being labeled as fanatical Zionists whether they agreed with or disputed current policies in the region.

She had read about increased anti-Semitism in Manchester and we thrashed out what might be understood as such and how people might interpret it differently depending on their personal history.

I was convinced that it wasn't happening to the same degree at home as the recent violent events in Europe, more that people were aware of the threat and took preventative measures against its possibility.

I confess I was in denial about the degree of anti-Semitism on the home ground then. I didn't want to accept that it was increasing in Manchester. Firstly, I hadn't read or heard about it, and secondly, I never liked the idea of ruining the myth of centuries of stability for the Jews in England compared to the miserable conditions endured on the Continent.

We returned to the office and had begun to read some more documents when we heard a siren warning of a bomb scare outside. Amira opened the window and stuck her head out into King George Street and I asked if we had to go to the shelter.

"No!" she said calmly, "but we'll just put our cardigans on in case we have to move quickly. Her casual manner made me laugh and she left the window open for updates. We were talking so much we didn't even notice the all-clear.

*****

In September 2022, just weeks after her 80th birthday, Arwel and I met with Amira in Tel Aviv. We wandered around the old Templar village at Sarona and ate pasta and ice cream in a new food market. I wanted to ask her face-face whether she would be happy if I put this chapter in my book. She wanted to thank me sincerely for my friendship. I thanked her too, of course, as we remarked on how far we had come.

Chapter 13

Tel Aviv talks to me

As you stroll along the streets in the city of Tel Aviv-Jaffa, it won't be long before you see one of thousands of feral cats that roam throughout the City. It can be a pretty ragged show as these strays take shelter under cars or bask in the sun on refuse bags or on top of an old fridge down some back alley. Some look healthy, others injured and malnourished. Occasionally you will see a one-eyed cat who may have been the victim of disease or a fight with a stronger contender. There is competition for discarded skin left by a fisherman in the harbour or the dirty water dripping from an air-conditioning unit in the suburbs.

A number of the breeds have been in the region since they were considered sacred in ancient Egypt, and today, these aristocrats sit upright and proud with haughty expressions, dismissing tourists who find their unusual pedigree an ideal photo opportunity. There is, however, evidence of other European breeds in the mix, since the British saw fit to bring in new varieties in the 1930s in order to combat a huge rat infestation.

One evening, I saw a youth climbing out of a skip with a kitten in his hand. It had been unable to get out after going in after some chicken scraps and the passer-by heard its faint cry for help. Not an unusual event, for they are mostly fed and watered by the public and in residential areas there are debates between those who want to feed them and those who don't want them encouraged.

Deliberations on how to tackle the cat problems go on in communities and in Parliament. Some funds have been made available for trapping, neutering, and vaccination, since carrying out euthanasia on a healthy cat is now illegal in Israel. A minority are being neutered or spayed in a long-term plan toward natural reduction, but since the estimated requirement of around a hundred operations per day is not being achieved, the birth rate still outnumbers the efforts of mobile clinics. The life expectancy of a street cat is said to be between two and three years, but their short lives do nothing to reduce the number of feral wanderers, as some females are giving birth to two or three litters each year.

Generally, the cats are very nervous around the people who want to tame and help them and this makes capture difficult. Organised spaces have been created in order to isolate some that have been treated, but when these quarters are infiltrated by the untamed that see the areas as an easy food source, the transformed cats are frightened away and the vicious circle continues. Another method to reduce numbers on the streets is to take kittens away from their wild environment as soon as they are born. These can then be offered to families for adoption and domesticated. It is a constant challenge, however, to find the kittens that begin their lives in derelict buildings, under the rocks on the sea shore, and in other secret maternity dens.

*****

Hanitai and I met for something to eat and to plan a trip one evening and he showed me where the old city of Jaffa met the new city being built in the earthy 20th century. This involved some discussion about Manshiyah and the Hasen Bek Mosque that some wanted to demolish in the 1960s, A local outcry, and dignitaries who believed its presence was important, eventually saved it.

It used to sit in Manshiyah, but now, from its minaret, the Arabs call for prayer and watch over the busy traffic on the wide boulevard where HaYarkon Street begins.

He asked how I felt to be back in Tel Aviv and I remember saying, after being away for 5 years, it was like I'd come home. I never knew why, but he said that was fine. "I know," he said, "Tel Aviv talks to you!" He was spot on with one line. The city that never sleeps - never stops talking.

We parked up outside the restaurant, adjacent to the Kishle. If I was near the Kishle; the old Turkish Fort, I had to go and have a look, especially as I'd read an article about it online earlier that day.

Hanitai hadn't heard that there was a proposal to turn the old prison into a hotel, though it looked like work had already started on the inside, behind its towering walls. In the dark, we could see something was happening as the wind blew a tarpaulin wrapped around a scaffolding tower.

"How luxurious do you think it will be in an old Turkish jail?" I asked him. I couldn't imagine it ever being anything other than cold in its appearance.

"This place, that became a British police station, where Mandate terrorists were held and interrogated. Goodness knows what these walls have seen."

He stood by me and looked up saying he hadn't noticed the renovation before or read anything in the paper.

"When it later became an Israeli police station," he said, "Nobody called it the Kishle. Nobody thought about the Turks much, it was just the police station by the Clock Tower."

"Oh!" I said, "The Clock Tower is Ottoman too!" He knew that, of course.

"You should be a guide." He said, but I didn't answer, just went off on a tangent about the old building.

The old prison made me think about Adolf Eichmann, the former Head of Jewish affairs for the Gestapo. He was kidnapped by Mossad in Buenos Aires and taken to Israel. His trial, in 1961, lasted for more than 3 months before he was hanged in Ramle prison.

"Would you like to stay here in a room where Mossad kept Eichmann?" I said. "Where he counted down the days until they hanged him? A 5-star luxury honeymoon suite built on Eichmann's death row."

"Oh! So this is a proposal then?" He said dryly. "You went round the houses with that one."

We both laughed and it certainly lightened the mood as we turned around and crossed the road to go to the Arab restaurant.

While reconstructing the prison, a cache of 50 rifles, found in the prison courtyard, was said to have been buried there by the British in the early Mandate days.

In the press, the designers had commented that as temporary residents, the British had made utilitarian changes inside the Kishle with no respect for the Ottoman style, making restoration more difficult.

This saddened me, but who knows whether the British were responsible for its demise? Israeli Police worked there for 4 or 5 decades after 1948 until they moved to their new complex about half a mile away.

We discussed British police stations in the area over dinner – as well as other things of course – we aren't total geeks. Hanitai drove me over to the Beit Hadar, (Citrus House) which may have been a Bevingrad, the name used cynically, especially by Jerusalem residents. It referred to British areas of Jerusalem that were fortified by masses of barbed wire against terrorist attacks.

When the situation became hostile in the late Mandate years, it was said that the British walled themselves in and surrounded every possible entry with fences and make-shift barricades for security purposes.

Then, it was one of the most pictured buildings in the press, showing contempt for the continued occupation, with headlines reminding their readers that: "The British live behind barbed wire. The British have rounded up themselves." It was believed to be impenetrable until the Irgun members dug a tunnel into it, the Administration saved by the Haganah member who lost his life when he found it.

On that evening in 2015, this enormous Bauhaus design dwarfed the brightly lit shops attached to its ground floor. It was a dirty grey, and only battered concrete was left. It looked like the bow of a ship, but with its front end softened, like a tugboat going nowhere. It stretched way back from the street, and when the shops ended, it continued into the darkness for about 500 metres.

The railway line from Jerusalem to Jaffa Port used to run beside it and, as a customs house, controlled the movement of goods trains. It is easy to imagine how imposing its presence was on this main arterial route into the city.

*****

Photographs of the time are black and white, or sepia, yet I have to visualise the Citrus House of 1947 as a smarter, possibly gleaming white construction in a new city.

Israeli Police moved in when the State was declared and stayed until the mid-1990s when the central police station opened on Alma Road. One of my favourite haunts for seeing old photographs is the Tzalmania photo house, the premises of the late Rudi Wiessenstein that, for many years, was at 30 Allenby Street, just as it bends to go downhill to the sea.

Rudi, Rudolph Wiessenstein, immigrated to Palestine from Czechoslovakia in 1936 and the shop is packed with old photographs providing a catalogue of the early years of Israel and before. The display of famous portraits in the window always gives the impression of a museum, and inside, are the originals of those used by many designers who enlarge them to the size of whole interior walls, in offices, hotels, and shopping centres. One of the most famous is David Ben-Gurion's declaration of the new State in 1948, later used on a postage stamp and first-day cover on the 50th anniversary of independence.

The next generation of the family who runs the shop today, leave keen browsers to appreciate the collection they inherited and assist in producing images of historical events they might have in their archives.

Some favourites, I found, were camel related, like the prints their hooves make in the soft sands of the Negev. Camel caravans are mystical to me and I love one especially. It's a photograph of a convoy walking along the shores of the Dead Sea with a backdrop of Mount Solomon.

Another, of them, carrying building materials to where the Yarkon River meets the sea in Tel Aviv, links a time when the British built a new port there. The Arab revolt in the late 1930s had led to issues in using the old ancient port of Jaffa.

In Jaffa, there were no facilities to anchor bigger ships and merchants had to row out into deeper waters to recover cargo.

It was through the eyes of Weissenstein that I first saw the layout of the stockade and watchtower fortifications in northern Israel and in kibbutz Hanita. Established in 1938 as a strategically placed kibbutz and subsequent training camp on the border of Lebanon and my good friend and guide, Hanitai, was given his name to honour the area. Here, Orde Wingate had the benefit of huge intelligence and played the army to its advantage. He hand-picked men and beat Arab incursions with his famous night squads.

There's so much to admire in his photography, like the barren and rocky landscapes where prickly acacia trees stand alone and the sharpness of their gnarly branches standout on their monochrome backgrounds.

The early years after Independence gave Israel shanty towns, tented settlements, and laborious road-building techniques with a brush and a shovel. Not even a hand roller was to be had on occasions and the concrete was patted down crudely. Different nationalities shared different techniques brought from Europe and often construction was archaic in the eyes of modern industrialists, but they used what they had on hand. Nevertheless, there were also the superior buildings of Allenby and Dizengoff Street, all dazzling in sunlight before the white city turned grey.

He had captured the faces of beautiful people sitting on the steep stepped alleyways of the Old City of Jerusalem and in Tel Aviv, smiling well-dressed ladies taking tea. There were so many random cafes along open sand, long before the promenade of today was constructed.

Here, the British spent their weekends, taking afternoon tea, playing tennis and swimming during the days leading up to World War II. Connected to this era, in the latter days of the British Empire, Arab ladies, whose husbands were sometimes Palestine Policemen, were seamstresses for army wives and edged garments with traditional embroidery. The higher ranks employed Arabs as gardeners, housekeepers, and British soldiers with familiar badges on their berets, posed with kibbutzniks, out in the fields.

Some portraits show expressions of hope and determination, while others are illustrations of the weariness of those who had little. There are furrowed brows reflecting upon the anguish left by events they may have endured. In this shop, Tel Aviv definitely talked to me.

*****

Wandering towards Yarkon Park, on a Sunday morning in 2000, I came upon hundreds of young soldiers waiting for their transport back to base after their weekend at home. Sunday is the first working day of the working week in Israel and I recalled the news at home a few months previously. A suicide bomber had detonated a device in the midst of such a crowd in a similar situation and seeing the crowd, I understood better how difficult the task of moving so many troops each week.

When I asked the Officer at the gate whether I could take a photograph of them, he was polite and helpful, but curiously cautious of my motives.

Part of me wanted him to refuse permission as I hoped he would prove competent and send me packing, just in case I might be a threat. He knows, I thought, as I studied his expression, that terrorists don't always look like terrorists and realised his response was largely be based on instinct.

Behind him were khaki-clad troops out in an open-air bus station, sitting on kerbstones, kit bags, and milling about chatting. His curious expression upon reading my proffered passport made us both smile as he seemed to have an idea up his sleeve.

"I cannot let you take a picture," he said in an American accent, "and I cannot let you pass this post. Please don't take a picture of me and the boys here at this checkpoint either."

Nodding in acceptance, I stood on a grass mound viewing a legion burdened by National Service and he perched on the edge of his table, my passport in hand. We exchanged no words for a minute, but must have been on a similar page as he suddenly surprised me by saying,

"Hey! I know - you can be part of an exercise. He joined me on my high point and pointed. "You see the trees along there between the road and the compound?" I nodded.

"There are guards hiding in there and if you find some as you walk along that path, you can ask them if they want to be in your picture. It's up to them then. They could be anywhere and no one will know the place."

He smiled sincerely as if he had solved my problem and also sensed that in some barmy way, the environment excited me.

"Will they shoot me?" I asked, which, seemed like a decent enough question.

"No," he said most definitely, "but they might shout until you say I have sent you".

I took my instruction and agreed to the interesting prospect of searching for soldiers. I bade him goodbye and he watched me go as I crept away warily and glanced back at him. He nodded as if to say, "go on then". Strolling on the outside of the patch of forest, I soon heard a Hebrew conversation and coming to a small opening, I saw two soldiers looking across the compound. One heard me immediately and turned around. I told him immediately, who had sent me and while listening to me intently, they agreed to the photograph.

The cheerful one, thinking this was a great diversion from the boredom, said,

"Wait! I want to put on my new sunglasses," and rested the butt of his Uzi on his hip so he could reach into his top pocket. This made me laugh, but his severe companion held his weapon upright and handy while the trendsetter straightened his attire.

I observed how vulnerable they were, a less than stealthy gunman could take them out, but I felt certain, would not get far afterward. Martyrs don't care though, do they?

They posed and I asked, though I knew the answer, "You can't stand closer together can you?"

"No," they answered in unison, so I took the photo with a five-foot gap between them. I thanked them and the pleasant chap moved forward to see me off as if I was a friend who had popped in for a coffee. As mad as it was, I felt pleased to have been a part of a change in their routine but gratified that they knew what they were doing.

Still thinking about this and having achieved my goal, I walked slowly along the grass verge towards the path and suddenly jumped out of my skin as another one came at me from the dense foliage and held me at gunpoint. He frowned as he shouted in Hebrew and with my hands raised; I quickly managed a reply in his own language,

"I'm English - and going to the park!"

There was a flash of fear and puzzlement in his black eyes as he ushered me towards the footpath with the barrel of his gun. He said something I didn't understand, but he never relaxed and I thanked the Lord that he wasn't as trigger-happy, as he was nervous.

On reflection, perhaps I should have said the officer's name again, but as one panicked novice to another, I was sure that reaching him in his own language was most important.

SCRATCHING THE SURFACE

It was my fault, I was rubbish at this - he was a kid and I had spooked him. I forgot there might be others. I felt sorry for him, mainly because he was more afraid than I was.

They all took it for granted that they would be robbed of 2 or 3 years of their life, simply because of where they were born. Not for the first time, I had experienced a reality check and I despaired at the whole situation.

As I crossed the wide road and went into the park, I reflected upon the sadness lingering under the skin of some Israeli soldiers I have met.

Another, I had met on the previous Sunday morning approached me on the beach. I was listening to music under a canopy after breakfast, glad to have the beach to myself. There was a nice breeze and a comfortable temperature and with my eyes closed, it was very relaxing.

I suddenly opened my eyes to see a young soldier, dressed in a dark uniform, looking down at me. His feet were wet as he had been paddling in the sea and he held his boots in his hand.

"Alright!" he asked, but in Hebrew. Then he said something else. I told him I couldn't understand and he just stood there.

I looked at my watch, it was almost 10 o'clock and he knew I was wondering why he wasn't with the rest of his unit, catching the bus back to base. Knowing what I was implying, he waved his free hand and marched off muttering something to me over his shoulder.

I wondered if he decided not to go back and didn't know what to do with himself. I was sorry because if he needed a friend, I was no use as I couldn't understand him.

Tel Aviv might talk to me more if I understood the language.

Chapter 14

The Road to Manshiyah

On Saturdays when most places are closed for the Sabbath, I love to eat lunch at a favourite Arab-run cafe in Jaffa. The walk down the promenade, which should take about 20 minutes, takes me over an hour after I set off from the big fountain at the bottom of Allenby Street. I have gathered so much history from this jaunt and learned something new every time.

I never tire of this walk - I love the place. There's a type of solitude with entrancing thoughts by the seashore. It's a Sabbath walk where you can lose yourself in memories of the past, even though others are doing the same with lots of children and dogs.

The place where the Arab village of Manshiya used to be, about halfway to Jaffa captivates me - historically and mystically.

British records state that in 1947, Manshiya was a very run-down suburb on the border of Jaffa and Tel Aviv. The smell was said to be so bad that it could cut the back of the throat. Not a place for sandals then in the rat-riddled squalor. I once saw a Mandate picture of the area where a dead horse lay rotting in an alley there.

To the British, it was officially out of bounds, unless a designated troop detail ventured there with armed reconnaissance vehicles, possibly in search of a member of the underground in a hideout. I have heard it said, off the record, that some ventured there for certain recreational activities, but it depended on whether you were prepared to face danger to satisfy a need. Army medics would knowingly supply the necessary remedy to resolve whatever was picked up.

In the late 1990s, I remember the run-down remains of a few Ottoman-style hovels that stood alone on the edge of wide-open parkland. Today, the bottom half of a large stone dwelling on a vast grass verge is the only evidence that a village was there. The original building would have been beautiful, with its arched windows and gable end staircases. The grand wooden doors have been restored and there is some wrought iron work left. The black glass of the modern Hetzl museum has been built inside its shell. One February afternoon, when the weather was particularly poor, I spent half an hour inside, standing by one certain window, looking out to sea. I watched the huge waves break on the jagged rocks outside; a luxurious, but angry view for a lost town that ended up as slum clearance.

I have visited the museum a few times to listen to tales of the battle for Jaffa, during the War of Independence. Girls on National Service who have chosen conflict-free opportunities, tell stories, both ugly and romantic, but filled with folklore and passion about the time the State of Israel was founded.

In my naive 1990s, however, these stories were not widely known among tourists. When I brought Colin to see the show in the old dolphinarium there, it wasn't a place where I learned local history.

Then - Colin photographed scavenging cats and carrion crows on the lawns in the shadow of the Hasen-Bek mosque; we knew nothing about the historical props around us. The dynamics of the locals were yet to be learned, and veterans from certain factions had yet to be encountered.

The area was different then, when the Shalom Tower on the other side of the Herbert Samuel dual carriageway, was one of the highest buildings in Israel, in the days before its 27 floors were dwarfed by skyscrapers. Colin, the young photographer, took a picture of it in the foreground of the mosque and captured his favourite modern hang-out with one of the oldest buildings in the area.

I didn't know then that from the minaret you could have watched the soldiers of Mandate Britain checking the goods wagons at Neve Tzedek train station before they entered Jaffa Port, less than a mile away. Today, the train station, HaTakana, has been renovated in Colonial style and is a good place for a Mandate imagination.

In pre-state Jaffa, oranges gathered from acres of orange groves were wrapped in monogrammed tissue paper and sent around the world in slatted plywood orange crates. This began long before the Jaffa brand was adopted by other countries. How many of those who sell Jaffa oranges around the world know the history of this variety? Neither do they have the treasured personal connection of their Father eating too many upon his arrival in Palestine and making himself sick. The temptation was too great for a young lad who hadn't seen an orange in England since before the war started in 1939.

With the sadness and romance of Manshiya around me, I approached the modern footbridge constructed in recent years, remembering how we used to jump over this dry wadi. Leaning on its balustrade, I have a raised view of where the old stream used to meet the sea and imagine the ghosts of families back to biblical times, washing their clothes and drying them on the rocks. A painting of the area from 1900 portrays a scene when the houses almost reached the water's edge, with women in long gowns and white headdresses. Fishermen look to be sorting a small catch on the ground. The pastel-coloured scene shows a terraced flat-roofed, shantytown, with orange groves beyond stretching as far as the eye can see.

The man-made beach today, worthy of any Mediterranean holiday club, has boulders around the edge at this point. I was always curious, as some rocks don't look as naturally formed as those that had been rounded off by the sea. I wondered where this scattering had come from until I compared a couple of maps with the aid of a graphic designer. He said it was obvious that some of the lands had been reclaimed and it all began to make sense to me.

During the late 1960s, the dilapidated Arab town of Manshiya looked to have been bulldozed into the sea to make way for the Charles Clore Park where thousands stroll today. The remnants of a village make a rugged sea wall that Jaffa's Arab families still sit upon and fish in the footsteps of their ancestors. Stray cats look for scraps and Israelis jog or practice the art of rock balancing with what might be the keystone to someone's front door.

In the mix of this rock pile, there is evidence of a rudimentary man-made mortar made from natural sand with shells visible in what was the old wall of a building. The imported sand of the new California-style beach has no shells in it today.

The park itself has undulating lawns and scattered palm trees and its 30 acres are sprinkled with desalinated water to keep it green. There isn't much decent soil there and if you search hard around the edges, you can see that the irregular turf is only a few inches thick. The grass is growing on a type of pond lining that has covered up the old town.

I seek out the past here and look for the town that once was and wonder why? If the British are not allowed to venture here for fear of those hiding in its smelly hovels, why does it feel like home to me?

It draws me in and keeps me there, giving me hours of contentment. This is why I can't walk to Jaffa in 20 minutes as others do.

Once you arrive on the terrace overlooking the Jaffa Port, there are rock gardens and benches placed strategically to take in the view. Gate posts on the new paths are parts of old door jambs, recovered for their Ottoman character. The retaining stone walls have the profiles of Arab arches within them. These look to be the tops of old window apertures embedded in the embankments; fossils of a lost village.

The owners of the houses on this stretch must have had lovely picture windows, and higher up the hill, the apartment owners in the new builds enjoy something similar, at a price.

One afternoon, I sat down on a bench, not far from the House of Simon the Tanner, where according to the scriptures, the Apostle Peter stayed. Just below is the small Jami'a al-Bahr, (mosque of the sea), who's minaret peeps a little higher than the sea lighthouse, partially hidden by tropical plants. The Turks used a French Engineering Company to design the lighthouse in 1865 which was largely renovated by the British in 1936 after they expanded the port. If you venture into the foliage and pull back the leaves, you can see skeletons of foundations, overgrown with beautiful landscaping. I cannot be sure they are all ruins, but the stones found along the tourist paths bear the same rough or soft holes, weathered by the sea for over hundreds of years. They are similar stones to those that cradle the Hetzl museum in the park. Some are so pitted that they have deep fissures, like coral.

A tropical garden stretches out on a hill above a row of more low arches whose original pillars may be partially hidden below ground. The planners have certainly made good use of ancient characteristics in the stonework. A knowledgeable mason could never deny that an Arab artisan once worked on them. On the maps from circa 1908, as Tel Aviv began and planners drew a line on the boundary of Jaffa, it was a representation of where new met old, where modernity met ancient. I naively believed in the early years of my study that this was a good thing. It showed that the footprint of Jaffa was untouchable.

As time went on I learned that people used to dwell in that gap and that the voids and cultural differences were a constant obstacle to progress in the eyes of developers. After the 6-Day-War of 1967, the rubble of Manshiya, left after the battle for Jaffa in 1948 was pushed into the sea. In the 1990s, the filling of the gap began with parks and hotels, and eventually, structures in Jaffa proper became part of expansionist progress to a huge degree.

For Israel, joining the 2 municipalities together to become Tel Aviv-Jaffa meant more opportunities to move into houses on the coast and revenue.

Within the scars of time on the main Yeffet Street, whose name was changed from Ajami Street, some elders who remember are still there. They will tell you they hid in the Orange groves and hoped to come out and carry on once the shooting had stopped. The majority of those who stayed in 1948 were sent to the Ajami district in the South of Jaffa, seen as a threat, and kept under strict control. Later, as the Arabs who were left in Jaffa tried to continue their lives within the new State of Israel, they found that they were joined by Jewish refugees who were seeking a haven.

The Arabs who left in 1948 were dispersed in all directions such as Lebanon, Iraq, Egypt, and Jordan, to name but a few new places of settlement. They were accommodated in tented cities and waited and waited to return to their homes. For the majority, this never happened and some families remain in refugee camps, 3 generations later.

I love Jaffa's terraces and the memories I have. It was the place we spent part of our first day in Israel, in August 1993. Colin and I walked around here with my friends Shai and

Amir and among the trees, we studied folk tales, how the land lay, and watched fishes swimming in the dock. I remember, when we returned to the hotel, Colin's pockets were filled with unripe dates that would never be of any use, but as an 11-year-old, it was a lesson and a collection he enjoyed. When I visit, I think about those days and usually sit in a familiar place for a while.

It was here. I hung out and listened to music on my walkman for a few hours shortly after my Father passed away. Old Jaffa is the nearest thing to old Palestine for me and has not changed as much as Tel Aviv since the Mandate days. From the bench, you can just about see the new road to the port that stretches along the sea wall and my Father recognised it in a photograph just weeks before he left us. He explained that a place I considered to be one of the most beautiful in the world, made him feel cold. It reminded him that on the road to the port, his comrades had to clean up after a stolen vehicle exploded. He described it as terrorist theft.

"It was a mess!" He told me. That's all he said, but I could imagine the rest.

Something else he said, quietly in the kitchen, that day. "You know, sometimes, when they were caught, they were knocked about a bit!"

"I know that Dad!" I said, "But it's done now, and they knocked you about a bit didn't they?"

That was it; our closing conversation on the Palestine affair.

Over 20 years ago, as I was sitting and thinking about that conversation, 3 passing soldiers stopped to chat and offered me some lemonade. They asked if I was alright and what I was doing there. We spent half an hour together and 20 nosey questions later, I told them that I had been thinking about my Father. They were intrigued by the story and they told me that they felt for him and others at that miserable time. They too had been told about the conditions for the British who were patrolling the ancient narrow alleys of Jaffa, describing it as a very unpleasant area. They agreed that knowledge of underground factions had been very vague and patrols couldn't have known who to trust.

One continued to explain that Old Jaffa had been saved by a few who wanted to benefit from it as a tourist area or make money from real estate, saying that millions of shekels had been poured into it in recent years.

Another soldier suddenly told me that he had the weekend off and asked if I wanted to go with him to Jerusalem to have lunch with his Mother. I nearly fell off my seat and declined politely.

"Why not?" He said, quite astonished at my refusal. "What else will you be doing?"

He was quite put out and his friends wandered off chuckling to themselves and muttered to each other in Hebrew. I was thinking, 'Don't leave me here with this stroppy guy!'

"My Mother is very nice." He continued. "Have you ever been to Jerusalem?"

I told him I had but was quite happy to stay in Tel Aviv this trip, even though I'm sure his Mother was lovely, and his Father, who apparently had a decent business in air conditioning.

His grinning friends strolled back, saying, "Come on! Get the message! Leave her alone!"

Stroppy replied saying: "She is just like Mary!"

"Who's Mary?" I asked, laughing and somewhat confused.

"She was a nurse who lived in our apartment block. She was staying here from England and was always on her own in her room. She was here for 3 months; working in the hospital in Jerusalem. We used to ask her to come out with us, but she was just soooo British!"

"Soooo British?" I repeated. "What's that supposed to mean?"

"Well, she just wanted to study and spend time alone when she was not working! You guys never mix with us." He thought for a minute then carried on. "Don't you think you are a little selfish? Do you not realise we want to speak to English people to improve our English? It's different than talking to Americans!"

This made me laugh and I was grateful he could tell the difference, but then maybe that was just me being so British.

They all gathered round again and took one hand off their automatic rifles to shake mine and say, "Shalom," eventually persuading their friend to shut up.

If ever I had a touch of melancholy, they cured me of it. He moves in mysterious ways!

Back in 2016, I walked downhill into the square to eat at my favourite restaurant and was happy to see the big resin camel that sits outside the street cafe.

I had eaten my homemade bread and many salads, including the best beetroots and red cabbage coleslaw with hummus and falafel. A German family of 4 was eating at the table next to me and we enjoyed some traditional music that was carried across the main square by St Peter's church. Two Israeli youths arrived with a small dog and talked noisily on their mobile phones as they settled at another table. The dog yapped at anything that moved in the square and they and the barking terrier generally spoiled the serenity we had had before. The family beside me looked uncomfortable.

The youths read the menu that was housed in an ornate wooden stand made from Olive Wood. They were arrogant in their manner, as they ordered, but the waiter seemed unaffected by their behaviour.

The dog jumped onto the table and from its high point, yapped at everyone passing. Eventually, one of the men lifted it onto the floor and gave it a menu to chew on.

I felt angry about their disregard for the owner's property and felt the situation was representative of bigger issues. After a few minutes, I had to speak.

"Excuse me!" I said, but they were making so much noise themselves, they didn't hear me.

"Excuse me!" I said again. As I did, a hand was placed on my shoulder from behind and I turned to see the old Arab owner behind me.

"It's fine!" He said smiling.

"It's not fine!" I replied. "The dog is eating your menu."

"I know." he said calmly, but it isn't worth it! It is best to just leave it."

He was like a profit of peaceful karma, I suddenly felt better about it as he continued.

"Would you like some mint tea and Knaffeh?" He brought me the best mint tea and a dessert I hadn't eaten before. It is a thin spun pastry soaked in sugar-based syrup and layered with white cheese and pistachio nuts. This is often served with vanilla ice cream.

The noisy men drank their coffee and left soon after and peace was restored. I have never forgotten the compromise made. In the general scheme of things, it was a small issue, but I wondered how often they put up with it.

Chapter 15

Rehovot

A memorable time was in November 2009. I would never have believed I could achieve so much in 3 days.

On tour with Hanitai, we visited the Ayalon Institute at Kibbutz Hill, Rehovot.

The land here was purchased from the Arabs some 60 years before the State was declared and is a Kibbutz from the time of the first Jewish immigration in the late 19th Century. Zionist organisations throughout the world purchased plots of land from established Arabs, bringing Jews from Eastern Europe to Palestine after 2000 years of Diaspora. Palestine was then under strict Ottoman Rule; that Britain saw fit to conquer in 1917.

Here I met Ohad, a lecturer at the institution, now an agricultural centre and business school. Ohad spent a morning with us, explaining how life there had changed little since the State was founded.

I learned that this old cooperative had always had, on the face of it, a tolerant perspective and worked towards a moderate association with the British. The history of the Kibbutz, under colonial rule, was entrenched in the work and mentality of Hagana and Palmach in the early 1940s and Ohad was keen to promote this.

It is, however, difficult to say whether the same cordial approach remained within these organisations during the shifts that took place, as communities merged at different stages, during British demobilisation.

As the State was born, activity became somewhat disjointed; more erratic and independent initiatives were apparent as Arabs invaded on all fronts. Nevertheless, the Hagana and the Palmach were, generally, classed as a moral army that tried to maintain harmony with the British for as long as possible.

The history of Kibbutz Ayalon is famous throughout Israel as an example of an informed and visionary community. When it came to monitoring the political situation, they were one step ahead and secretly preparing for the time the Arab League would move in as the British moved out.

The famous enterprise here was a basement room dug some eight metres underground to establish a bullet factory with the soil discarded secretly a little at a time in the fashion of any secret tunneller. The workshop was disguised under a laundry room and a bakery, these being occupations that would require a chimney and as such, would allow ventilation without arousing suspicion. The cellar was filled with scrap machinery that had been brought from Poland in 1938 and taken by ship to Beirut. In 1941 it was craftily transported on British vehicles by Jews who were serving soldiers. It was left dormant until 1945 when the manufacture of ammunition began in readiness for the inevitable war on the ground.

Next to the Rehovot Science Park, on Kibbutz Hill, stands the Ayalon Institute, which tells one of the fascinating and mysterious stories in the history of the struggle for the establishment of the State of Israel. Here, beneath the ground, and right under the noses of the British, a factory was created for the production of 9mm bullets for the Sten submachine gun, which was the personal weapon of Palmach fighters. The factory lay eight metres below the ground and was the size of a tennis court. The task was assigned to the members of the Scouts, A group, who were joined by others, a total of 45 young men and women. The site operated under complete secrecy from 1945 until 1948, a period in which over 4 million bullets were produced.

(Photographs can be seen at ayalon@shimur.org.il)

Under the umbrella of the Council of Conservation and Heritage Sites in Israel.

The giraffes, so nicknamed, were the only ones privy to what was going on underground. The factory workers would eat breakfast and leave the canteen each day saying they were on their way to work in the fields. This ploy avoided suspicion for a while until questions were asked as to why agricultural workers looked so ashen and unhealthy. Those employed on munitions hardly looked like farmers who spent their days outdoors.

We climbed down a spiral staircase that led to the factory and I was shown a small booth, not much bigger than a telephone box, where primitive sunray lamps had been installed. Each worker was required to spend 15 minutes a day acquiring a better skin colour. At the end of the day, the workers would scrape their shoes on a hard surface to remove the gunpowder and small metal shards taken on by the leather and this wore them away quickly. Further suspicion ensued when the kibbutz cobbler realised that certain members of the community were having their shoes repaired regularly.

Constant shrewdness and caution were needed to continue the illegal activity, not only keeping inside knowledge away from the occupiers but ensuring careless talk didn't happen in their close-knit community.

The laundry was not only tending to the dirty washing of the kibbutzniks but also providing the British Army with 24-hour service and they had to ensure the noisy, old-fashioned appliances inside the washhouse drowned out the machinery underground.

The soldiers loved to visit, as they were always certain of a good meal and a welcome bottle of beer to quench their thirst in the horrendous heat. It was the policy of the kibbutz to keep them sweet with good food and the excellent, freshly baked bread that was being used, together with a strong washing soap, to mask the smell of gunpowder. Once or twice they were almost caught out by a random patrol and the community leaders discussed a way to stop the British from popping in unannounced.

No names were mentioned, but it was a cunning man from the canteen who asked the patrols to let them know of visits in advance as there was nothing worse than warm beer and it would be better if they knew to prepare some food and chill drinks before their arrival. This suggestion was gratefully received by the soldiers and eliminated, to some degree, the element of surprise, providing the opportunity to cease ammo-making until after the visit.

"Such, jolly nice people!" I can hear them saying.

Another couple joined us and we sat down on some packing cases and sandbags, placed to make the room historically authentic, and looked at the engineer's drawings of how the munitions factory was designed. This was followed by our own little debate about why the Stern Gang, LEHI, had continued to blow up British trains, vehicles and installations after November 1947. They were aware that demobilisation was underway and the British would be leaving the country in May 1948.

Neither, Hanitai nor Ohad could understand why the LEHI had blown up a train outside the back gates of Kibbutz Hill on 29th February 1948 as it slowed down on the approach to Rehovot station. While the existence of the factory was not common knowledge, we agreed, maybe with some naivety, that this 'run away faction' must have had little respect for the inhabitants of the kibbutz to put them in such danger. An American lady in our little gathering told us that it didn't matter who died in their pursuit of the British:

"They couldn't rest until every one of them had left, whether they were packing up or not!"

It seemed that they wanted to show the world that they had 'seen off' British Colonial Rule. Some didn't believe that they would ever leave, given the promises they had broken in the past. There was general disappointment in the country and some, even in the more moderate organisations, felt personally let down after fighting with them conditionally, the British had gone back on their word to keep the Arabs sweet.

Hanitai came back at us with a more positive view and from someone who was around at the time:

"Don't get too hung up on everyone being evil and against the English," he said, "LEHI were just 900 men; there were many thousands here who were grateful to soldiers who had helped them. Many things were going on in this orchestra and LEHI was the piccolo; you didn't hear it very often, but when the piccolo plays, it does so very loudly. The piece is very complicated."

He constantly tried to teach about the different factions and mentalities, but sometimes I felt that he believed we would never get to grips with it. My Dad told me that the soldiers were so tense in a thankless situation, that in a 'them or us' scenario, they would shoot first and ask questions later. Troops were afraid to walk the streets and there was the constant worry of not knowing who to trust. More difficult for many who found themselves in a situation with no actual knowledge of what it was all about.

I was pleased to learn that in this place, there was evidence of some sort of decent liaison between the Jews and the British. It also became more apparent that the methods of the extreme freedom fighters were not popular with the general public. I also began to understand the confused mindset of those who had just arrived in the country, often illegally and didn't know the whereabouts of the rest of their families, missing since the Germans had moved across Europe.

The British, allowing entry to only 1200 refugees a month, didn't allow sufficient recruitment for a new nation that needed an army to fight an impending Arab invasion. It seemed that there were many on all sides that had been dumped in a God-forsaken land of strangers. Some of the natives went about carrying out their personal agendas. The British, still in Palestine representing the end of the Empire, were just doing as they were told and waiting to go home.

Showing us photographs of the train wreckage left after the explosion in February 1948, Ohad explained how injured soldiers were brought from the blazing train and received attention from the kibbutz doctors. Some of the people working in the munitions factory below had received the coded 3 light warning from the sentry box at the front gate as the explosion happened and climbed the ladders to ground level very quickly.

They covered their work clothes with white coats as they ran down the dirt track to help carry the wounded away from the incident. British newspapers related news of the attack on 1st March 1948 describing the carnage as a result of 3 land mines under the Cairo to Haifa troop train, being activated by a pusher at 9.45 a.m. A 4th mine had failed to explode, saving another packed carriage, but locals had described the orange groves littered with wood and limbs.

The reports mentioned confusion as assistance arrived when the British thought that more terrorists were coming out of a nearby wooded area. Fortunately, 2 girls managed to get through and convince the soldiers to stop shooting. The British officially thanked the people from surrounding areas who came to help as they couldn't call in for assistance after the telephone lines had been cut.

Ohad stressed the character of the kibbutzniks at the time:

"If you are injured, you need help whoever you are."

He also stressed assuredly that the manufacture of ammunition was intended for the inevitable Arab invasion and not to fight the British.

"We were doing what we had to do under the noses of the British, but it was never the intention of the people here to make them suffer."

While travelling with Hanitai I was privileged to be labelled as someone who had learned something about Israel before my visits and he sometimes spoke quietly in Hebrew to the people we met. I think the mysterious conversations were complementary as I was treated as more than a novice on certain subjects. The first few times it happened, I suppose I was a little paranoid, but eventually flattered to be treated more as an equal, or more so, less of a threat.

This became apparent again as we were leaving Kibbutz Hill. Ohad, escorting us back to our vehicle, suddenly asked me about our plan to go to the British Cemetery at Ramle. He asked to see the poppy posy I was taking there as he had only ever seen poppies on television in November. We weren't solemn as he looked at it, but he was thoughtful before speaking again.

"Would you like to go down to the railway line and see where the explosion happened? I can get the keys and open the gates at the bottom of the hill!"

The thought of encountering such a reality unnerved me a little, but I was very grateful for the opportunity and agreed.

He went off to the office and left me standing on the spot with Hanitai, I was a little apprehensive. As I write this, it's as if I'm there again with the hot sun beating down on me and the packed sand beneath my feet, anticipating a visit to the exact spot where 26 of our lads were blown up by terrorists.

With my Dad's voice in my head telling me to hold it together until the remembrance service is over, I felt a mixture of panic and honour as Ohad came running across the dusty car park with the keys. He seemed pleased that he was contributing to some more of my research and in some way building a bridge.

I went to the passenger door and opened it, which confused Hanitai, but I was collecting a poppy cross from my other bag and told him so. We walked down the dirt track together, between well-established olive bushes, but didn't speak until we reached the gate in a ten-foot boundary fence. I saw the railway line that still carries passenger and goods trains in and out of Rehovot station today.

A smooth modern train crawled in front of us and came to a halt waiting for the signal to enter the station just around the bend. We waited in the trees as members of the Stern Gang had done 60 years before and when the train had gone out of sight, Ohad opened the squeaky gate.

We walked on new ballast laid on sandy dunes and I asked where it had happened. Showing me the place, I looked around for a minute, at the hot polished metal of the lines and the sparse grasses that grew out of the desert land. I embedded the little wooden cross into the hard sandstones and we stood in silence for a minute. Ohad stood beside me and Hanitai wandered off for a minute as he does when his emotions get the better of him.

I was very pleased to have been able to do this – another gem that I would never have dreamt of.

We turned to leave and I made the same journey as the injured and dead had done, back up the dirt track. Ohad told me that he knew that my Father had been in Palestine and asked whether he was still alive.

He surprised me by explaining the difficulties the British had encountered and sympathised with their situation, especially on the coast and the issues of displaced people and illegal ships.

I agreed: "It was a miserable situation for those having to board ships that were transporting women and children. Sometimes it was a big surprise to find such cargo when you had been told that the ships were full of troublemakers who were just coming to join the Irgun and kill some more of your friends. Some soldiers didn't want to carry out certain orders. Just as many Israeli soldiers don't today!"

We had surprised each other as he told me, he had never really thought about it. We both despaired at the difficulties of dealing with displaced and desperate people, trust issues, and fear of who you might be dealing with in new and difficult situations.

I likened the British soldier in Palestine in 1947, to those on the border today. They might also get up in the morning and say,

"I can't do this anymore!"

"Occasionally British soldiers were absent without leave, rather than insight a mutiny," I told him.

"The elders in England tell me, Palestine was a dirty, ugly war, but my Father later despaired for the displaced people when he heard they were drowning in the Mediterranean and sympathised with those who had to fish them out or guard them in the displacement camps in Cyprus."

We were by then back in the gardens and looked to see Hanitai, who hadn't walked back with us, but a few paces behind and was now checking out old ploughs, wooden forks, and other hand-made agricultural tools.

"We had these at home when I was a boy!" he told us. He was reminiscing about his childhood in the Kibbutz and the mood seemed to lighten again.

We watched him as he moved over to check out some old and rusty milk churns.

"Do you know what these were used for Julie?" he shouted

I thought it was a trick question or a quiz', so said in quick succession, "Carrying milk; carrying ammo; blowing up the King David Hotel!"

This shocked him and I don't know why, we all laughed at such black humour. None of it was funny, but it seemed to say: It happened, but we're here now!

When we were back in the Land Cruiser, Hanitai told us we were off to an Arab cafe in Ramle that makes the best hummus and pita bread, but seemed preoccupied, away with his thoughts somehow and I asked him if he was ok and he said.

"I think it is very sad that young men have to face such awful deaths when they are just doing as they are told! I wonder what the people of England think of us today!"

"The majority don't have an opinion about that time," I told him. "Whatever happened in Palestine aren't things we talk about much in England. Many have no idea about our time here.

If you are thinking about bitterness towards the enemy, I think we are more likely to talk about the Japanese. I know gentlemen who would refuse to travel in this vehicle. Palestine is known as a forgotten war and I believe my Father reached a place where he wasn't bitter. Time makes you see things differently; he could see the other side more in the end!"

"Well he should have been bitter!" he said quite emotionally, "it was absolute balagan. Some people went too far!"

"Absolute what?" I asked him.

"Balagan!" he repeated. "Have you not heard that before? It means chaos, everything messed up, and no control. It's an Arabic word and is generally used to describe the Middle East!"

"Years ago," I told him, "When I first learned about things that happened here, I wasn't this calm. I used to shout about it, and especially after he died, usually to my Mother.

Sometimes, I was so angry and I couldn't think about that period without getting upset. I suppose that's why she wanted me to leave it alone. By the time he'd gone, I was too close to it to leave it alone.

I had already started digging.

My Dad warned me, more than once, "The Jews will break your heart, they'll never let you in." and I wonder whether they broke his.

"And have they broken your heart?" he asked looking thoughtfully at his passenger.

"The situation, from start to finish, breaks my heart," I told him. "I don't think the Jews have ever tried to do me any harm intentionally. But you can be a peculiar lot!" He nodded in agreement as he stopped at the traffic lights.

I continued, "At first he didn't want me to go to Israel, he couldn't understand why I had been fascinated with the Jewish People since I was in my teens, and then, he wasn't impressed when he found out I was reading the Odessa Files."

He said, "Don't start reading about the Holocaust, you'll never sleep at night!'

"My earliest memory on the subject was when I was about 14 yrs old. My Mam, Dad and I were sitting at the breakfast table one Sunday morning."

I told them I had had a strange dream that I didn't understand.

I explained how my Dad and I were standing on the footplate of a steam train that was crawling along a shoreline. He was wearing khaki shorts, long socks, and boots. Behind the train, there were soldiers working on the railway line. On the beach, a group of children was dancing in a big circle and I asked him if I could go and play with them. He said 'No! Stay here with me.'

My Mother was as puzzled as I was.

My Father got up from the table and said,

"You've been to Palestine. Forget it now and don't go there again."

It felt like a taboo subject and we didn't speak about it again, but it looks like I didn't listen to his advice.

Hanitai was thoughtful as he was driving, but didn't say anything else for a few minutes, but then told me about an early memory of his own Father.

"The English were very nice people, they did lot of good things to help us." He said.

SCRATCHING THE SURFACE

One Friday afternoon in June 1946, a British officer came to warn Hanitai's Father about the impending operation to arrest all leaders of the Underground. His village was close to a British base and the officer asked who the commander was, which eventually brought him an audience with his Father.

He was informed that the operation would commence at midnight. There was a curfew from 6 o'clock so there was no way they could get a message to Tel Aviv to warn all who resided there. They couldn't drive on the roads for fear of being stopped and felt sure that the British would be listening to any telephone calls.

Someone called the hospital and advised that they had a small boy who had been bitten by a snake and they feared for his life. Hanitai was appropriately bandaged ready for the ambulance to collect him and his Father and he left for Tel Aviv, having advised the driver of the desperate situation.

On the way, they were stopped by British soldiers who opened the back doors of the ambulance to see the young boy on the stretcher. When his Father explained the situation:

"The soldiers were perfect gentlemen and wanted to help me!"

After the checkpoint, they continued the journey alone and headed for the house of Ephraim Dekel, a Hagana Commander who was Hanitai's Uncle. Before midnight, they were able to warn some of the leaders of the impending raids, but not all. Many of the high commanders were able to flee without being apprehended and Hanitai stayed with his Aunt until the operation was over, some three days later. Some

Palmach members were killed as the British rounded up people and weapons on the following Saturday.

His Uncle, Ephraim Dekel was born in Russia in 1903 and moved to live in Israel in 1921. He set up the Intelligence Service, The Shai, in Tel Aviv in 1934 and headed it until 1946. Underground intelligence was established before this, The Shai was formed nationally in Jewish Palestine in 1940. Dekel monitored British radio and telephone communications, with other Shai members. Together they worked on deciphering British codes that normally changed weekly. In 1946 he was sent to Europe to assist in the escape of Jews from Europe. In Europe he was also in charge of the secret arms-purchasing efforts for the Hagana underground militia in Palestine.

Suddenly, out of nowhere, we had our own balagan in the centre of Ramle. It started to rain – and boy did it rain. Everyone just stopped for a few minutes and waited until they could see through their windscreens again and then crawled away through standing water.

Our conversation changed to the weather as it always does with the British, until we parked up in a strange alley surrounded by shanty buildings that we, in Manchester, might refer to as derelict. I surveyed the remains of a breeze-block wall as we pulled up beside it and wondered where on earth we were going now.

The rain had stopped and we had to avoid the craters on the road surface that were filled with water, up until then, it had been a glorious day, and the sun was coming out again.

Walking along the broken road surface of a very poor street, some Arab women with small children walked towards us, but they didn't smile back, just hung their heads as they passed. It was a rough area around the place we had chosen as a car park, but it seemed to improve a little further along the road. Near the cafe was a small church with a square bell tower similar to some I have seen in Bethlehem.

Thinking how quaint it looked among the rubble and believing it to be a Christian Arab church, generally under the denomination of the Greek Orthodox, I took a photograph. It had an open bell tower and the bell hung on a rope like a chapel in the wild-west. Among randomly placed buildings in various states of dilapidation, I found a little tumble-down house draped in an abundance of purple flowers. Further along, there was and huge earthenware vase, it was straight out of Alibaba and big enough to accommodate a genie and I couldn't pass it without taking a picture. Hanitai allowed me to stroll and gaze in wonder at the beautiful things amid a partially broken town.

Inside the restaurant, which was like a canteen with a long counter along the back wall, we were so out of place as we sat down on crude metal chairs.

There was no way you could creep in either as the legs scraped on the stone floor and it seemed as if everyone stared at us.

I was a stranger in town, but Hanitai was well versed in the procedure.

He was in command and gave the order, in Hebrew, to a teenage boy who approached us, also asking if I could use the toilet. He then turned to his phone to see if he had any messages.

"It's in there!" the expressionless young man told me, pointing in the direction of the kitchen. I ventured slowly around the corner behind the counter and met with the cool black eyes of an elderly man wearing pale grey cotton from head to foot. He was leaning on the wall smoking a cigarette.

"Is there a toilet?" I asked.

He said nothing but dismissed me into the area behind me. I had to walk through the kitchen as the toilet was in a small room in the back corner. The cooks were all men and they didn't look up. I didn't expect the single toilet to be decorated with beautiful blue tiles, or that there would be sweet-smelling hand wash on the sink. It was a nice surprise.

When I came out, the impolite smoker had gone, but in the doorway, I came face-to-face with another man carrying an old oil drum. He didn't move and looked at me as if I was in the way, so I stepped aside to let him pass.

He said nothing, but I saw the drum was half filled with chickpeas.

'That's my lunch,' I thought and prayed for the continued health of my stomach.

Sitting down, the order had arrived and Hanitai beckoned me to, "Eat, eat already," like a Jewish mama and I surveyed a table filled with a feast.

We had falafel and tahini dip and big dishes of hummus; swimming in oil and topped with chickpeas, topped off with flatbread. I was hungry and ate plenty, washing it down with bottled water. Hanitai ordered some hummus to take away and it was brought to him in a plastic tub with a lid.

Communication with the Arabs was sparse and I felt tolerated but well-fed. It was a good experience and though they seemed pretty cool toward us, it gave me more confidence to venture into Arab restaurants in Jaffa, where I found the owners much more talkative.

I thought more about the past and their lives today. Is this how it was when the British went to a cafe? Has colonialism changed hands? Are the beautiful things, I see, remnants of an Arab village where genie pots used to line the way?

Were the buildings repaired with, make-shift, breeze blocks once fashioned completely, in the Ottoman stone I saw at the bottom of their walls? I had a lot to learn.

Chapter 16

Ramle Cemetery

When we arrived at the Ramle cemetery, we were disappointed to find the gates locked. I could see Hanitai's mind working overtime as he went on reconnaissance around the stone house by the entrance and tried to look over the perimeter wall.

I was resigned to defeat and suggested we come back on another day, but he didn't answer for a minute as the cogwheels in his head kept turning.

"We'll go over the wall!" He said suddenly, and with that, he was gone – over the wall.

"Oh no", I thought, "he's on manoeuvres and I'm left standing here!" I couldn't even see over the wall. There was no consideration for my inadequacies; Israelis think everyone is a soldier because everyone has been in the army and there's no excuse for lazy softies.

I looked around and in a corner, where the wall went off at an angle, I saw a mound made from composted garden waste. Standing upon this gave me a 3-foot start and I could see him chatting to someone in front of the stone house.

"Oh good I thought, he's not watching!"

I managed to get a foothold in the rough fascia and was grateful for the stone's irregularity, also for the blessing of higher ground on the other side. Sloth-like scrambling got me over and I strolled over to him as if it was the most natural way to enter a cemetery.

"Where have you been?" he asked impatiently.

Introducing me to the 2 gardeners, he told them how I came from England and it was very important to me to see the graves. I learned this with his later translation from Hebrew and they welcomed me and asked us to stay as long as we wanted. As they walked off along the manicured lawn I realised my priority.

"Get them to open the gate Hanitai!"

Laughing smugly, he shouted the request, and they obliged with great kindness.

I saw that the cemetery sat in the middle of an abandoned plain, but nearby was a small white mosque complete with a beautiful minaret.

In this Arab town, I saw through a mesh fence, topped with barbed wire, the vastness of the cement factory for which Ramle is particularly known.

I later learned that this flat ground was close to the site of The Battle of Station Junction, in the aftermath of the Battle for Mughar Ridge in November 1917. The railway station, originally in Turkish hands marked a split in the main Damascus, Jerusalem line and branched out towards Gaza, Jaffa, and Beersheba. This strategic operation involving the 7th and 8th British armies and Australian forces was important in the South Palestine offensive. However, from where I stood, I couldn't see any remaining railway lines on the parched soil.

Inside the cemetery, the headstones of many nationalities spread out before me, commemorating the dead from 1917, and with thanks to the War Graves Commission, I am providing statistics.

> World War 1 – 3,300, World War 11 – 1,168,
> British Mandate for Palestine – 525
> Unknown from World War 1- 964
>
> Burials by Nation:
> The United Kingdom 3608, India 528, Poland 272,
> New Zealand 94, France 77, Australia 71,
> High Commission Territories 58, Italy 41, Africa 41,
> South Africa 35, British West Indies 23, Arab 12,
> Yugoslavia 11, Czechoslovakia 7, Belgium 3,
> Seychelles 2, Norway, 2, Canada 2, Turkey 416,
> Germany 31.

Among those buried in Ramle are the 2 British sergeants, Mervyn Paice and Clifford Martin, killed by the Irgun in 1947, in response to the death sentences carried out by British Mandate authorities, on 3 of their members.

We walked around quietly for a while, both drinking in names and eras represented. Hanitai helped me to assess the layout and find the headstones representing British Mandatory Rule for its 30-year period, the last one buried had been killed on 9th May 1948. This was poignant I told him, as it was my Father's 20th birthday.

I asked again:

"Why did it matter so much to kill someone else on the day before they were due to lower the flag? There were only a few of them left by then."

"There was no need at all," he said, "they just had to make a point!"

We were saddened by the number of British men killed during demobilisation between November 1947 and May 1948. They were in a row by the fence and a soft breeze blew in from the Judean Hills in the distance.

We spent a while looking at the regimental insignia on the headstones and with this, had a refresher course on beret badges. We talked about Field Marshal Montgomery and the fact that he wore both the badge of the Tank Regiment and another of a Field Marshal on his beret. I explained that he was generally a law unto himself.

Each plot was tended and had an individual shrub or rosebush, and with additional rows of flora and fauna gracing random flower beds, it made a restful English garden of remembrance surrounded by barren land.

Finding the resting place of a German, Hanitai asked why we would bury one of the enemies among us. He talked about how we were known for bringing injured enemy soldiers out of the desert and nursing them in local hospitals and thought it was strange to bury them here if they passed away.

I didn't find it peculiar, but suggested Israel's enemies were not Jewish and would need to go to an Arab garden, even though on reflection, some Arabs and Turkish soldiers are buried in Ramle cemetery. The cenotaph in a War Graves resting ground allows for different denominations in its design. Nevertheless, it gave us something to talk about and the reactions of those who make decisions in the field of battle are far removed from standing here peacefully with this veteran.

Our solitude was suddenly broken when a group of 4 Arab youths appeared outside the high fence. As we walked past them, they shouted, "Shalom!" and we returned the greeting not expecting what followed. They began to laugh and jeer at us loudly and I imagined they were launching insults in our direction. The mood changed, but Hanitai just held his ground, watched them, and despaired.

"What are they saying?" I asked.

"Never mind!" he said and turned his back on them to walk away.

"What's going on with them?" I asked, stumped by the language barrier. I slowly followed him as the noise from the boys became louder and they became more animated with their gestures.

"They are Arabs; they do that, just leave it!" He said quite seriously.

I'll never know what they said, for my commander had spoken and he meant it.

He asked if I wanted to lay my poppies and volunteered to get them from the car. He went off and told me to wait where I was away from Arabs and not to go on a peace-keeping mission. They continued for a few minutes, but I was distanced as I strolled across to a row of people who had been sleeping there since 1947. I looked back to see them walk off, as kicking the dry dirt, they went toward the town.

Hanitai gave me the poppy crosses and held onto the posy of poppies as I placed the small wooded stakes into the ground at the end of the row.

"You should come here in November." he said. "All the dignitaries come here for the service. Sometimes there is a piper."

"No, I think I prefer to be here when it's quiet, it's a better environment for thinking."

At this, he nodded his head understandingly.

We walked towards the white block cenotaph engraved with the words: 'Their name liveth forevermore'. And handing the posy to me, he produced a small poetry book from his pocket.

"If you wouldn't mind, I'd like to read a poem as you put down the flowers," he said humbly.

I thought this was a lovely thought and it suggested to me that he had personal reflections of the challenges faced by the British in Palestine.

I was overwhelmed and grateful for the heartfelt words of this new friend, and felt sure my Father would have appreciated them too. He would have been so pleased to know that we had visited a place where Tommy may have been placed and have a poem read to him by an Israeli officer.

> In Flanders' fields, the poppies blow
> Between the crosses, row on row
> That mark our place: and in the sky
> The larks, still bravely singing, fly
> Scarce heard amid the guns below
> We are the dead. Short days ago
> We lived, felt dawn, saw sunset glow
> Loved and were loved, and now we lie
> In Flanders' fields
> Take up our quarrel with the foe
> To you from failing hands we throw
> The torch; be yours to hold it high
> If ye break faith with us who die
> We shall not sleep, though poppies grow
> In Flanders' Fields.
> *Lieutenant Colonel John McCrae 1915*

I thanked Hanitai for his sincere reading and saying it was a pleasure, he wanted me to instil in my mind that the methods adopted by terrorists, or freedom fighters in the 1940s, were not approved by everyone. He told me he felt confident that the care of the British cemeteries in Israel would continue and would always be regarded with respect.

Chapter 17

On the Gaza border

There are French Jews in Ashdod. Many Jews are fleeing Europe again in 2016, following recent alleged attacks by fundamental extremists who believe they represent true Islam.

Having chosen a permanent move to Israel, many French families have settled in the area south of Tel Aviv in the new cities of Ashdod and Ashkelon. According to news channels, world consensus may be that they would probably be safer staying in France rather than building a new life so close to the unsettled Gaza border. Nevertheless, it seemed the main deciding factor was that Europe was, and still under threat from a new anti-Semitism. At least, in Israel, they see shared solidarity and a locally acknowledged need for the inherited contained community.

Flocking to the Holy Land at Prime Minister Binyamin Netanyahu's personal invitation in his undertaking to protect world Jewry, by building a security wall, seems to have been received as a paradoxical opportunity to be safe.

The Western World continues to fight the turmoil created by those that are duty-bound to commit actions of grave terrorism and atrocities against religious freedom. It is little wonder that millions of unsettled and displaced people have no idea which way to turn and question whether their hitherto settled existence is in danger once again.

Ashdod is a very modern place, said to be among the top 6 cities in Israel and sees much of the state's imported goods passing through its modern port.

The Ashdod area is mentioned in the Bible, as Ashdud, a place where the Philistines lived. The modern city has grown up near the site of the, pre-independence town, following the Arab-Israeli War of 1948.The British Census of Palestine taken in 1922 shows that over 2000 Arabs lived in the town with 11 Christians.

There is evidence that there was a Persian khan on the main trade route through the ancient town, with a huge hostelry where caravans of camel-riding traders would have rested. On approach, the khan may have looked like a palace or fort, with a central courtyard flanked by animal stalls. The first evidence of Jews buying land in the area is said to be 1945 when British records quote the presence of Jewish homes for 290 people.

Today, the city has a mass of modern apartments, some overlooking the sea and others edging wide boulevards named after famous Israelis, such as Menachem Begin and Moshe Dayan. There is a large shopping and leisure complex and a marina to accommodate about 600 vessels at anchor.

Lately, despite the uncertainty of peace in the area due to missile launches from across the Gaza border, tourists are visiting here and more and more Israelis are taking the short trip from Tel Aviv to visit families who have set up homes in the many new builds. Apart from the newly established French population, communities have developed with immigrants from Georgia and Morocco. The land was officially acquired by Israel as part of the 1949 armistice agreement after the Egyptians gave up their temporary foothold.

The traffic navigation, WAZE helped us on our journey, keeping us on the right track and we heard there was a 5-kilometre tailback from Ashkelon due to an incident and the Port Traffic build-up becomes apparent. Heavy haulage begins to build up and slow down and the drivers start to weave in and out instead of waiting patiently. Some vehicles wander on and off the hard shoulder, our vehicle included.

Sometimes I feel a bit uncomfortable with some manoeuvres, based on what is acceptable at home. Grinding to a halt, Hanitai translates the traffic bulletin telling us that a lorry has shed its load on this route and we are expecting delays and a diversion at the next junction.

While waiting we discuss whether you can tell the age of the car by the number plate. The Israeli government has decided to stop this practice and the system is quite random now.

"So, the car in front," I am told, "could be very old or brand new."

Political party posters have been hung onto the gantries with string and a huge folding banner of Binyamin Netanyahu flaps about in the breeze. Another contribution by some cynic of the political system has placed another one saying, "Trust God!"

Thinking practically, my concern is that one might fall onto a windscreen and cause an accident. Telling Hanitai why this wouldn't be allowed at home and he sees the danger and nods.

"We haven't time to worry about this!" he says calmly, "we have bigger issues!"

I understandingly accept that. We are quite laid back about the situation compared to the impatience of those around us, though he mentions that the delay may affect his schedule for the day.

I watch a goods train, running parallel with the highway; shimmering in the heat as it passes by smugly with no regard for the chaos beside it.

Before long we are diverted onto a lesser know country road which is inadequate for the volume of traffic and we crawl along for half an hour chatting and listening to the radio. The benefit of the diversion shows me some beautiful villages and the spring flowers that only stay for a few weeks in the spring before the soil dries up. There are miles and miles of, black rubber, irrigation pipes going across the fields and farmers are planting with modern machinery similar to things that might be seen at home.

Suddenly, Hanitai's impatience took over; we were an hour late and he pulled over into the hedgerow and got out of the Hilux to get something out of the boot, which he calls a trunk, in favour of Israeli Americanism. He returned with an iPad and logged onto a field map website and told me,

"We'll use the field roads and we will complete our mission if it takes us until midnight!"

Admiring his determination, I prayed that he didn't want me to map read, as I failed miserably at this subject at school and my sense of direction has not improved since.

"Here, take this." He said and I looked on a screen at a map of purple and green that meant nothing.

Fortunately, he didn't look at it again; it must have been a refresher course because he knows this land like the back of his hand. No problem!

He soon found a hole in the hedge and off we went across an already bone-dry field, soon moving onto a narrow dirt trail, whose edges were churned up by tank tracks. These had probably been ravaged by tanks during Operation Protective Edge earlier in the year. It hits home that this is where it all happens.

This is the real connection to the conflict and the daily war watching I see on television. The varied channels, with different opinions I watch at home, either show Israeli security measures as justification for airstrikes, or the miserable conditions for the Palestinian people. It goes on - just over there somewhere. It is daunting for me, as we carry on and eventually reach our destination via military short-cuts.

*****

In the Black Arrow memorial ground and park on the edge of no man's land by the border of the Gaza Strip black letters have been engraved in Hebrew on pristine shards of white granite. The names of strangers to me, of course, but Hanitai pointed to them one by one advising that he had fought with them in the Battle for Suez in 1956.

"This man I knew, and this one; and this one!"

Sadness veiled his expression and the heavy heart of a veteran soldier filled the void between us as he, no doubt, thought about the miserable times. In Israel where, since the country's birth, there has always been conflict on one border or another, combatants are linked to reflections of their personal skirmishes. Hanitai, the retired second lieutenant with an army service that spans the age of the State, is a meticulous historian and very connected companion.

Silence fell for a moment and I left him alone with his thoughts and strolled to an excellent vantage point to look straight into the Gaza Strip. I was not alone for long, however, as my bodyguard was soon beside me, thoughts of fallen comrades set aside as he was watching my back today. At first, I felt that he was always in my space; my protectorate never left me to my own devices for a minute, but I was soon mindful that I was within feet of a buffer zone open to random ground activity.

Through army issue binoculars, it was quite overwhelming to be there, looking into the strip and seeing well-known landmarks.

It all looked strangely familiar to me after watching the area for years, via long-distance, media perspectives. How long have I been comparing one report to another and considering the lop-sided views of journalists? I was, forever hoping, that the world would, with analysis, see things from both sides. Physically it appeared not to have changed much for decades, but it was, now, politically unrecognisable from the Yasser Arafat days of the 1990s.

"Some may not have had a good word for Arafat," I said, "but do you think that it was a case of, better the devil you know? Would you say that his successors are worse?"

He shrugged hopelessly, balancing his sunglasses on the top of his head.

"I just wish more people knew that the situation here revolves around mostly decent people who just want to get on with their lives. You know, when we cleared Gaza of Settlements in the name of 'Land for Peace', look what happened. The Road Map to Peace is a mess. The Settlers moved out so that the Palestinians could build their own lives and look at it! Hamas moved in and make it awful for their own people."

As an observer, I had no intention of interrogating my guide in search of who should take responsibility for the reported desperate situation in which the Palestinians found themselves. I was resigned that neither of us was an authority on the true conditions since this narrow stretch of land, with a population of one and a half million people, (estimate in 2015) was fenced off by the Israelis after Operation Cast Lead at the start of 2009.

Only recently, in the same year, history had repeated itself with missiles raining down on Israeli towns in the area. The inevitable retaliation from Israel, this time in Operation Protective Edge had proved to be different. After years of combat against mobile missile units and then another ground offensive, things had changed here, with the discovery of Hamas tunnels burrowed a long way under no man's land and coming out inside Israeli kibbutz' communities.

The land between the Strip, and the place we stood in, was farmland that stretched out as far as the perimeter fence on the other side. This, being a no-go area, seemed like such a waste and I despaired at the impact it must be having on people's livelihood, but could see how occupying such a sizeable space would hinder Hamas' capabilities. It may limit the launch of rockets hitting Ashdod and Ashkelon and reduce the likelihood of soldier abduction, but it is wasteland and tragic to see in a very narrow country and a densely populated Gaza. I was further saddened to learn that people had been shot at for venturing into their own patches of land that border the perimeter fence inside Gaza.

Indeed, the whole world tends to question whether the measures to protect the population in this area are disproportionate. Having just passed some properties that lay victim to the latest Kassam rockets and seeing the groups of soldiers now needed, in case a terrorist appears at the entrance of a hidden tunnel on the village green, I understood.

Did I have to resign myself to the fact that awful tit-for-tat reprisals would continue beside the debates on human rights forums until some sort of permanent ceasefire or peace is achieved?

I asked Hanitai about the duties of the soldiers in the lighthouse-shaped observation towers; sitting alone for hours on end and looking out through camouflage netting.

"In the tower, there's like a small kitchen area", he said, "Where they can make coffee and keep food. It's not great, but they change them around after about 6 hours. They can shoot at those whom they think are a danger to them!"

"Or even those who aren't?" I said, despairingly, "How do they know?"

I wondered how such a fraught existence between 2 Peoples could have reached any type of agreement on demarcation and wondered whether orders would be vague in an ever-changing situation, coupled with the added complication of ever-shifting personnel.

"What are the consequences for the soldier if he makes a wrong decision?" I asked, "There's no second opinion is there? No time to call in!"

"I don't know!" he said, "It's a long time since I worked with young soldiers on guard duty and I'm too old to have been involved here. I am thankful that I have never had to work around the settlements or guard a kibbutz. My duties as a tank commander have always been with squadrons or training people in armoured divisions."

"The situation certainly feels bigger than both of us standing here," I said.

Nodding thoughtfully, he agreed and told me that he wished he had the answers for the Middle East and me. "Everyone gets so tired!" he said wearily, and who wouldn't after a lifetime of it?

We stood quietly for a while watching 2 Israeli reconnaissance vehicles patrolling slowly along the service road between the fences of the buffer zone.

"They're keeping apart to ensure that any damage inflicted on one vehicle won't affect the other aren't they?"

"That's right!" he said, surprised that I had some sort of military insight. "How did you know that?"

"British basics really: Land mines on the road in Afghanistan; don't walk too close together around the streets of Belfast; a general rule I suppose. I bet we taught you how to do it." I said smugly, trying to lighten the mood.

He laughed and immediately reminded me of the feeble engineering of a sunken pontoon bridge we'd seen across a dry wadi earlier in the day. My excuse that it was built on sand 70 years ago made no difference; he insisted it was a poor job done by British Engineers. It was good to have banter.

I sat down on a concrete tank ramp, used to bring battle tanks from low loaders should immediate deployment to Gaza be required, visualising how its arrival would disrupt the tranquillity of the place. I imagined the sound of its engine as it tracked down the ramp, maybe going straight through the wire mesh fence and across the field, throwing out a cloud of dry dust as it cut up the sandy soil.

I wouldn't be intimidated, as tanks are old friends and I am quite used to them, but I would keep out of its way, only too aware of its fighting power. Easy for me to be untroubled, they don't live in my back yard, and when they did they never posed a daily threat.

Looking back towards the meandering patrol, something suddenly dawned on me and I was saddened.

"Hanitai, my Dad was driving too close to the ambulance in front when the terrorists blew it up, wasn't he? If he'd kept his distance, maybe the windscreen wouldn't have hit him in the face."

"Maybe," he shrugged, "who knows – in war, we make mistakes."

He made me smile as his tone had a stereotypical Jewish undertow with a 'what can you do?' inflection as he flayed his arms out.

I immediately realised that this was a futile debate now. No wishful 'if only' or reprimand to the old man, just odd that it had occurred to me there and then, on old Palestine ground.

My mentor carried on:

"In war, people make lots of mistakes, like the Irgun themselves, they should be sorry. What's the point? If they looked at getting rid of High Commissioners or other people who were making big decisions – fair enough, but what they did was stupid. If you want to get rid of the British, you use some sort of strategy that will hurt the top man. What was the point of picking on a young driver who was just doing as he was told?"

He stopped to think again, "It was all chaos you know, these people just wanted to be a nuisance so they could say – 'we saw off the English."

Hanitai was raised on a kibbutz; his late Father was a Hagana commander during the last days of British Mandatory Rule and he had always remained reasonable where the British were concerned. He did, however, feel let down by broken British promises, but insisted that negotiation would have resulted in a better deal than the grim times that preceded the founding of the State. Like his Father, Hanitai always embraces the old founder's mentality of the kibbutz youth movement, the Palmach and the level-headed Hagana, rather than the hard-line aggression of the Irgun and LEHI.

Beside one of the most controversial buffer zones in the world, I found a few minutes of contentment in the chaos. The April sun was warm and we appreciated a slight breeze coming in from the Negev. Quiet enough for a lizard to appear a few feet away from us and while I have no experience with reptiles, this one seemed remarkably big, basking on a rock. Standing perfectly still on long-clawed toes, his pale brown scales glinted in the sunlight. He was more alert than any of us, as his eyes moved on a ball in their sockets.

"Wow! He's beautiful," I whispered rising slowly to my feet, "I'm going to take his photograph."

"I wish you luck with that," Hanitai whispered with some amusement as I crept around the other side for a better view.

Almost there, I lifted my camera slowly.

"He's seen you," he said, knowing that the effort was hopeless and as I tried to get him into focus on the digital screen, he was gone. I turned to see Hanitai chuckling, amused by my naiveté at believing I could outwit a creature whose wisdom covers millennia. I was not only a novice soldier here, but realised that my companion had long since resigned himself to the futility of trying to creep up on a lizard.

"It's something you just know," he told me, "like the Israelis can't sniff out water as the Bedouins do. I don't know how they do it; they are like a horse or a camel. This is why the English used to take them out on missions. The Jews lost their knowledge of the land and what lies beneath it during 2000 years of Diaspora. We had to learn again. Sometimes we are successful with it and sometimes we are not. Like the land we have seen, some of it is green and some of it is bad. You just have to keep trying".

The lizard was neither Jew nor Arab, yet the land was his. His ancestors had been around since long before the arrival of any Semitic culture or monotheistic religion. In light of our reflections on the past, our discussion on the present and an unknown wonder on what the future might bring, we envied the lizard's simple, yet superior existence and called him Solomon.

Back in the vehicle, Hanitai told me it was time to eat something and drove to a garden and picnic area very close by. It was one of my favourite March weather days at about 20 degrees, sunny with a light breeze, and just the right type of day to sit on a bench and procrastinate for a while.

Hanitai set about preparing the usual spread of old East European fair. Strudels, bagels and he passed an avocado for me to peel and mash-up for the sandwiches. Handing me the lemon he had cut in half, reminded me: "Don't forget to put plenty of salt on!"

Over the years we have become accustomed to this treat on any of our stops in the wilderness. After my chores, I sat down at the table dressed with a blue table cloth, which he always insisted upon, because I'm British. I made ready with my tea bags brought from home, now desperate for some boiling water and a brew. He screwed his nose up at it and poured out some of his strong, undrinkable coffee.

Settling down to eat quietly in this favourite spot of the Western Negev, with the rumble of a tank somewhere in the distance, I felt a peculiar calm just knowing they were around. Hanitai talked to me about the field roads that had helped us make up time and how army maps can often be useful if you have the right vehicle, but sensing that my map reading was inferior, he hadn't encouraged me to do anything but watch and learn.

Suddenly the calm for me was broken by the sudden nearby clatter of an automatic weapon. Seeing me, wide-eyed and lifting my head and looking to him for instruction, he smiled wryly:

"It's the firing range behind the trees!" he told me taking another bite of his sandwich. "Do you think these guys would be crawling about calmly if Hamas were coming?"

He nodded his head to gesture that something was happening behind me and I turned to see 2 jeeps creeping in. It was apparently lunch time for the patrol and they were coming to the same picnic site to eat.

The soldiers pulled up and took out various plastic boxes from their land rovers. The clatter of mess tins and young men's Hebrew chatter filled the air. I bet he knew this would happen, I thought, I wouldn't be surprised

They pottered around a big round table that had a fixed bench. Some sat on the seats, one leaned on the side of the jeep and one with a telephone headset seemed to be stocktaking and dishing up rice and breaded chicken, but he didn't warm it and they tucked into it cold. I was surprised to see that they did the same with the tinned spaghetti and made a comment about cold food.

"They're 18-year-old lads who have been out all day, they're always hungry and they don't care what they eat!" said Hanitai, who had seen it all before.

"Can you see all the gear they are wearing?

They have to keep it on all the time.

Stab vests and jackets and the ammunition belts!" I looked over to see what they had with them as well as automatic weapons.

He continued, "There's a joke that is always told in training. I'll tell you!" He began:

"One soldier said to another, 'when you get home from manoeuvres, what's the first thing you do?

I make love to my wife, he replied.

Then what do you do?

I make love to my wife again!"

Then what do you do? Asked the first soldier again.

The other one said, "I take off my gear".

We both laughed as he told me that sometimes, letting me into a secret, the soldiers tell jokes about the British, usually about them being posh or polite. Or the fact that they think about things too long over a cup of tea. "It's more the old guard than the young ones." He said smiling.

"I've got a joke you'll like then," I said, and began.

"There's this posh lady in England and she's expecting twins and genie comes to see her."

"What's a genie?" He asked.

"Erm, a man that lives in a lamp and when you rub the lamp, he comes out and asks you what you wish for," I explained.

"Oh like in Aladdin?"

"Yes, that's right. So this genie asked the lady – if you could choose a special quality for your babies, what would it be?"

"Oh well, said the lady -They must have manners and are very polite!"

Anyway, after 5 years of the lady being pregnant, the babies don't arrive and the doctor decides to give her a caesarean to see what's going on. When he opened her up, he saw 2 little boys in bowler hats saying, "After you - no after you - no after you - no after you!"

Hanitai loved the joke and said he'd remember it for his friends as it was the very sort they liked.

"Jokes about the British gentleman; Yes we love those," he said.

Afterward, he tried to get me to eat more, but I 'politely' declined as there was always too much, he asked if I wanted to talk to the soldiers. I insisted that I didn't want to get in the way, but he muttered something as he walked away towards them, shaking his head and wittering about me - my not wanting to be a nuisance.

I started to clear up as he introduced himself to them and then they all seemed to grasp the idea at once, shouting me over to join them and they tried to get me to eat chicken and drink orange juice. I explained that Hanitai had already provided a feast.

A young stout lad with very olive skin, still eating spaghetti left his plate and stood up to move the tripod-mounted machine gun and offered me a seat. He placed it in front of me and asked if I wanted to look at it. Almost before I answered he was pulling it to pieces and asking me to look through the detachable sites.

"You need to put the Red Cross on your target. Here you do it." Within minutes, there I was, the virgin soldier who can only shut one eye, looking out through the olive trees and across into no man's land. I was grateful that I was only handling pieces and not the whole thing, surrounded by long belts of bullets now spread out across the table.

He eventually clicked all the parts of the gun back together and his colleague, a taller chap in a black woollen hat, asked where I was from. Hearing that I came from Manchester, he shouted in Hebrew, to his friend who was looking at something on his mobile phone. Coming to join us, he told me that he had a 5 year-old brother who wants to be a goalkeeper for Manchester United when he grows up. Soldier 3, with a thin face and designer spectacles, told me about his crazy kid brother who was always wearing one football kit or another.

They had only just finished basic training, so they hadn't been around during Operation Protective Edge some 5 months before, and didn't want to be part of another skirmish either. The tallest of them, with a broad smile and maybe the joker of the pack, said that with a bit of luck, they would be out of the way before it all starts again.

"Maybe, he told me, "If there is another war here in 2 years, I will have been sent somewhere else?"

"Who knows?" I said, "They don't have to happen every 2 years, even though there does seem to have been a regular pattern since 2009. How do you know? You might not want to leave the army after your service.

You may want to stay."

He grimaced thoughtfully, "I doubt it now."

The others were just hanging about chatting and Hanitai had left me with them and gone to carry on with our clearing up.

Soldier 4 continued; in hear-shot of everyone else. "I'm home-sick already, I want to go home!" I told him I was sorry, but he was stuck with it, just like everyone else. I asked him if it was just a case of missing home or was he unhappy with what he was doing?

He went on to tell me that he usually had a gun mounted on a tripod, but it was broken and in the workshop. He told me that he liked the technology and that computerised triggers were safer for everyone when you could fire the gun on top without getting out of the vehicle.

He was laughing again now. "It's always better if you don't have to stick your head out of the window. If you can see the enemy – the enemy can see you!" He told me as if it was something we all had to learn as new recruits.

Thinking about how much responsibility he had, I offered him a sobering question:

"When you are running on adrenaline, would it be easy to fire in anger or panic, with all that at your fingertips? One move can change the mood of the People around here and it escalates pretty quickly."

"No!" he said earnestly, "It's a serious weapon and there would always be a discussion before it was fired. I promise you, I have only ever fired in training. We would all rather be somewhere else, so we are not going to make things worse for ourselves."

I believed him, and as the others slowly gathered around, I saw they were nodding in agreement and I thought, as I often do, it's a shame they have to sacrifice their late teenage years.

After a thoughtful pause, the brother of the future goalkeeper asked where I had been on my travels with Hanitai. When I told them that I had been to the Occupied Territories earlier in the week, a few eyebrows were raised and they asked where exactly I had been.

I was a bit stumped after mentioning the big towns, but told them how I saw the difference in settlements on each side of the country.

"On this side of the country, everyone in the kibbutzim is nice and hospitable, even though they are dodging missiles, but in the West Bank, the Settlers told me to get lost."

This amused them as they all agreed that they tell them to get lost too, even though they were supposed to be taking care of them. As they were showing great interest in my travels, we established that it would be best for Hanitai to explain.

I shouted across to him and he waved his ok and got the map and a highlighter out of the passenger seat. Within a few minutes, they were all gathered around him as he explained our expedition. It was all a bit technical for me, especially as it was in Hebrew, but I noticed the respect they gave him. One sat cross-legged on the table beside him and another on the other side peeled an orange and piled the peel on his dirty plate as he listened. Heads bowed over the map on the table they hung on his every word as if it was a briefing and I could tell that he loved teaching them.

I went over to the duty chef who was banging a piece of a paraffin stove on the table and blowing into the burners which seemed to be blocked.

"Is it broken?" I asked.

"Yes, we need a new one I think!"

This one wore a khaki bush hat and earphones with a microphone attached. Hebrew conversations were coming through loudly on the vehicle radio and when the soldier spoke, I could hear the exchange on the land rover's radio.

"Are you keeping in contact with the patrol to make sure they are safe?" I asked.

"Yes I've got them, he said confidently. "Don't worry about the others on the border, we are always in contact. You need to learn Hebrew!" he said, as if it would be better if I could understand the communications better and I felt pleased that I was a trusted party.

He gave up on the stove and threw it into a box and I gathered a few of the plates still on the table. He started to put them into the box with the clean mess tins, like a young lad who might be great on his radio, but his kitchen skills were lacking.

"Do you have to use these plates again?" I asked.

"No, we've got lots!"

"Why don't you put them in the picnic site rubbish bin, then all the mess tins won't be covered in sauce?"

"Ok." he agreed. "Good plan!"

His face beamed at me as if I was a useful, but fussy Aunt and he proceeded to gather all the disposable stuff and took it to the green bin on wheels in the picnic area. He was just heading for the last pieces of rubbish when the wind blew and a plate landed face down on the map. There were cries of disgust as the bits of spaghetti drew new roads on the map and another soldier who hadn't spoken previously tried to flick it off with his finger. They laughed as they shared some Hebrew banter about the situation.

"It is always good to have some lunch left on the map!" the tall comedian in the black woollen hat told me. "You might need it later!" My goodness, how we all laughed!

Time with my unexpected lunch companions had been great. I would never have dreamed of joining a patrol and couldn't have done so without Hanitai. He always made special experiences fall into my lap.

I keep the map with me here as I write, sauce stains and all, as it brings me closer to the memorable day with the cold pasta brigade.

*****

Hanitai and I left the soldiers. He drove slowly, down a lane that I assumed, went north toward Tel Aviv's main highway. We entered another wooded area and came to a compound filled with reconnaissance vehicles.

4-tonne trucks and wide flat beds were parked inside high wire fences topped with barbed wire and a check-point by the gate.

The entrance was open and a few Merkava tanks were parked in the lane, while others troops milled around the area. One soldier, in dark green, denim overalls stood with one leg on each side of an open turret. He had his hands on his hips and shouted across, to one of his buddies who had just climbed onto a tank by the gate. This reminded me of the days on the tank park in Germany, with British Army of the

Rhine, when there was always banter, laughter and the similar smell of diesel.

"That's strange!"

Hanitai said, thoughtfully, looking into the distance towards a wooded area beyond.

"What is?"

"Down there, can you see?

The barrier should be closed to the path through the trees – it is open."

We both looked down to where the tarmac became a track and Hanitai remained pensive.

"Where does the path go to?" I asked beginning to wonder what was going on.

Suddenly, with a rumble on the ground, 2 tanks came dashing out of the compound and went off toward the open gate – quickly followed by 2 of the wide jeeps with mounted machine guns.

They fled into the trees and out of sight. The others in the compound didn't turn a hair and carried on with what looked like regular maintenance.

"It leads into Gaza." He said, "I wonder what's going on?"

"Oh my God, Hanitai! Don't say they are going into Gaza with all that stuff. Please don't let them be going into Gaza."

I felt sick as we both sat and thought for a moment, Hanitai looking round to see if anything else was about to happen.

"I don't know what they are doing." He said earnestly, "I've not seen that before. Maybe they are training."

He was calm, but I was perplexed, even taking deep breaths as we sat in waiting for a few minutes.

"Maybe we shouldn't be here. We might be in the way." I almost insisted.

"Just wait a minute." He said. "It doesn't look like anymore are going."

He started the engine and turned the vehicle around, but after a short distance, he stopped again.

He got out and went to the boot, returning with binoculars.

"I know a road by the fence. Do you want to go and find out what's going on?"

"I think we'll be stopped!" I said, wondering what on earth we would be doing next. I hesitated.

"We can go and see - it's up to you. You just have to remember, if you can see the enemy, then the enemy can see you." He smiled smugly, as if it was a dare. I smiled too. He didn't know that I had been told the same thing, just an hour ago, by the others.

"Come on! We'll see what we can see." He said.

At that moment, I felt surprisingly calmer. Maybe the panic had subsided after the initial shock of the troops suddenly being galvanised into action. Once they had disappeared into the buffer zone and others hadn't followed, I decided it must be a practice run.

We hadn't heard of any incursions on the news. No rockets were raining down on us. There weren't any iron dome missile interceptors set up; that I could see. As I said earlier; it's too soon after the last flare-up. I was doing a good job at convincing myself. I was getting more and more settled in my train of thought.

We were soon approaching a narrow road that ran down the side of an enormous and densely wired fence. Concrete posts set equidistantly, close together, ensured there was nothing flimsy about it and off it went, stretching out into the distance.

This must have cost a fortune, I thought. It's a massive expense to build it; maintain it; watch over it; with a forfeit of liberty on either side. A sacrifice for those who are fenced in; those who can't plough their fields in the buffer zone; not to mention the loss of teenage years for those on National Service. The biggest thing though, is the unnecessary loss of life.

On our left, we passed 2 white, modern pill boxes and Hanitai parked quite near one, so they could see straight into our vehicle.

"We're being watched." I told him.

"That's ok he replied, I'm making sure they can see us."

I looked around at the heavily barricaded areas, and at the tank tracks furrowing a land that wasn't used much. In the month of March, Israel was still green after the rains enabling heavy movement to churn up the ground.

The occupants of the tower, about 20 meters away, watched us and chatted to each other. Hanitai, was already looking through his field glasses, and then offered them to me.

"Look over there," he pointed." There's a clump of trees and above them, there's camouflage netting. If you look through these, you will see a Merkava's gun, just showing above the net."

Taking the binoculars, I saw what he had seen. With some relief!

"There you are," he said reassuringly, "they are just training."

With that, he waved at the soldiers in the tower, before we drove away. I asked him why they just allow us to meander near the fence.

"If they want to know who I am, they can find out in a minute." He wasn't perturbed at all.

He was, however, so pleased that he had been able to show me something of the conflict at close quarters. We had had the best of days in his eyes.

Showing me the real thing was always his mission. I was, as usual, amazed at what I had been privileged to see.

Chapter 18

The Negev

There are many houses that are close to the buffer zone fences. I saw evidence of military movement in the tracks that have been left behind and children ride their bicycles along them and play ball not 100 metres from a high-security wall. This one has been painted with blue arches to make it look more cheerful. For about 500 metres, its mural looks like a blue and gold Moroccan palace growing out of the sand.

I walked along through the dried-up foliage for a few minutes, Hanitai strolling close behind me when I came across an old ammunition box. I shouted to him, hoping he would catch up. He bent down and dusted off the sand and revealed white Hebrew lettering stamped on the side.

"Has it been left her from a recent conflict?" I asked him, but he shook his head.

"No, it's old and it's empty," he had already concluded. "This is of British design and would hold shells for a Centurion tank. Everyone has ammunition boxes in the attic; it's a common thing for storage. I think someone has dumped it here."

We decided he was right as further along we found a duvet and the frame of an old bicycle. Turning back on ourselves, we came to a gap in the wall and a modern pill box that was tall enough for the guard to look out over the Strip. It was built like a white plaster windmill without sails and had a black windowed cone on the top. The guard inside looked down through the camouflage netting and waved. We acknowledged him and his boredom.

"This is a modern pill box," Hanitai told me, "and they are portable. The concrete ones you have seen before were left by the British and used in the war of 1948. These are of a modern material. Some are not in use today, but still, have netting and the guards move about. The mobile units who fire the missiles from the Strip into the towns of Sderot and Ashkelon are not really a problem to these lookout posts; they are too close, but snipers could be a problem. So we cover them up and move about from day to day."

I reminded him of a visit we had paid to this area before, where at a gap in the wall, there's a section that's been made into a peace wall. The wall, painted French blue, looks like it is covered in fridge magnets. You can make your plaster mould into whatever shape you would like to be on the wall. There are lots of doves, flowers, rainbows, and Hebrew messages.

He said he knew where I meant and asked if I wanted to go back, but I told him I was happy wherever we went.

Later, we stopped to talk to a couple of soldiers, one from Haifa and a Moroccan Jew from Beersheba who told me that the kitchen inside the tower keeps them going for their usual eight-hour shifts, but the length of the shift can depend on the current situation.

"We are meant to hold the line until the reserves and the regular army get here; things change from week to week."

Some are now watching over the Kibbutzim because there might be tunnels underneath the buffer zone and sometimes the locals feed them.

"We are never without supplies and towns are close by when we finish!"

The Moroccan was very trendy, I remember, but I couldn't see his eyes for his mirrored sunglasses. He was about 5 feet 7 inches tall and apologised for his poor English. Hanitai had asked him to, take off his glasses for a photo, but he's said he looked better with them on.

They were young, and strolled about kicking dirt; hindered by their kit and weapons. I remember as I looked at their gear then, in 2016, how much it seemed to have improved. Some of the guns I saw in the 1990s were quite worn and scratched. I have noticed changes over the years and while I have little knowledge of the types they carry, I can see the difference from those that 30 years ago looked a little better than an old Sten.

Nobody knows what is going to happen from one day to the next, let alone looking for a long-term plan. The situation is worse, of course, when hostilities break out as they have several times in recent years since the Strip was fenced off.

This is an area where Hamas terrorists came out of tunnels into the back gardens of the civilian population and a new form of fear had to be absorbed.

The security forces had put so much effort into covering all possible entrances. Most of the random missiles sent over from Gaza are being intercepted by the iron dome missile interceptor, and the kindergartens by the fence have been lagged in breeze block. The residents have perfected getting into the bunkers in less than a minute, once the siren sounds and everyone feels as secure as they can be. Then, you learn that everyone has been blind to the degree of activity going on underground.

I used this in my research about 1947, when Irgun fighters were tunnelling under Tel Aviv to get into the buildings of the British administration. War is awful in every era!

All out war against Hamas, is always followed up with the war on the reputation of both sides.

For those in the Gaza strip, who in the eyes of the world, are being bombed, disproportionately, with a threat to civilian life, there's the question of whether safe houses are being used to store ammunition and whether they are oppressing and putting the lives of their own people in jeopardy.

In a broadcast, I heard something peculiar while watching an interview with a Palestinian journalist on Sky News in 2020. He explained that no warning was given before the jets dropped their bombs. They appealed to the Israeli Air Force to ensure civilians know the Israeli targets.

This is extraordinary warfare to my knowledge, but maybe there's a suggestion here that some sort of dialogue exists between them. I'm not condoning attacks on civilians, but I found the concept quite bizarre.

Nevertheless, the propaganda war comes through with every ugly skirmish. Some channels interview the Israeli population and others show pictures of the injured in makeshift hospitals inside Gaza. However deep the anger or measures to say which side is to blame; both sides are traumatised. In 2016, the media blamed the American administration, but in, 2021, Trump has gone, together with his ally, the unmoving Netanyahu and someone else is being blamed for not finding a solution after the latest hostilities.

The world looks for those who are responsible or contributing to the repeated patterns. Who is supplying arms to either side? Fingers pointed at those who have allowed Hamas to re-group after their weaponry was depleted last time.

Israel, in her defence, may insist that her neighbours don't want peace, but desire total destruction of the Jewish State, and a response might come from others saying that she has no right to exist in the first place.

Some reporters focus on the plight of the Palestinian people and base their dialogue on the partition vote in 1947. They focus on an expansionist Israel that took more land in the second catastrophe of the 6-Day-War of 1967. The Palestinians appear and say they won't negotiate until the Settlers are evicted from their land in the West Bank and that armistice borders of 1949 must be are acknowledged. An avenue of debate moves to West Bank issues and the unrelenting issue of Jerusalem saying the Palestinians must have half of the city as their Capital in a 2 State Solution.

This proposal is according to agreements stated in the now, outdated, Oslo Accords of 1993. How hopeful we were then when a road to peace seemed to be going somewhere.

The pattern is similar each time things erupt and the world calls for some sort of restraint or a cease-fire for time to think.

It happens! A cease-fire is agreed for 72 hours while 'experts' try to persuade the Knesset to find some compassion. Meanwhile, the cease-fire is broken, and both sides blame each other for firing the first shot.

It seems hopeless, more hatred manifests from this situation, and the baggage of the past becomes just as heavy for the next generation.

Dogma reigns under fire, while the demoralised withdraw into themselves and resort to a perpetual state of mind, analysing their personal history and the welfare of their families.

There seems little hope at these times, either for people being bombarded with missiles or those living in constant fear on both sides as history repeats itself – we're all back here - hate stalemate again!

Peacemakers say, 'We can't give up!' While speeches from leaders across the rest of the Middle East, often enveloped in their particular turmoil and under scrutiny for less than democratic methods, ignore it; the extreme call for Israel's destruction, but who as ever really wanted the responsibility for the bewildered Palestinian People.

Looking at the tunnels that cross the Gaza/Israel border, we have to accept that urban confrontation is back, and generally speaking, Israel's problem is no longer the worry of huge military operations. I talked, in my earlier explorations about multi-national Arab armies on her borders, but today it is more about being caught out and trapped by surprise in face-to-face terrorism.

Hanitai and I don't debate things; we both know the situation, and one-liners and a companionable silence seem to be enough.

"You know Israel!" he says these days, for we have discussed things often enough over the years. An expression speaks volumes as we sigh wearily, pause, and carry on. I couldn't have found a better guide, knowledgeable companion, or bodyguard if I had searched for years.

*****

In the Negev one day, I came upon an old fir tree that had failed in existence; toppled and prostrate on barren land surrounded by its remains. Its cones and tiny needles, now brown with age, were scatted over a vast area of white stone-riddled sand and any desired souvenir crumbled to dust like used tinder between my fingers. As fragile as the history it watched, tangled and symbolic of a time long ago, the vast skeleton was beautiful in the matching amber light.

Just beyond the tree, I found the remains of a small factory and inside its rudimentary frame; wells were dug deep into the ground.

Hanitai told me that the factory structure had been achieved when the British brought sand from the beaches of Gaza and I could see that this method had produced shell-dashed concrete. The basic aggregate mix lay in ragged blocks all around us among other shrubs that had not survived in 'bad land'.

He explained:

"Not every part of the desert blooms, but in some areas where the British hung out, water sources were underground.

Learning about the sand from Gaza beaches made me realise how the beaches in tourist hotspots are man-made. A few miles up the coast in Tel Aviv, the tractor pulls along its trailer with attached combs and automatic litter pickers every morning, making the beach like a deep piled carpet.

As Hanitai set up the primus stove and got out a box of apple cake, I had to admit that my adventure wasn't anything like Lawrence of Arabia may have experienced.

I was there with a bodyguard and the luxury of a four-wheel drive vehicle packed with goodies. I probably couldn't get on a camel, let alone travel a hundred miles on one.

We talked about what it was like then before the desert bloomed.

Were these concrete roads and sandy tracks here on the way to Gaza when the battle raged between the Ottoman Empire and the Arabs?

As General Allenby made his way, did he know the secret agenda between the British and French governments that were on standby to undermine all Lawrence had strived for with his Arab hordes?

Unlike Lawrence, I didn't walk across the landscape between Arab villages in my youth or become akin to the language and culture. It was an overdue search for historical facts that brought me to the same territory; today contested between the Israelis and the Palestinians.

I was just playing at it! I am not the product of a middle-class upbringing where boys were trained in public schools and universities to run the British Empire.

I am the aging daughter of a working-class dreamer, who, himself, came to see the real thing after being taught in a classroom where the map on the wall was coloured in red patches that showed the British Empire.

"The map showed us what was ours!" he used to say,

My Dad never forgot the surreal mysticism of the landscape and we often sat together after tea, during my thirties, discussing the book by T E Lawrence, Seven Pillars of Wisdom.

Unprecedented writings for me were the imagination ran wild with the gore of an Arab war, poor hygiene, unthinkable cuisine, and even sexual depravity. Fighting the Ottoman Empire in the desert was not pretty. Some descriptions came across as pure evil, even in the horrible way the Arabs treated each other.

Sharing this precious piece of my past with Hanitai, I explained that I had visited Lawrence of Arabia's house in England and described it to him.

We visited Clouds Hill, where T. E. Lawrence had kept a small cottage just before his death in 1935.

We found the house hidden in the woods, at the foot of a steep, shrub-covered embankment. There it was, looking every bit the house of a forester, as it had been, long before Lawrence was born.

Inside a garage, he built himself to store his seven motorbikes, a television was set up and his life story was being narrated with some old films to accompany the dialogue. I was content to sit on a polypropylene chair, under a corrugated roof, with some of his belongings, in happy anticipation before entering his own space.

Here, I was experiencing the man himself and not the polished, Peter O'Toole in the movie.

We crossed the threshold through a small door in the white plastered walled cottage and came upon an austere room, where an elderly gent greeted us with a cheery, "Hello!"

There was an armchair for an upright man, an old oak fireplace and many books lined the walls, with a reader's lectern randomly placed.

This had been his bedroom, his library, and was now a museum. Sketches of Lawrence and pictures of Arab acquaintances are hung on the walls. A strand of light streamed in through a single window and illuminated the cowhide cover on the divan. I spotted metal debris on a low shelf - pieces of a railway line with some rusty nuts and bolts.

In a lengthy explanation, the old gent talked about the souvenirs from blown-up trains in the desert and described Lawrence's association with the Arabs as someone mentoring a backward People.

He explained their excitement at encountering dynamite for the first time and the 100-year-old pieces reminded me of the bloodbaths I had read about.

I wondered whether the peace and tranquillity of the place was not just a luxury to Lawrence but a necessity after all he had experienced in the Middle East.

When asked, the guide disregarded the idea that Lawrence had been killed by a mystery man in a black car. He did, however, say that he, 'Scott', the name he was using to avoid celebrity status, had been spotted on this Brough motorcycle, travelling at speed after leaving the post office in Bovington. He said the story had come about after two journalists came to the area and wanted a headline about his recent association with people who were particularly against the establishment.

A report from two cyclists, he had avoided before hitting dense scrubland, had supplied details contrary to any mysterious plot. Not wearing a crash helmet, his injuries included a fractured skull and resulted in his subsequent death, some six days later.

On the first floor was the best room of all; warm, bright, and welcoming under a skylight window. The huge fireplace at one end was decorated with a trident candle sticks in heavy silver and above the cornice was a picture of a young boy sitting on a beach and looking out to sea.

This was an all-purpose room used for writing at the grand desk, listening to music on the gramophone, and generally entertaining friends.

Here we met a lady who had a self-made catalogue of information about her hero.

"I love guarding his things!" she told us.

She talked about all the assignments he might have partaken had he lived beyond 46.

"He could have been an advisor during World War II, or written so much more, as I believe he planned to do."

She showed me her favourite painting of Lawrence wearing Arab robes and his famous headdress and said it emphasised his piercing blue eyes.

Above the staircase was a pencil drawing of General Allenby. The contents of the museum showed empathy for both sides of the conflict. The Colonial thinkers were there with the Arab leaders that figured in the Arab revolt against the Turks and successive British occupiers.

SCRATCHING THE SURFACE

I delayed having to take leave of the rural retreat by relishing in the tranquillity in the garden. I looked up towards the top of the woody embankment, which I'm told, was a mass of rhododendrons in Lawrence's day. I stood for a while, in the space of this mythical legend and pondered. A motorbike flew by noisily on the road above. This made me smile, as romantically, I imagined it could be the ghost of this invincible madman.

In the little churchyard of St Nicolas' Moreton, surrounded by unspoiled Dorset countryside, I sat by his graveside. In the beautiful August sunshine, I watched a ground beetle, who dared to wander across his chest, taking shade under the leaves of the peach rose bush planted there.

It didn't feel like the spiritual resting place of an indomitable wanderer.

"He's not here," I said. "I bet he's gone back to the Levant to be a nomad in the desert again!"

Hanitai, still listening intently, took my romancing on the chin as I told him that I believed Lawrence's times in Palestine were probably nearer to the Egyptian border and that he would have taken a more easterly route to Jerusalem. Nevertheless, even if he didn't go to Gaza as General Allenby did, I think he must have passed this way in one life or another. Maybe it was just the other day in a flowing white robe and riding a horse. Somehow, I think he would prefer his Arab attire, and a horse, to his uncomfortable officer's uniform and an open-top car. Anyway, a flat hat and putties just don't paint the right picture for me.

I wonder if he despairs today and what would be his opinion on the partition he didn't survive long enough to see. Would he consider more betrayal and still be siding with the Arabs 2 or 3 generations later?

*****

Carrying on with our journey, we passed agricultural land and what looked to be acres of carrots growing along the roadside.

"Do you like carrots?" He asked.

"Yes, I do. Why, what are you going to do now Hanitai?"

He stopped the land cruiser on a dirt track and getting out of the driver's seat, he proceeded to find a plastic bucket he had somewhere behind his seat. In less than two minutes, he was filling the bucket with water from his supply and pulled carrots from the ground.

"We can't take the carrots." I said, "They belong to someone else."

"They have many," he replied, "and anyway, soldiers watching the Strip can help themselves to carrots, it's an unwritten law! Today you are watching the Strip."

The carrots had a huge bunch of green leaves attached to the top as he passed them to me like a big bunch of flowers.

Within minutes, we were off again, going along another lane, where we encountered a flock of sheep wandering in front of us. They were very woolly and were great colours, of black, brown and grey. Not far away, there were a few tents from a Bedouin camp as I was told that they move about a lot at that time of year, looking for pasture for the animals.

We had to stop as the road was blocked, but I couldn't see anyone by the tents, just an old battered Nissan van, and a huge satellite dish, so maybe they had Sky television. This baffled me a bit in such a remote location.

"What shall we do now?" I asked, thinking Hanitai would probably turn the car around and go in a different direction.

"Oh, here comes the shepherd now!" he said, but I couldn't see him. I was expecting a man in a long traditional cloak with a crooked staff, but I couldn't see anyone.

"He's up there," Hanitai said as he pointed towards the hilltop.

What a disappointment to see a thin man wearing jeans and a tee shirt, riding on a black donkey. He was riding bareback and his legs were so long, his feet were dragging on the floor.

"Him?" I said, with obvious regret.

We watched as he approached his sheep, which numbered about 20 and as he did so, the donkey caught sight of our vehicle and became very vocal.

It spun round about three times, threw the shepherd on the ground, and ran away into the field. I had to laugh as the poor man got to his feet and looked at us as if it was our fault.

"I'll help him move the sheep," Hanitai said, getting out again.

"This'll be good," I said.

He looked at me through the open window as if I was a cheeky child and said. "Eat your carrots and don't get out."

The young Arab, with his black outfit covered in dust, waved his arms about as Hanitai had a chat with him.

Of course, by now, they had both walked through the flock and they and the donkey had dispersed the sheep. They were everywhere, but now with a clear road we were soon on our way again. The shepherd had had enough of our help.

Seeing the Bedouins and the way they live, you associate the aroma of animals, sweat, and a general unpleasant smell as a link to disease. I am spoiled, never had to rough it and I am always thinking about the bug that will give me a stomach upset. Hanitai understood what I meant but was too much of a gentleman to call me soft, on that occasion anyway. Instead, he told me with a knowing smile that I could cure everything I might pick up by drinking camel urine. Apparently, Camel's urine is good for skin diseases, drying up abscesses, sores, and dandruff. It is said to be a good hair conditioner. Not only does it make the hair shiny, but it assists in new growth at the early stages of baldness. Personally, when in the desert, I usually give up on my hair, but good to know that you can also use it for cleaning sand from the eyes and toothache, should you be unable to find a dentist and be all out of over-the-counter painkillers.

The Bedouins are no longer held captive by their elders as folklore would have it. Some marry out, travel the world, join the Israeli Army or attend college or university with their Jewish neighbours.

The disappearing values might come from internal conflict, together with the changing patterns of life caused by the occupation.

Some want to live as their forefathers did; at one with nature in the quiet lands of the desert and being told that they are not allowed to wander in a certain area causes great upset. They want their ancient villages recognised and respected and don't want to be paid off or placed conveniently into Israeli society. While the government plays the health & safety card saying new areas will benefit families living in slums with no roads, facilities, or services, the Bedouin may not want to live in a nice apartment with a kitchen. Their culture keeps them under the stars where their roots and long-lived traditions have allowed opportunities in agriculture and rearing livestock for centuries.

*****

Making our way back to Tel Aviv, we stopped at the Erez crossing at the northern tip of the Gaza strip. This is the major border crossing between Israel and Gaza.

Kibbutz Erez is on one side and the Gaza side, the Palestinian town of Beit Hanoun.

The building itself is like an enormous hangar with facilities for the passage of cargo into Gaza.

I had been there before, I think in 2009 when the metal fortifications and barbed wire fences were strewn with Israeli flags, ribbons, and pictures of Gilad Shalit, the soldier was kidnapped during a cross-border-raid, and was kept in captivity for 5 years between 2006 and 2011. Negotiations were ongoing for years until he was exchanged for over a 1000 Palestinian prisoners, some of whom were on life sentences for their terrorist activity.

On the Saturday afternoon I visited, it was quiet with few vehicles at the crossing and I saw a beautifully dressed

Palestinian lady who seemed to be waiting for her transport. As we drove past her, sitting peacefully and alone, I took her picture.

We headed for the exit to leave the compound and a security fellow in a suite ran across and flagged us down.

"Oh, here we go!" Said Hanitai as he slowed down and the man came and stood by my window.

I opened the window and he immediately said.

"You were taking pictures of the compound."

"No, I said, I took one picture of the Palestinian lady sitting on the bench."

"No! You took pictures of the compound." He insisted and holding out his hand demanded, "Camera!"

"It's a phone," I said passing the phone to him. "And don't delete all my photos because I've been out all day and this isn't necessary."

He found the last picture of the lady and deleted it. Then he spent a few minutes looking at other photos. As he passed it back to me through the open window, I showed him the front of my passport to show him I was from the European Union.

"No need." He said and waved his hand for us to go.

Hanitai had said nothing while this inquiry was going on, but as we drove off, he said: "Good job! You handled that very well."

After a few minutes, he laughed and said. "That'll teach you to mess with national security!" Which I believe was a sarcastic jibe at the chap who had stopped us on a slow news day.

Chapter 19

Latrun

We had a great picnic bought from a cafe owned by the family of a Catholic Arab in Ramle, the best hummus, pita, and falafel you could wish for, made from fresh chickpeas and before our very eyes. Not dry falafel we might buy from the supermarkets in England with a need for me to add beetroots and tomatoes as a treat. He and his friend, a Greek Orthodox worshiper, were Manchester City fans and wanted to talk more about Manchester and where I lived in relation to the stadium. One explained that he had a degree in English and loved the opportunity to speak it and asked me to explain what a Protestant was.

He had never understood how they came about in the Christian church or why people from the same religion were fighting each other, about religious issues. Having discussed its Royal beginnings, we chatted about the connection in football, and how in big cities where there were two football teams with a connection to the Catholic Church or the Protestant church.

When they asked if people from either side married each other, it brought out the complexities and variations in different cities and family opinion.

It all seemed a million miles away from Ramle, but I think there was some empathy with those who had come across an adamant religious mentality. Speaking to them, I sensed that familiar feeling that they were envious of anyone who had enough money to travel. Together with this fact, it was likely that they would be expected to live up to family expectations and traditions.

Back on the road, Hanitai explained that the fresh fare we had doesn't last long and it is best to eat it on the day. He added that in Israel you can also get the long-lasting variety that is full of preservatives, but why bother, when you have the real thing just down the street?

"It's good to support local people," he added. "Some of these families have been providing the community with their own personal recipes for over a hundred years."

It was good to hear that he had absolutely no problem with supporting the Arab community and I asked if I had imagined the questioning expressions as we had entered. I felt as if there was an air of suspicion and it took them a few minutes to weigh up the situation.

"Listen!" He said, as he and other Israelis always do when they want to get a point across. It isn't considered rude to start a sentence with 'listen' as it might appear aggressive in the United Kingdom.

"These are Arabs in Israel; they don't know what trouble will walk in the door. Peaceful people, but the situation makes them very wary. As you saw, they are the good guys, just making a living, going to church, and watching football."

I felt good to have been part of bridging a small gap; maybe ridiculous in the general scheme of things, but I was happy to see some harmony in a hard-of-hearing orchestra.

Driving out of Ramle, Hanitai was having a good moan at the driver in the vehicle in front of us, who was meandering all over the road. "Look at this! I bet it's a woman!"

I looked at him with some derision as he had already informed me that he didn't trust the woman on the WAZE machine after she had sent him down a few dead ends. I told him that the device couldn't account for a constantly changing border control and didn't cut any ice. He changed it to speak English and asked me to navigate just to prove he was right. An amusing moment for him was when 'the WAZE woman' instructed us to 'turn left at the next roundabout'.

"At the what? At the next what?" He shouted at me and the WAZE woman.

"Roundabout!" I said.

"What's a roundabout? Is there a fairground near here?"

After some confusion, we'd missed the turning and he was trying to convince me that it was a silly name for a circular road. So this time he blamed the English.

"There are some funny things in English!" he said. "Like Reading power station!" – he pronounced it Reeding.

"Reeding?" I said. "It's called Redding!"

"Exactly!" he said. "You just can't make your minds up! A power station is named after a town and the word is also used when you are reading a book. We always call the power station Reeding!"

I had to admit that the Reading power station in Tel Aviv Port had been given a name enough to cause confusion among the locals.

He was grumpy at the traffic as we travelled towards Latrun, but soon back in his comfort zone as a teacher as we veered away from Route 40 toward Ben Gurion Airport and I learned that we were in the area of the old Lydda Royal Air Force station in the Biblical land of Lod.

Our diversion later took us to the old German Colony of Wilhelma, so named after King William II of Wuerttemberg. Cruising along a straight, tree-lined road, I heard that the first German Templers arrived in Haifa in the 1860s while Palestine was under Ottoman Rule. They were an offshoot of Lutherans who believed in the second coming of Christ and wanted to set up a home in the Holy Land.

Upon arrival, they encountered the same challenges as the early Zionists, converting malaria-riddled areas and draining swamps some ten years before the large-scale immigration of Russian Jews who were fleeing persecution and pogroms.

They remained patriotic to their homeland and greeted Kaiser Wilhelm II with enthusiasm when he visited Jerusalem in 1898

Many Templers returned to Europe and died fighting for Germany during the First World War. When it ended in 1918, Palestine was governed by the British, who after seeing an end to Ottoman rule, saw the Templers as alien enemies. Many left Palestine and the British interned most of the remainder in camps, seizing their property and life-stock.

They were allowed to return in 1920, but by this time, the Jews were relying more on the British for general modernisation and expansion of towns and cities.

In the 1920s the Templers had their own vineyards and worked under the umbrella of the German Cooperative

Culture Society in Palestine. A wine label from this period states 'Deutches Weina Wilhelma – Sarona Palestina' and the archives show that in the orange groves and warehouses under a similar jurisdiction, the fruit bore the old tissue paper wrappers promoting original Jaffa Oranges under a German banner.

An era ensued when life was peaceful for them and relationships between everyone were most accommodating. Tolerance was promoted in schools where Germans, English, Arabs, and Jews shared the same classrooms.

Shops advertised their merchandise in German, English, Arabic, and Hebrew and all nationalities used the highly recommended Templer Bank. The German-Palestine post office stamps bore the head of the Kaiser and 'Jaffa Deutsche Post' insignia. It was a German community, under British Rule in a predominantly Arab country.

During the 1930s, Germany was changing and the Templers of Palestine began to follow the national Socialist path, especially the young, post-religious generation who were drawn into the views of the Nazi party as its influence swept through the community.

*****

As we sat at a table eating our picnic, at the monument of the Alexandroni Brigade at Latrun, peculiar sounds interrupted the peace as we contemplated things that had happened there.

I heard some sort of farm machinery working in a field behind the trees. A tractor perhaps, no doubt, would have been a familiar sound there while trying to find a way into

Jerusalem, when it was under siege during the War of Independence.

It would be towing vehicles on perilous, crumbling ground or pushing things over the side into the valley below. The trucks that didn't make it, with their wasted supplies tumbled into the gorge for the Arabs to commandeer on foot.

Here, in a vast expanse of rough, undulating land, at a strategic post that had seen the conflict of centuries, I thought I heard the echoes of voices. Was my imagination playing tricks on me? Were they the ghosts of past wars? Perhaps the voices on the wind were Crusaders of a thousand years ago, or British Tommies guarding the prison camp behind me talking as they patrolled the fence.

I imagined the old transport flitting up and down the short lane to and from Latrun police station, just a stone's throw away, ferrying those detained back and forth from the camp.

The eerie noises might just have been the sound of distant traffic bouncing off the hillsides. It was a sad, soulful, but beautiful place in a serene light. I didn't tell Hanitai what I was thinking; he seemed to be in the mood for a mission, not a soulful debate.

The area is a satellite of Jerusalem where the Jordanians and Israelis fought a bloody battle in the 6-Day-War. It was here, in the War of Independence, future Prime Ministers such as Yitzhak Rabin and Ariel Sharon led brigades in a primitive army. The early Israel Defence Force was brought into being from the factions whose members had been detained in Latrun Camp behind me.

Jordanians had moved into the old Tegart police station of Latrun as the British moved out on May 8th 1948. The city was under siege and 100,000 Jews were starving there. The main road leading into the city was built in a valley controlled by Arab forces that were well established on the hilltops on either side.

They set up and mined heavy stone roadblocks in order to stop convoys from reaching Jerusalem. Israelis found that they were blocking the way further with any destroyed vehicles leading the convoy.

They had open trucks or converted British reconnaissance vehicles with slatted or mesh metal coverings to stop bullets and hand grenades. The vehicles that failed in the 8-mile-an-hour convoy still sit as memorials on the roadside embankments of the new modern Highway 1 going into Jerusalem today. They represent those who were ambushed and had nowhere to run and died on the way.

Battered buses fought through, transporting hundreds of soldiers to this place.

Some who were experienced and some who had just come from Europe had no battle experience and may have been Holocaust survivors who didn't understand Hebrew.

Palmach forces navigated along what was just a path, south of Latrun and walked to Tel Aviv without venturing on the main Jerusalem highway to find some way of getting supplies to their people. A few kilometres away, the dangerous and often impassable Burma Road of Israel was built on the hilltops while fighting Arab forces.

Something is certain, in an echo chamber like this; you would have to be experienced to know where the gunfire was coming from; behind a boulder or from a clump of trees.

As you bedded down with sand and shards for a ground sheet and tried to fight back, the land would move and rubble would roll down onto your comrades. The heat would be felt through your clothes as you tried to crawl for safety. You might find the young inexperienced combat of your new brigade frustrating as you all tried to make the best of things with limited, homemade ammunition.

There was a personal connection to my mentors in all I had learned on this day out. I heard that Hanitai's brother had fought with the Rabin brigade and Amira, as a little girl, had visited Latrun detention camp with her mother. The British believed that her Father, the Brother of Avraham Stern, must have some information or connection to the activities of the Stern Gang. He was kept there for 8 months. She remembered holding her mother's hand as they showed their papers at the gate and sitting across a table wondering why he wasn't allowed to go home with them.

As I walked toward the old brick gatehouse where my friend, Amira Stern, entered the Latrun Detention camp with her mother, I saw all that remains in an open field.

Just along the old lane the British Tegart police station, built in the late thirties following the Arab Revolt, still stands in an ideal position to keep watch over the Tel Aviv – Jerusalem Road. It is now a military museum and the Israeli flag on top of the building can be seen for miles. It was always an imposing building and the flying flag shows all in the area, just who is in charge of this statement outpost. It was the British in the 1930s, the Jordanians from 1948; and now, since 1967, the Israelis.

Just before we left, we drove to where the gates of the detention camp used to be, and leaving the vehicle, I ventured a few metres over more rough land to look through the aperture where a guard would have looked out and checked the papers of visitors.

I envisaged a young lad in khaki shorts and a shirt with maybe a black beret, maybe a red one. Another, perhaps older and in charge, sitting at the army issue table sighing about the situation, and the weather and wondering when the authorities were going to sort themselves out, release this God-forsaken country, and let him go home.

Chapter 20

The West Bank

At the West Bank Community Settlement of Ateret, some 40 kilometres North West of Jerusalem, Hanitai suddenly told me we were only 4km from a coffee stop. I looked at what seemed to be a very modern settlement and from the hilltop nearby.

I was assured that on a fine day, we would be able to see the airport from here and with the country being so narrow, it was important to keep this land so that aircraft had enough space to stack and turn round. Given the inhospitable neighbours in the Arab world this was the only route as it was better for Israel to manage aircraft without flying into the airspace of other surrounding countries.

The prospect of Hamas or Isis moving into the area as Hamas had done when Israel moved out of Gaza, would not only result in further restrictions, but would enable them to attack Israel from the East as well as the West.

We spent some time watching an exercise under way involving the Army, the Fire Brigade and the Settlement Police. This involved small aircraft who have to fly low underneath the red pod markers on the telegraph wires. These warn all flights of their recommended height while they are turning back over Israel proper. If there is an aircraft in the air, every service needs to know about it as an unidentified plane could induce panic. The small ones today were practicing flight for when they have to extinguish forest fires.

We carried on along narrow lanes; smart buildings seemed to pop up from nowhere. These were new Yeshiva, High and Primary schools, and a Kindergarten. All were serving other Settlements in the area. It was a day when we travelled around the Ramallah area, taking in sights and places where I had heard of events that had made the international news channels. Stoning at bus stops and knife attacks the places where the Settlers marched on the hills stating claim to the land of the Bible. The setting Mediterranean Forests unchanged for 3000 years. Small trees clinging to natural terraces on the sides of steep valleys; and flowers, yes it was green, because it was March.

Seeing the new City of Rawabi being built on the other side of a field made the competition for the land all too real. There was a Palestinian flag sitting on a nearby hill side and being told that Ramallah was only 15 minutes away, made me aware that it could be dangerous.

At the entrance to another Settlement, the guard with a gun was doing his shift from the rota to save the inhabitants from a Shahid. A word, I am told, used for a Muslim martyr or sometimes referred to as Holy Man.

They mean a suicide bomber which is why the random Palestinian employees, have to leave their cars outside the gated complexes and walk to the site where they are working that day. They are parked outside the heavy mechanical, yellow gates and display green on white number plates as opposed to the ones registered in Israel which are black on yellow.

The irony is; the Palestinians are working on building sites and constructing new or extending settlements that they disagree with and are seen by the world as illegal.

At the gate, it may say, this is the land of Benjamin, or Gad, thus taking us back to the tribes of Moses, for on this soil, the tribes arrived after their Exodus from Egypt and lived on the land that God gave to Abraham.

In this area, the Settler motto is: "Not one inch!" describing the amount of land they are willing to give to, or back, to the Palestinians.

In poorer Settlements along the way, they have just arrived and are living in cabins or shipping containers that sit on wooden or metal stilts.

Standing by them on remote hill tops, in nature, you can hear the twittering birds and the whirring of the fans on the air conditioning units often sitting on the ground underneath the unit.

Considering it is a land that is drenched in anger, and peppered with the make-shift habitats of those who have just decided they have a right to be there, it is very quiet today.

The long term prospect that has to be considered is whether the Bible map philosophy will prevail or will Israel have to look toward long term peace.

Is Israel living with a siege mentality because they don't want peace or taking a realistic stance given the instability of the greater region. The issues always go back to what happened in Gaza when they Jewish Settlements were evicted and the area was given to the Palestinian Authority, only for Hamas to move in within a year. It has provided the ideal area for the nurturing of terrorism and the fanatical, harsh ruling and unreliable neighbours outweigh those who crave a more peaceful and improved quality of life.

Hanitai drove into a well established Settlement and he said we could get out of the car. 2 men who were gardening nearby, one with a wheel barrow and another giving orders, stopped to talk to us.

They had pistols in the back pockets of their jeans; placed like any other tool in case they should need them; instead of a ball of string or a trowel.

They asked, in Hebrew, if that was our vehicle at the gate. I decided it would show a fine command of knowledge to say nothing and turned to watch the children in the playground behind high mesh fences. I was sure that Hanitai would translate for me after the event. They asked him immediately, who he was intending to vote for in the up and coming elections. Or maybe, tried to bully him into saying he was going to vote for their right-wing supporter Naphtali Bennett.

Hanitai agreed with whatever they said, thinking it was for the best. They asked who I was and he explained I was English and studying the region. At this point, they accused him of bringing a spy into the camp; an English journalist who wanted to see how the land lay and would go back and report to the BBC.

"No!" I heard him say, "She's a tourist!"

To this one dismissed us both aggressively with a wave of his hand and I picked out words to the effect of:

"Take her back to the beach!"

I was mindful of being on their territory. They didn't want us there. I had ensured I was respectfully covered apart from my hair, having considered the environment before I left the car. But what did they care? They had made their mind up. I realised almost immediately; it wasn't all about me; they were permanently angry people because of the situation they were in. These guys meant business and I knew already that they would defend their territory to the death.

I strolled away and looked across at more randomly placed Palestinian flags on high points. I wondered how the situation could ever be solved when nobody trusted anybody.

At the bottom of the embankment I saw the dogs tethered beside their kennels and the metal cabins by the fence where the soldiers keep watch at night.

An Orthodox Jewish lady was walking up the dusty lane inside the electrified fence and we waved to each other, exchanging a cheery "Shalom!" as she went by carrying the laundry.

Hanitai came to join me, embarrassed that his kin had been so rude, but he knew I would take it in my stride. We had talked about regional paranoia often enough.

I clicked my tongue to attract the attention of the chunky Labrador dog who lay in the shade of a huge olive bush, but he lifted his head with only slight interest and went back to sleep.

"They've trained the dogs to be inhospitable too!" he said.

"They look well cared for with the big kennels!" I told him.

"Oh yes, they treat them well, they are all around. They took this idea from the British." he said, "They make a big noise at night if any one comes along."

Looking out from the embankment made me think of the old Exodus film to which I had been introduced many years ago. Paul Newman as Ari Ben Canaan rescued the children from situations like this in 1948.

I shared the thought with my mentor.

"It's like an old film, where there's little ammunition and the kibbutzniks are waiting for reinforcements. At night, someone would be here with a faulty Sten watching for a white keffiyeh (head dress) moving in the darkness of the shrub land. It's like the ideal place to pop them off as they creep in!"

He nodded. "That's just how it was! Today, the soldiers would arrest them?"

"I worry, in case the settlers might shoot them first." I said knowing it was likely.

He shrugged and shook his head and I took this to mean he didn't really know what might happen any more than I did. Anything was possible, but I just hoped they wouldn't come across for everyone's sake.

We stood looking out as we often do to think and take in the scenery. To me it was a new thing; I couldn't believe I was actually there. For Hanitai, it's what he has known for more than 70 years. I believe he looks out at the ever changing, yet never changing landscapes, revisiting events across the years in his mind. He sees so much more than I do.

Through field glasses we looked out at the outskirts of Ramallah and the new Palestinian City of Rawabi. I was shown the concrete shells of apartments which had never been finished and told that Yasser Arafat was having these built for his soldiers, but they had been like this for years.

I later heard that negotiations with Israel had failed regarding water and electricity supplies to the new city. There are always 2 sides to the story.

Hanitai and I got lost in talk about Arafat's death and whether he died of natural causes or not. We knew little about this either, but had heard that there wasn't any evidence that the Israelis had poisoned him when the body had been exhumed and re-examined. We just had to agree that it was a crazy country and who knows what goes on.

Across the valley, Rawabi was springing up out of the sand in a wave of high rise buildings somewhat camouflaged in the same colour as the sand. Mechanical cranes and JCBs seemed to be in operation and through binoculars I could see that it was littered with Palestinian flags, stating that the territory is theirs. Where we stood, at our remote outpost, the blue and white Star of David blew in the breeze as the Israeli Settlers stated the same thing.

It was a rare treat when Hanitai told me that in spite of the Settlers attitude towards me, they had agreed to let me use the communal ladies toilet. This was good as they were few and far between on our journey that day.

When I came out of the little stone building, Hanitai had been approached by one of the elders of the community. He was a small bearded man and the fringes of his prayer shawl seemed to go on forever, past his knees. I walked past them both and readied to go; only to be told soon after that the conversation had been similar to the one he had with the other Settlers we met earlier.

This gentleman, however, quoted from the Torah to remind Hanitai that the land of the Bible belonged to them based upon the tribal confederation and he should be voting for the right party.

The sad thing is that if it was decided in some future agreement, to hand this land back to the Palestinians, I think there would be civil war there. The soldiers would have to move the people from the settlement as they did in Gaza in 2009 .There was only about 3000 people there; I believe there were nearly 400,000 Jewish Settlers in the West Bank on that day in 2016. It is a number that is increasing every week.

I couldn't believe how angry the Settlers are towards their own people. There is no reprieve for either side on the outskirts of Ramallah. Every time they look out, they are reminded that the land is occupied by someone whom they think should be somewhere else.

If Jewishness is measured, there are many concentric circles from the hard core centre and the Settlers frown upon anyone who isn't observing the faith in an ultra Orthodox manner. They don't see the Jews who take part in a lesser religious observance as real Jews for they don't aspire to the same level of faith the Orthodox believe was intended for Israel, either 5000 years ago or when the new State was established. This is a brief explanation, for I can't speak for them all, but you can feel that it is a dangerous place which is constantly simmering away. At the bottom of the hill from the Settlement gates, there is a small army base where the big guns sit in wait.

It's a, just in case, armoury and while each soldier has his own mind and his own opinion, they have to do as they are told under current policy. How many would rather not be there protecting the Settlers, who sometime turn their aggression on their military guardians and yet do what they want under the umbrella of military protection. There would have to be a totally different way of doing things in the West Bank than was taken in Gaza. Borders would have to be redrawn in the event of withdrawal to a border drawn in the sand. It seems very unlikely. Realistic options to me are to advocate peace that a 2 State solution could be agreed upon.

Nevertheless I doubt there will ever be total acceptance or recognition of the State of Israel by all the Palestinians. Hamas as the main player, totally refuse to recognise Israel. Waiting for peace to happen isn't an option though? How long can everyone go on managing the conflict and making the same mistakes? I don't have the answers, but have seen history repeat itself time and time again.

Back on the road, we found ourselves discussing what might have happened if the Golan Heights had been handed back to Syria and agreed that Isis would probably have been knocking on Israel's front door by now. He explained how different it was now compared to my visit in the 1990s and said we'd go and have a look at the war from the Golan Height one day if I wanted to.

Driving back down the hill, through the big steel gates and reaching a more modern road, he stopped and at sharp elbow to take us back on ourselves, to the sign saying Ramallah and stopped

"It's 7 minutes in that direction to the centre of Ramallah if you fancy hummus!" I noted the precision of the statement, there was nothing casual about how long the journey would take us.

"Are you serious?" I asked in amazement.

He laughed: "No just wondered how crazy you really are!"

We didn't pass the warning sign at the entrance to every Palestinian town or village. A tall red sign which is written in Hebrew, Arabic and English:

This Road leads to Area "A" Under the Palestinian Authority, the Entrance for Israeli Citizens is Forbidden, Dangerous To Your Lives and is Against the Israeli Law.

We continued along more roads that had been built between the Settlements, at great expense and of which were varied in quality. Some were just crude concrete; some dirt tracks to a newly formed illegal settlement which consisted of just a few cabins. I was told that there wasn't much hope for these random groups who have virtually decided to park themselves, provocatively, on disputed land. If negotiations eventually lead to handing back territory these are viewed as even more illegal, than the huge illegal ones supported by the Government.

We arrived at a peculiar stopping point and Hanitai, who normally drinks coffee, asked me to choose a tea bag from the selection in his plastic box. We ate apple Barakas (small pastries) and drank English breakfast tea without milk. He really hated it and said he'd never try it again.

The recreation ground was part of a Settlement that overlooked a very beautiful area and beyond the building site in front of us; we could see all the way to Beersheba. I'm sure this unspoiled land is a wonderful wilderness that holds many stories of Bible and history.

Sitting on our bench, eating cakes whose recipes had travelled across Europe to Palestine with the Eastern European founders who have been moving to Israel since the late 1880s, he asked:

"What do you see here?"

"I see an extension to the Settlement behind us. These are the ones that Netanyahu tells America and the rest of the world that are no longer being built."

He nodded, somewhat defeated, but I think more at the hopelessness of the situation than taking any side.

"He says they are for extended families that have grown up and need somewhere to live." He said.

I disagreed. "I don't think so. More likely cheap houses for people coming into the country; the man tells lies. He shoots himself in the foot. Does he think the world can't see what he's up to? I honestly think he doesn't care."

Hanitai's mobile phone began to ring and he reached into his back pocket to answer it, saying:

"If this is Bibi now, I'll tell him what a disappointment he is to you!"

Hanitai, with all the wisdom and weariness of his years has been watching political chaos all of his life.

I watched the heavy plant vehicles moving about on the man-made flat areas where Palestinian workers were building dry stone walls to mark out the garden boundaries.

A pile driver noisily hammered away making the foundations of the customary concrete safe rooms, now mandatory in new builds. Everything about the properties gave a far more permanent feeling than the make-shift communities I had seen in the hills earlier in the day. A new different noise began and I stud up to look over the ledge beneath to see what was going on below me. Another JCB connected to a nibbler was chomping away at an orange rock surface and threw up a cloud of dust over the picnic area as I threw my English breakfast tea into the sand. Bibi had ruined my tea with his building site. A small price for me to pay in the general scheme of things, I thought.

I was surprised to find a new friend at this point as a Golden Retriever dog brought me a rock and danced about in front of me, wagging his tail in anticipation, waiting for me to throw it.

I launched it across the croft and he fled after it. Picking it up, he must have realised that it was too hot to play fetch and he strolled back and lay down under a tree behind me. I noticed that someone was washing their car outside a slightly older house and it seemed the dog belonged to him. I found this domestic scene in the middle of such a wilderness to be so far removed from my own life.

Hanitai finished his call and we packed up to leave. As I was getting back into the vehicle a kerb crawling chap stopped and opened his window. He spoke to me in Hebrew, but I didn't understand. Hanitai walked around to translate for me. The man was asking us if we were interested in buying a new house. Confirmation, if ever I needed it, that the houses were not being built for the extended families in the Settlement. Cheap housing with a beautiful view was on offer here, for anyone it seemed.

We were planning on heading for the border now, we had to go back across the green line to get to Tel Aviv.

A lane ran between two agricultural fields and an old Arab lady strewn from head to foot in black, walked along carrying a washing up bowl filled with vegetables. It seemed she was miles from anywhere and I wished we were in a normal world where we could offer her a lift, but we dare not.

"This is very sad," I said, "How strong she must be to undertake this back breaking task?"

How fascinating would it be to listen to her story, as it would to talk to the very olive skinned shepherd on the side of the road, who sat on an old wooden box with his white donkey by his side?

However, with my companion, I knew I had to be grateful for what I was seeing. We parked at a safe distance to look at a beautiful old breed of sheep with their long ears and goat-like frame. Hanitai always stopped so I could see the animals. Once, in a safer place, he took my camera and headed off over a ploughed field so I could have a picture of some donkeys. When he shouted, "Come here donkeys!" They all ran away. He said they didn't know they were donkeys, they had never heard the English word before.

However, in the West Bank, we weren't so crazy and we had to keep them at a distance because our car has Israeli number plates. The Palestinian may see us as a threat rather than a friend and we have to follow the code of not approaching strangers with the windows open. I don't know how often these peaceful looking people have to bear the brunt of those who strike back at the occupation, but as a guest to both parties, I have to do as I'm told to avoid any confrontation.

Even as I write this, I pause to sigh at the sadness of this hostility in a most beautiful and peaceful of settings. The shepherd may as well be on another planet, for I'm sure he wouldn't want to be bothered with me and I cannot take any chances or even wave lest it be construed as some sort of mockery at his situation. I'm wearing the wrong brand, the SUV is grand and so we must respectfully drive by. Our behaviour must also be governed by the tales of random unsuspecting travellers who have been targeted before.

I thought a lot about our journey into the West Bank when I got home and really wanted to go onto Palestinian land after seeing Ramallah in the distance. I couldn't go there with an Israeli so I researched Palestinian tours and found someone who could take me there.

Chapter 21

Ramallah Palestine

The Ma'al Adumim block is situated in the West Bank southeast of Jerusalem. Just a ten-minute drive from the city, commuters use Highway 1 to make the circa 7km journey on a daily basis. The new road, running through a series of tunnels, has improved the journey time of Israeli citizens whose vehicle number plates are registered with the State.

This area was mentioned in the book of Joshua (15) as a borderline between the Tribes of Judah and Benjamin. Linking the Jordan Valley with the Judean desert has always been of strategic importance in the defence of Jerusalem.

The area between this block and East Jerusalem is commonly known as the E1 gap. The gap has given rise to ambitious planning space and proposals have been changing for as long as I have been party to any information about the area. I am personally unsure whether the long-term plan to close the gap between Ma'al Adumim and East Jerusalem is a fact or a myth born of continually changing borders, disagreements in Knesset coalitions, or numerous failed agreements with the Palestinians since the Road to Peace began with the Oslo Accord of 1993.

I do know that Palestinians are still being dispossessed of their land, illegal Israeli construction seems often to be overlooked and according to the Palestinians, planned resources maximise the needs of the Settlers and thwart those of the Palestinians.

In Ma'al Adumim Settlement at the time of writing in December 2016, accommodates some 40,000 according to my Palestinian source. Despite the government saying that the Settlers are Ultra-Orthodox and claiming the land God gave to Moses, only about a quarter are strictly religious.

In 1915, the British reported this as an area of Industry, a picture from the Bible where the Bedouin wander. Since the founding of the State in 1948, there has been constant change.

The 2016 borderline was considerably different from the original partition agreed by the League of Nations prior to the War of Independence, Nakba, in November 1947. Neither does it resemble the cease-fire line of 1949.

It varies again from the green line following the 6-Day-War of 1967 and wanders in and out of the various zones set down by the 1993 Oslo Accord signed between Yitzhak Rabin and Yasser Arafat on the Whitehouse Lawn. The expansionist Israel that was fighting for her life at her birth still exists in the hearts and mentalities of those who want to take advantage of the offer of a new life and those being swayed by real estate and an opportunity to live in the real Holy Land.

On the outskirts of Jerusalem, our driver, Osama, who had picked us up in Tel Aviv, introduced us to Yamen, our guide for the day. We had to change cars from a vehicle belonging to an Israeli Arab, to a car owned by a Palestinian because of the roads we were going to travel on.

He explained to us, "We used to go around, via East Jerusalem, from another road that takes an hour less, but we are not allowed there anymore. We'd rather have recognition or the rights of everyone else instead. So, to get to Ramallah from Bethlehem takes 2 hours, when it's less than one hour the other way."

The road we took to Ramallah was steep and wound through the arid desert hills. We were told that lots of accidents happen there when the weather is bad because trucks and tankers that deliver water struggle.

"Sometimes they meet each other on the bends and then can't back up or back down."

The road surface was new and decent enough, but the road markings were poor and he had to put on the brakes often as some were taking bends wide, ignoring the speed limit and meeting us head-on, as we made our way up the twisting incline.

We passed through a few villages as he told us that land and property became more valuable along the new road.

"Some are happy and some are sad about the changes, its okay from a business point of view." He said.

While there are those who want to reap the benefits of passing trade, others wish it was as quiet as it used to be. The road had been gifted by American aid in an effort to improve travel for the Palestinians in the West Bank zones where Israelis don't normally travel.

We were treated to a loud rendition of Hotline Bling, some dance music by Mohamed Asaf. Drake 360 degrees or something! Well forgive me if any of this information isn't correct, but I'm not well up on the Arab top ten of 2016.

We did have a laugh though, as Yemen tried to get me and two other ladies in the car, to sing along." Yollah Yollah yollah!" This encourages anyone to set off, move along or hurry up.

We were shown stretches of newly organised Settlements, Bedouin camps, and the more random cabin setups where the Ultra-Orthodox had just moved in. The Palestinians believe that the Jews won't rest until the Settlements reach the wall and join up with the rest of Israel and that they are expected to leave to make room for them.

"Don't get me wrong!" The guide said, "Jews have always lived here, but they were only about 5 percent a hundred years ago. When you get to Hebron, you can speak to the people there and see how they feel about things.

He continued speaking at high speed, so much so that I couldn't grasp it all at once. He was desperate to get his point across.

"Before Oslo, there were only 80,000 Jews in West Bank Settlements, but since then the numbers have increased to 600,000. These are illegal; they are built against international law. The Jews brainwash people all over the world to take their birthright trip and come to live here. Many are religious Jews and live on welfare from the government, with the soldiers protecting them; it costs millions of dollars every day to keep them here.

Most religious Jews refuse to do army service. They are offered cheap housing in the Occupied Territories and those who are not biased or religious when they arrive are influenced by the leaders of the community. There are twenty-six illegal settlements in the Gush Etzion Circle, he said, "What I call the death circle because people fight each other here. You can see the soldiers, the snipers who protect the Settlers as they go to the big shopping mall here. They have taken the land and, as you can see, at every opportunity they put an Israeli flag on it. In some areas, the Settlers are a law unto themselves. They are always armed and uncontrollable. There are watch towers and the soldiers watch over us – sometimes its worse when they don't as the Settlers are armed. ``

As we passed through Bet Oman we were told that there is a protest here every Friday. The Soldiers are always close by, but this doesn't stop the settlers at the top of the hill from opening their tanks and letting the sewage flow down the hill onto our land. Sewage from settlements flows down the valleys to destroy our crops and contaminate our land. They have a total disregard for our health.

In Ramallah, we walked around the market that was a magnificent display of beautiful fruits and spices. The aroma was fantastic as the stall holders shouted to each other and emptied ladies' choices into their baskets.

The clothing on sale looked to be cheap in price, but that is, of course, relative to income. I spent some time at a scarf stall and chose a couple that cost about £7 each.

In a dark doorway, I saw a man in a long black robe, who was sitting on a low stool counting money and asked what he was doing. I received a quick and vague reply about them dealing in their own currency, but it felt like he didn't want me to know.

Around us, it seemed like most of the youths were wearing the Keffyah, the trademark dog-toothed headdress worn by Yasser Arafat. A few wore them on their heads, but most wore them draped around their shoulders. We were soon made aware that this wasn't their usual attire, but they were preparing for the opening of the Arafat Museum and mausoleum and that there was always a parade on his birthday, which fell on the following day.

We stopped at the Bank of Palestine as the ladies needed to get some cash. The machine wouldn't accept their card, so Yamen took them inside the bank to see if the cashier could help them.

I asked if I could stay in the square and watch the crowds and when they had gone I looked up at the old stone bank that had its name engraved in the stonework over the door. It felt to me like the British would have done this in days gone by, as it was very typical of a design at home.

I leaned on a handrail and watched everyone chatting, shopping, and the boys who were excited to carry out their plans for the parade. A young girl in a long gown stood beside me on a mobile phone and I was surprised to see that she was wearing a lot of makeup with bright red lipstick. She was beautiful enough without makeup.

She was the only person who really paid any attention to me. I was there, in an Arab town, the only woman without a head covering, the only white blonde, and nobody seemed to bother at all. I hoped visitors were not unusual and generally accepted, but it was a surprise after years of being told I couldn't go there. I would never go alone however; I was on an organised Palestinian tour.

The shops in the high street were fascinating, but everything was happening so quickly and we weren't allowed to browse in the Palestinian boutique shops. We had to keep to a schedule and had a lot to fit in.

We passed a coffee shop that amused us as its name was Stars and Bucks, and the colour scheme was the same colour as that well-known brand.

In the ice cream parlour, we stopped for a toilet break and some refreshments. The owner had left his home in West Yorkshire to open up a cafe in Ramallah. I didn't get a chance to ask him much about his decision as we were suddenly disturbed by a loud knocking sound from somewhere behind his counter. The young Arab youth went to investigate, with a screwdriver and this gave me some concern.

It turned out that one of our ladies had locked herself in the ladies' room and couldn't get out. She was flabbergasted when the door eventually opened, to see an Arab youth standing there with a large screwdriver. The Yorkshire man said, "That's always happening!"

When it was my turn, I hurried and didn't lock the door. I didn't want to be left in a toilet in Ramallah while Yamen dragged the others on his finely tuned march.

When we reached the street, we stood on the footway to hear the next part of our plan, and our impending trip to meet others in Bethlehem before we had lunch in Hebron.

An old lady came up to me. She was quite short in size and wrapped in a fancy Arab robe. As she placed her hand on my arm, I noticed she wore an elaborate silver ring on each finger. She looked up at me and said, "You are a very beautiful lady!"

I was quite shocked, but replied, "And so are you!" She hugged me and went on her way.

"That was nice!" Yamen said.

"Yes, it was," I replied. "Do you think she's got bad eyes?"

"Oh definitely," he replied.

Under the huge mural of President Mahmoud Abbas, we all had a good laugh at my expense before going back to the car.

Trying to find a quiet road to get out of Ramallah was very difficult and Yamen drove into Lion Square. This square has seen much change over the years, from being a dirt track at the beginning of Mandate, then being turned into a roundabout with a huge monument of Lions guarding it until 1967. The Israeli authorities moved the lions, but they were returned after Oslo when the Palestinian authorities took them out of storage. Its name is Lion Square or Al-Manara Square and represents bravery in the Lions and some distinguished Arab families from the past.

This is a meeting place for those who want to make a point; hunger strikers have taken their tents their and collaborators have been shot there. A place used as a political stage and forum for anger as well as celebration.

Yamen hit the brakes hard as we came upon a crowd of youths with Palestinian flags, placards and banners making statements in Arabic I couldn't read. The young men were shouting like tribal warriors and waving their fists in to the air, wearing their keffyiah's. The precondition in me, panicked, as the only thing missing, in my mind, was an automatic weapon being shot in the air.

As the car stopped, I said with some anguish.

"Don't stop here!"

He was already well ahead and was turning the car around before I had finished my sentence. We didn't talk much about what was going on, and just took the comment that they were preparing for Arafat's birthday and the opening of his new museum, at face value.

We were going to Bethlehem to meet some others from another group. Many years ago, when I visited the area with an Israeli guide on a trip to see Christian Holy places in Bethlehem and Jerusalem, we took the quick route along an Israeli main road between the ancients, Jerusalem and Bethlehem; I remember seeing the small Tomb of Rachel, which pre-dates the Second Temple

Today, however, I believe it is surrounded by breeze-block walls and has strict security since divisions following plans from Oslo, placed it on Palestinian land. Alternative walking routes had to be sourced so that the Orthodox Jewish Community who attend the Tomb for worship, don't have to pass through Palestinian neighbourhoods.

We saw many minarets on new limestone mosques as we entered Bet Sahour, Yamen told me that he lives in this town and pointed up a steep side road.

"The name means Shepherds town," he said, "but we don't have sheep now, only old shepherds! This area used to be 80 percent, Christian, before Oslo in 1993, but many have left since. I think now that only 10 percent are Christians."

The ladies who were with us had requested a bathroom stop and he suggested we stop at the house where they had been staying with a Palestinian family for the last few days.

As they entered the house, Yamen decided to play a trick on me after I asked about a small workshop in the building next door. I could see lathes and piles of olive wood and asked if this was a typical place where the famous wooden souvenirs were made.

"It is yes, but you can't buy them here."

He seemed to have a brain wave and within seconds was saying, "Right, hold on tight, you're being kidnapped!"

"Oh not again!" I said as he revved the engine, did the quickest three-point turn I've ever seen, and sped off down the road.

"Where are we going? I asked, "the others will be worried when they come out and find us gone!" He didn't answer, just laughed and agreed. I wasn't worried honestly - and made light of it.

"Yamen, when you come back with a camel instead of me, there'll be hell to pay, I'm telling you."

"You said you wanted to buy a cross in Bethlehem, didn't you? In a tone that meant, shut up moaning. "We won't have time when we get there as we'll have to swap cars again and join the others for lunch."

He laughed and sang loudly in Arabic along to the song on the radio and we were soon outside the Bet Sahour, Souvenir Store, the name of which also has a memorable rhythmic ring.

"This is my friend's shop - he'll give you a good deal."

He was out of the car and staring into the window of an unlit, closed shop before I could gather myself.

"It's closed!" I told him as I strolled over.

"It's ok; we'll make him open it." With this, he banged on the window, and Joseph Kassis, owner, and Manager opened the door as slowly and calmly as a Bishop in comparison.

Explaining who I was and what we were doing, at the only quick pace that Yamen worked, he told me he was now leaving me with these strangers and he'd be back in five minutes.

"Five minutes?" I repeated, looking at all the lovely goods and wondering how I would ever manage to find anything in such a short time.

"Yes!" he said, "tell him what you want."

Joseph, with great reverence, shook my hand and welcomed me. Within minutes he had taken out crosses of gold, silver, and some fashioned from precious stones. He explained the difference between the crosses of Jerusalem and Bethlehem. There were plain crosses and crucifixes and I even had time for my head to be turned by a selection of carved camels.

Nevertheless, I decided on a green pebble pendant inlaid with a traditional gold cross, just in time to hear Yamen banging on the door again. He was back with the ladies, who had come out of the house somewhat confused at not finding us there.

An assistant calmly unlocked the shop door, to the sound of the crazy Arab shouting, "Yollah! Yollah! Yollah!" because he knew telling me to hurry up - would wind me up.

Joseph kindly, and calmly, gave me a gift of a picture postcard of Mary and Joseph with their donkey to keep me safe on my journey.

As I paid, I quickly chose a small tile, engraved with a picture of the Angel Gabriel for a dear friend who had been unwell. We were out of the door back and on the road as I told them about my purchase and strange experience.

Chapter 22

Hebron

We visited a glass factory in Hebron where the family had been running the business for a very long time. Hanitai told me that he bought some glass from the factory shop years ago when he was a soldier, it was then under Israel's jurisdiction and he was patrolling the area. They use recycled glass and motor oil to manufacture their pieces. I learned that all the blue and white, Mediterranean-looking pottery I have at home, bought from Jerusalem and Jaffa, probably came from this factory, and we visited the 'paint a pot in Palestine' workshop at the back of the building. There was an opportunity to buy lots of pretty things in the shop until we were reminded that we were on a tight schedule and our hosts, the Palestinian family in Hebron, were expecting us for lunch on time.

We proceeded on the bus we had changed to in Bethlehem where we had joined another tour group that was considerably larger than ours, and in all, we now made 15. We were a mixed bunch representing the whole world, but all were adept in English. No surprise in finding that people from other lands were speaking far better than most of the English speak foreign languages.

The guide explained that we would see the peculiar setup in Hebron which is split between Arabs and Jewish settlers and is under the control of the Israeli army – as peacekeepers. According to the press at the time, 1,500 soldiers guarded 500 Settlers, but numbers change every day, especially among the Settler population. The town is split into Zones with checkpoints.

The Tomb of Abraham building was divided into 2 after Baruch Goldstein, born in New York, but who had lived in Israel for about 10 years, entered the Abraham Mosque (Cave of the Patriarchs) and opened fire on a group at prayer; killing 29 Palestinians and injuring 125.

He was battered to death by survivors and denounced by many Jews in Israel. Yitzhak Rabin described him as a degenerate murderer.

The building is split with a separation wall down the middle. The Jews enter their synagogue via a staircase at the side of the building and the Muslim entrance is along a path that winds around the back of the building.

Many Jews were gathered on the steps, reading their prayer books and waiting to enter. We were asked if we wanted to go alone as the guides weren't allowed, but seeing how busy it was, we decided to go into the Mosque.

Palestinian men lined the route and they said, "Thank you for coming to this place. You are welcome here."

We were given a grey hooded cloak to wear and left to wander on the vast Turkish rugs, red carpets, and various coloured mats. The tiled walls were my kind of thing. Black, beige, cream and pale pink tiles are arranged in various geometric patterns. There was so much room to walk about, it was so cool and it was remarkably peaceful. It was as if chaos could have been miles away.

In the house of a Palestinian family, we sat on sofas and cushions around low occasional tables and ate chicken and rice, washed down with bottled water. Unfortunately, we didn't see the ones we wanted to thank for lunch. We could hear that there were women in the kitchen, but they didn't come out to see us.

When I asked Yamen if they would be coming out so we could thank them, he shouted in Arabic and we thought he was calling for them to join us. Immediately, they sent the young children through to meet us. They had been peeping shyly around the door to look at us until then, but they ran in on hearing the invitation.

We talked among ourselves about the women who had prepared the food, saying it was a shame we hadn't met them, but didn't pursue it.

After lunch, we went out into the street and wandered around the old shuttered marketplace, now known as the ghost town. It used to be a thriving market where a community worked together, but over time, it has been closed and heavily fortified checkpoints and empty alleys are all that can be seen until you reach the designated Arab market on the other side of the clanging turnstile. The armed guards search everyone going through, either manually or with the equivalent of airport security scanners.

I came across a paratrooper, standing by a wooden guard hut. He had been watching us as we ascended a stone staircase that was attached to the apartment complex.

"Hi." He said, in an American accent. "What's going on?"

"Hi." I replied, "We are a tour group and we've just had lunch at an apartment."

I mentioned how quiet it was and he said, "It is for now!"

He was a volunteer who had gone to Israel especially to join the army; he said he wanted to do something for the country of his family's roots. He was ready for a posting to the Gaza border and had less than a year before he had finished his service. When I asked if he would consider staying, he said that he would prefer to go home and find a job now.

He continued asking me questions,

"Are you all English?"

"No," I said, "there's some who are French, Scottish, American, and Canadian."

He nodded and asked where else we had been, and hearing we'd been to Ramallah, asked what was going on there.

I told him about the parade preparation, he knew it was going to be Arafat's birthday. When I told him that people were gathering in Lion's Square, he asked if they were quiet. I told him that they were shouting, but I didn't know what they were saying.

Hearing this, he said, "Excuse me a minute," and contacted someone on his radio, and told them what I had reported. I'm not sure how I felt about that.

We exchanged best wishes and we carried on. I walked back to the group outside the block, only to find a crowd and a loud commotion going on in the square.

Yamen explained that the group causing the disturbance, and drawing much attention from the soldiers, were members of an organisation named, 'Breaking the Silence'. A group of ex-combatants who have served in the Occupied Territories is determined to illustrate how government policies are enacted by Israel's defence force.

A television crew had surrounded the former IDF soldier who was speaking into a microphone. He was being hounded by local Settlers who were trying to shout loud enough to drown him out. Someone from the crew stepped in to push them away so the interview could continue. This encouraged even more animated anger and they jostled and shouted over the heads of the film crew, presumably to put their side of things on the television screen.

I couldn't understand the angry Hebrew conversations, but Ebbed, from a small market stall, came over to us and tried to get us to feel the bump on his head. A surreal moment, until we learned that he was trying to draw our attention to a ring-leader Settler who had recently turned over his stall during a tantrum and hit Ebbed on the head with some of his own merchandise. Yamen, our guide, remembered the incident and agreed that this Settler was always a force to be reckoned with and generally caused havoc when he appeared.

We continued to watch the crazy scene until they gradually moved off through the ghost town, past the checkpoint, closely followed by a military jeep.

Our tour group stood watching in silence trying to absorb the situation as jumbled accounts of past experiences from the

Palestinians rained down on us. They desperately wanted to tell us what life was like for them.

I leaned my elbow on the counter of the juice stall beside a huge mound of pomegranates and looked around at the mix of people. There were 3 soldiers with automatic weapons who had strolled down to take a closer look; the crowd of market holders shouting loudly in Arabic; a tour group of 15 people from around the world, including me; a group of Orthodox Jews walking to the Synagogue, to their half of Abraham's Tomb.

A young Arab teenager, wearing jeans and a white tee-shirt, came and stood beside me. As he turned his head to look at me, I saw that the colour of his eyes was almost black and mysterious. He put his hands in his pockets and sighed.

"This is my life!" he said miserably and resignedly. Immediately, and to my surprise, another voice spoke quietly behind me.

"And this is mine!"

I turned around to see that the second voice belonged to a young Israeli soldier, who had nothing to smile about either; they were both equally fed-up with the situation.

I admit that while I wasn't afraid before I saw the soldier, I felt safer with him, subconsciously feeling, that I knew more about his situation than the daily life of the Palestinian youth. They didn't say anything else, just slowly walked away from each other.

I didn't want them to separate, I would have liked them to talk to each other – but thought it unlikely somehow. It crossed my mind, however, that the soldier's dismal predicament would be relatively more short-lived. He was probably waiting for the next troop rotation.

I later learned that the Breaking the Silence interview was reported on the local news back in Tel Aviv. Included in the gathering was Evgenia Dodina, an actress from the play, 'A Simple Story', who had joined the crew on a street tour of Kiryat Arba and Hebron before going on stage in the local area. She had been encouraged to learn more about the situation as there had been huge controversy about this theatre group deciding to do a production in the West Bank theatre.

During the tour, they visited the grave of the murderer Baruch Goldstein, located in Kahane Park in Kiryat Arba, a short distance away. At the end of the day, the Breaking the Silence team quoted on their website:

"Dodina understood, after the tour, that the unjust daily reality in Hebron cannot be concealed. A curtain can't be drawn on such horror."

Several left-wing creative and academic professionals had previously protested the decision of Israel's National Habima theatre, to perform, A Simple Story, written by Shahar Pinkas in Kiryat Arba, Hebron.

Chaim Weiss, who teaches at Ben Gurion University in Beersheva, quoted:

"The willingness of the theatre, its workers, and actors to take part in the normalization of the occupation by turning Kiryat Arba into yet another town where they perform is very troubling. Was it the financial difficulties the theatre is facing and the hope that appearing in Hebron would cause the Culture Minister and other Ministers to support them, that led to the decision on performing in Kiryat Arba-Hebron?"

I was told by a friend in Tel Aviv that Culture Minister Miri Regev (Likud) was alleged to have issued a directive whereby theatrical institutions that perform in Jewish communities in Judea and Samaria (Jewish towns in the Palestinian Territories) will receive a 10 percent increase in their state budgets, while institutions that refuse to include these communities in their schedule will suffer a 33 percent cut. The Israeli Civil Liberties Association had appealed for a directive from the Supreme Court.

Calm was restored in the street and all went quiet again. A little boy sitting on the kerbstone began to shout, "Juice, Juice," and rising to his feet to approach me said, "Juice, ten shekels."

This seemed like a great idea, and I and another member of our party agreed to have some. The boy shouted to one of the adults to come along and work the old press, it took some effort to squash the 3 pomegranates needed to fill one large paper cup; and it was delicious.

3 smaller boys had been sitting quietly with the juice seller. They had thick black hair and observed everything in order to become the next generation who might find themselves in the same situation. I wondered whether their environment, parental advice, and even boredom would teach them to make a difference. Would they be influenced by violence or peaceful negotiations? They were beautiful children and I wanted a photograph as I waited for my drink.

I learned, however, that whatever their impending political stance, they didn't want to be part of a freak show. When I asked if I could take their photograph, they couldn't speak English, but upon seeing the camera, automatically put up 2 fingers. It was like a trap. "Let's smile sweetly until she gets the camera out!"

They rolled about on the ground, with laughter, so I laughed with them but felt quite sad. A kid's prank was fair enough, but I wondered about their future and the opinions they were being taught. I also thought about the fact that no girls were playing in the street with them. Maybe they were up in the kitchen with their Mothers.

We went back through the checkpoint towards our minibus, but stopped in the bigger Arab market to chat with a few who were selling. They pointed out above the arcades to show us that they had to put mesh coverings over the alleys because the Settlers in the apartments above their shops, emptied rubbish onto them. We could see the nets were weighted with waste.

"The soldiers - just watch them!" A man said, "They don't do anything about it.

We had to make sympathetic noises, but didn't have much time to say anything else as we were led to our bus.

Back on the bus, Yamen talked to us via his microphone.

"The old Hebron in Ottoman times was beautiful, but now it is famous for the trash left by the settlers. People don't shop in Hebron anymore, it has suffered since the market became a ghost town and people prefer to go shopping in Ramallah.

The media lies are no guarantee that you are getting the right story. I am pleased that you have come to see for yourselves. I live in Bet Sahour now, near Bethlehem, but most of my family are still in the Aida refugee camp where they have been since the State of Israel began.

In this area, you will see them digging out the limestone from the quarries and if you build property around here, this is where you will get your limestone. Let me know if you are buying a house, I know how to get you a good deal. In this area, there are 25 factories producing limestone blocks.

"Here you will see where the olive trees have been destroyed by the settlers."

We looked upon a field of small stumps where the olive trees used to be.

As we looked out of the window, he explained:

"An olive tree is like a baby, you have to water it and look after it properly for the first 3 years, after that, it will look after itself in all kinds of weather. We treasure them; some have been in the fields of our families for hundreds of years. You can see that these were very new when they were destroyed."

He paused as we travelled. "I must tell you though, that the best bananas in the country are grown in Jericho, they are beautiful, you must try them."

On the way back to Jerusalem, we passed the perfectly proportioned conical hillock of Herodium.

This is one of a dozen centrally heated palaces where the neurotic King Herod built a palace as a bolt hole. According to Josephus, Herod is buried here, but excavation in 1962 was unable to provide anything to support this.

The minibus stopped so we could get out to look upon the remaining stone columns. There was something dark about it and it was easy to imagine, with the help of Hollywood movie reflection, and the Bible as a historical document, how he might have ordered his army of soldiers to go out and murder baby boys from this place.

I could visualise Roman soldiers galloping on horseback, or marching in sandals over the surrounding rock-strewn hills. Looking up to where the odd illegal cabin now sits and the Bedouin still dwell in tents lower down the slopes, I thought about today's wise men, on all sides, still trying to avoid danger.

On one side, are the displaced local victims of a regional ruler, who, in their eyes, is protecting the Jewish People to a hugely disproportionate degree and encouraging world Jewry to take up their birthright to return. On the other hand, the Israeli government is justifying its current footing to protect its returning people in a ridiculously self-centered fashion. While covering a minuscule patch, in comparison to the Roman Empire, or even current Arab land in the Middle East, the region manages to keep the world focused on both pro-Israel and pro-Palestinian interests.

Within Israel proper, the shift in feelings is frequent and often frustrating. It causes continual debate between the left and the right as they negotiate what to do for the best. While they procrastinate, the plans become outdated because there has been a change in the situation. They are not often visionary ideas and may not take into account the knock-on effect of each culture or the different needs and factors of many denominations.

Chapter 23

Going Home

After being at Ben-Gurion airport for nearly 4 hours, this economy flight is 15 minutes late for take-off and hoping now that Manchester comes soon, I happily reflect upon my very busy week in Israel. It wasn't until I got to the airport that I felt the tension and nervous energy in the State, but the security team were very serious and I was interrogated about a box of Turkish delight I bought from an Arab deli in Haifa.

"This is your Captain speaking. Will everyone please take their seats? We already have to paddle like mad today because of a head-wind that will put 20 minutes on the journey."

The Ultra-Orthodox are asking if people will swap seats so the men are not sitting between 2 women. Stewards are telling them that they can't and there's an argument. It'll all calm down in a minute and the prayer books, sandwiches wrapped in layers of cling film and iPods will come out.

As we took off flying straight out to sea to avoid the airspace of Israel's neighbours, I strained to look back to where the Mediterranean meets the sands of modern Tel Aviv. I hoped, as always, that I would be back soon.

SCRATCHING THE SURFACE

In the old Hagana headquarters this morning, with my head in 1947, I should have been better connected with the current situation when I had to stride over a group of young paratroopers who lay on the floor with a map. The museum is also a training centre and with their kit bags strewn all over the place, it was a bit of a clue that they wouldn't be going home for dinner. Another was lost in conversation on his mobile phone and sprawled across the staircase and I had to tap him on the shoulder to get him to move so I didn't fall over his highly polished red boots. In my last few hours before I met my airport taxi at midday, as normal I had taken a last walk in the street. Leaving my luggage in the room behind the hotel reception where, Daniel had told me, some guests leave stuff for a month and go on tour, so it would be fine for a couple of hours.

I had expected the morning to be quite uneventful, but the call of the streets proved fruitful as usual and apart from my last chat with the archivists at the Hagana museum, the lady I met on Ben Yehuda was very positive as she handed me a business card and we chatted about the promotion of her new taxi company.

Her employees were dancing on the back of a flat bed vehicle on the side of the road and had rigged up a noisy speaker system that could be heard 3 streets away.

Walking back towards the shore, I wondered whether the Mandate would remain in the street names even though the buildings from that period are slowly being demolished.

I sat on a bench and looked out towards the horizon and a man rode up to me on his bicycle and initially spoke to me in

Hebrew. Having apologised for my poor language skills, he immediately replied in a well educated English accent. I learned that his Father, now in his 80s, but originally from Egypt, had been an English teacher in London. He asked me if I knew the name of the street I was sitting on, there on the promenade and was surprised when I said, "Herbert Samuel." Apparently the Israelis call it the Boardwalk and don't know its real name.

Sitting on his bicycle, he kept me company during the last quarter of an hour of my time in Tel Aviv. I experiencing the usual mixed feelings; desperate to get home and feeling sad at having to leave. In this short time he took the opportunity to show me his racism and venomously vented his spleen about the immigration of Africans. He was negative about Israel's future since it was suffering from various 'cancers'.

When I tried to lighten the mood by telling him the bench on the promenade was a favourite place, he told me I was braver than he was as he wouldn't dream of going into the area at night, especially in winter when nobody walked there. He explained how some Arabs had recently beaten a man to death and I was grateful he didn't work for the tourist office.

I described briefly, the changes I had seen since my first visit in 1993 and he joined in giving me some reassurance that I hadn't imagined the difference. I questioned him about suggested racism and he confirmed that both were rife in the country: "Rife with black asylum seekers and rife with hatred for those who walk among us like cancerous sores on the face of our society".

He then moved on to an enlightening speech about what the United Kingdom should do about immigration, as he articulately described again: "The multiplication of Muslims". He warned me that, long-term, Israel would not be the only country overrun by the mentality of Islam. When he continued to say that he sympathised as we had enough trouble with the Irish, I questioned his up-to-date knowledge of Britain and wondered whether I should just be aware of his mental instability in general.

From his saddle and with his feet ironically placed on the ground, he portrayed the passion of a revolutionary, conveyed the eloquence of a poet, but the irrationality and adolescence of someone who just loved the sound of his own voice.

In this, I sensed an unfavourable character and when he gave me his card so I could keep in touch and meet when he was in Manchester, I thanked him, but sensibly in my mind, knew I wouldn't be following up the invitation.

Upon my return to the hotel, Baruk asked if I had seen the key to my room as it was missing and I realise that it was still in my back pocket. He also told me that the 'metal specialist' was coming to fix the window in my room where it rained in and seemed sorry that I was going home just as the weather was changing. He apologised for the fact that I had endured a great flood in what the Israelis were calling the worst storm in ten years.

*****

The taxi driver was very excited about sharing his opinion of the current political situation on the journey to the airport.

Just when I thought the mission for me was over, this journey turned out to be another highlight as we shared some dialogue. His parents had originally come from Argentina, but he was born in Israel in 1963. He was an unusually, calm and coordinated driver for an excitable chap, I was so engrossed in his conversation that I hardly remember looking out of the window.

Having picked me up promptly on Allenby Street, we were soon talking about whether I had achieved all I wanted to. Truth is, I never do, and always have a list of things to do next time. I started by telling him that I couldn't believe how bad the weather had been.

"Just like everyone else!" he said, "This has been the worst February for ten years."

I explained that I had been hit by a sandstorm on the Boardwalk, the window in my hotel room had virtually fallen out and the canopy from the front of the building was resting somewhere round the back of the Opera Tower. On Tuesday morning, I had to get into a taxi directly from the pavement because the streets were flooded and the outlet gates to the sea had been opened to let the excess water down a freshly dug channel on the beach.

"It snowed in Jerusalem!" he said agreeing that it had indeed been very unusual.

He continued: "The Boardwalk isn't really called the Boardwalk you know!" he was referring to the local name for the promenade.

"I know it's called Herbert Samuel." I said.

"He was British!"

I nodded, knowing that he was about to start fishing like a nosy neighbour and he didn't disappoint.

"How did you know that?" he asked.

"I've been lost in British Mandate for a lot of the week," I answered.

"And where did you find it?"

"Well not so much in the streets these days, it's disappearing. Many of the old Bauhaus buildings that were cafes along the sea front in the forties have been demolished. I have seen many photographs though and historical documents."

"The Mandate is still here," he said, "It's still in the names of the streets!"

"Yes but for how long? Change happens here, I've learned that. It wouldn't be the first time you changed all the street names!"

I wasn't intending to accuse, but that was it! I pulled a pin on a grenade and he was off!

"What! There was nothing here before – our land is a miracle!" He said, looking straight ahead and I wondered whether the statement was tongue in cheek. While I thought for a minute, he hesitated, and then carried on. "Ok then, but the Arabs left because of propaganda and didn't come back!"

This was a test, I could see that now. He looked at me.

"Yes," I said, "all the gates were open and don't tell me, it was years before you realised they weren't coming back, so you thought you might as well live in their houses!"

"Ok," he said smiling, "If you want to play that game, I'll be the Jew and you are the Arab, let's see whether we will be any good at achieving peace!"

"Go on then," I said, "We'll give it a go; achieving peace in 20 minutes!"

"You Arabs started it, in Hebron in 1929." He began

"That wasn't me," I told him, "you can't say we're all the same. I didn't mind you building a kibbutz or 2 then."

"Then the trouble started, the British moved out and you all ran away!"

"Yes because the Irgun went into Der Yasin and other places, and those they didn't murder sent the word that this will probably happen to your village too!"

"Well I'm sorry about that – but that wasn't me either. I was ok living with the Arabs, we just wanted a homeland and to save all those that the British wouldn't let in! We didn't know who to trust did we? Since there were Arab armies attacking us on every border. They wanted to wipe us off the map before we were on it."

"Yes well, you made sure those who belonged here didn't come back, you carried on building walls and fences didn't you? We couldn't come back and you changed the laws to punish absentee landlords! Then in 1967 you had to take some more!"

He became animated then!

"You were all planning to wipe us off the map again and shouting it from Egypt!"

"Not all of us, some of us were afraid to refuse in case the Egyptians won and took over. All you did after the war was isolate the ones that didn't have a say in the matter and create even more refugee camps!"

"Well we never asked for Yom Kippur! That wasn't us!"

"Yes fair enough, that was a bit of a shock to me too."

"We gave back the Sinai and then Gaza – and look what you've done with that! You've got Mickey Mouse in the kindergarten teaching the kids to hate Israelis."

"Well we can't get in or out and you stop the boats coming in and we can't go fishing!"

"Well Hamas only import fish – do they?"

"That's all I want to do, feed my family!" I said.

"Pity everyone doesn't just want to fish and grow fruit!"

"Oh and maybe go to the Al Aqsa mosque now and again." I added.

"Well we didn't start to intifada!"

"Oh no? Did Sharon not break the rules and wander about where he shouldn't have gone to insight a riot?"

"Well he won't be doing it again will he?" There was a lull, but I thought how easily it would be to come to blows if the argument was for real.

"Ok!" I said, "I'll be me now as we're not very good at this are we?"

"Nobody is," he said wearily, "this is a typical conversation. We can't get past the bitterness and move on! So what shall we do?"

"I don't know", I said, "maybe we should all go to sleep for a hundred years and see if we wake up in a better mood."

Granted we had laid it on a little for effect, but even pretending to debate the peace process wasn't pleasant, so imagine what it must be like when you are carrying the burden of your personal past. The baggage of history increases daily across 3 or 4 generations.

He continued: "I am worried about the situation. I like it less and less each day. I'm not angry at you. At least you come and see what it's all about instead of deciding the Israelis are just bad. If we, say, 6 million Israelis are doing such bad things to the Palestinians, where are the 50 million of their Arab brothers? Why don't they come to help them?"

"Islam isn't a vast nation in the Arab world like the Jewish Nation of Israel." I said. "Islam is broken into pieces with many who have their own agenda. These days Judaism isn't just a religion, it is always connected to Zionism by the ill informed and sadly that shows everywhere across the world. No one is allowed to be just Jewish any more. Even though some would rather disregard the Zionist banner, you are made to wear it like a prayer shawl."

"Well at least we all look after each other in a crisis!" He paused for thought. "It's true then, your universities are as biased as the BBC?"

"Well I can't speak for everyone, I'm sure there is room for some rational thought, but there are definitely pro-Palestinian entities on campus". I nodded admittedly. "There are many in the Jewish community in Manchester, however, and throughout the world, there are those who are working very hard to represent the people of Israel as varied. I have always asked myself why you don't promote yourself"

"Too wrapped up in everything going on here I think. We wish some of the big names would side with us sometimes instead of everyone hating us. What you do is only a piece of the sea! But thank you!"

He agreed with my comment that the government of the State were not faultless angels and I was just about to have a go at the right wing politics when the car slowed down and stopped.

A soldier knocked on the driver's window and he opened it.

"Oh," I said surprised, "What does he want?" The soldier looked across at me.

"We're here already; this is the checkpoint on the outskirts of the airport. She's English!" he told the soldier apologetically as if it would explain all eccentricities.

"Oh right!" said the soldier, in Hebrew and we all laughed. Not sure what at, but then that's Israel for you. I gave him my passport and he winked at me. Cheeky young beggar, I thought – but he was quite cute.

The driver carried on to the terminal and we agreed that we had enjoyed our journey in the usual, futile full-circle and not even scratched the surface. Wishing each other the best of luck in all we have to do, we shook hands and bade each other: "Shalom!"

In the later part of 1800s, the prayer of, 'Next year in Jerusalem' accompanied by a 2000 year yearning kept by religious communities in Diaspora, wasn't the only pull towards Israel. The socially motivated, tired of constant adversity wanted a homeland for Jewish People to nurture their own national laws and rights.

If there was ever an original nationalism among the Jews scattered around the world, after being driven out of Israel by the Romans around CE 68 (Common Era) (68AD), they had, over time, become a very diverse group of wanderers. History shows that they eventually met prejudice and intolerance wherever they had settled.

The Herzl museum in Jerusalem shows the fulfilment of his romantic vision as a success story from the first Zionist idea until today, but this early format wasn't the ideal everyone imagined on their pilgrimage to the Holy Land.

The strict Orthodox in Eastern European villages generally opposed Zionism, but some believed in Herzl and the movement he promoted as an alternative to their own harsh conditions. Looking at the State's Orthodox communities today and the religious weight that has influenced various laws that superseded those left by the British, maybe they thought they would inflict 'the true meaning of Judaism' on the masses once they had a foot in the door.

It was never going to be plain sailing for those who thought they would bring along their own proposed systems, faith or philosophy, however, if anyone was hoping for a unified existence, living under their umbrella, they were to be disappointed.

By the late 1940s, the new Jewish refugees of the late British Mandate period could have managed their own internal war of words, and local harmony was further complicated as they were threaded among Palestinian natives they had not expected to find living on the hallowed sands.

The native Palestinians didn't agree with the impending partition granted by the League of Nations in November 1947 and this soon reignited Jewish Arab clashes that could not be resolved under Mandatory rule.

Hostilities were rife during British demobilisation and once the British left and the State of Israel was declared, all out war broke out within 24 hours. As the old Jewish underground became an embryonic Israeli Defence Force, drawing on the knowledge of varying mentalities and those on individual missions for survival in the aftermath of the Holocaust, the region was soon dealing with the invasion of 5 Arab armies who wanted to destroy the new State.

During the first week, an ill equipped army was fighting on all fronts with bands of radical revolutionaries either clearing out the Palestinians, or if, so far untouched, the majority of Arab citizens were terrified enough by their own spreading propaganda, to flea in fear.

There are many adaptations of the Arab catastrophe of 1948, and we know that from those who fled, thinking they would go home after the dust had settled, only a few were allowed to. As a consequence, the world remarks on and often defends, the dispersed Palestinians more than any other refugees on the planet.

In Israel today, all denominations communicate with a modern version of revised classical Hebrew, known as Ivrit. This common language is used today in the debates they have about the way the State should be run, just as the new immigrants did in the original mosquito riddled settlements in the 1880s. If anything, the 'never unified' visions of the pioneers, now blurred and somewhat mythical, have been forgotten by new waves claiming the right of return.

Children are of paramount importance in Israel and are fortunately allowed a childhood far removed from this history, but on a daily basis are faced with the conflict of today. Once they reach 18 and drafted into the military, they learn the spirit of the founders as part of the army training. During those 2 or 3 years service, they decide either to take on an in-depth sense of Zionism and devote their life to the military, or get their obligatory service 'over with' and return to the changeable history making that is, living in the State of Israel – a very small, yet influential sliver of the Middle-East. It must be remembered however, the sense of family and duty will draw them back in times of crisis and there is a huge reserve force that keep up-to-date and attend refreshers until they are around 40.

These days, some of the defence force regulars are Orthodox Jews, Arabs, Druze, Bedouin or volunteers from around the world and like the general population itself, present a mosaic of different nationalities and philosophies.

There are still Jewish Orthodox communities dotted around the globe who are waiting for the Messiah to arrive before they go to Israel. Those still in Diaspora, who keep the 613 commandments received by Moses at Sinai. Not a strict rule for all however, as some go for Bible study in Jerusalem and debate the pages of the Holy Books, then go home again.

Some may despair at the behaviours of the concentric circles that ripple out from the religiously strict hardcore; Reformists; Liberals and Modern Orthodox, to name a few – again their own description may waver depending on their Rabbi and the committees.

The West Bank Orthodox have returned to find Messiah in the soil beneath their feet in the land of the tribal confederation; walked upon by Abraham, they are descendants, with his blood line or converts who have returned to the original code of life.

East Jerusalem and the West Bank again, is threaded with those who stretch the green line towards the Jordan River and are labelled as Religious Expansionists.

There are those who claim the right of return and want to take advantage of cheap real estate as the right wing government continue to approve building in the Occupied Territories.

One side often sees the other side as an embarrassment. The strict don't see various groups of incomers as 'real Jews' because they who have knitted modernity into the original rules. The modern with different lifestyles, may be saddened at the fanatics who are unapproachable, requiring increased defence and cause additional problems for the Palestinians.

This is a vague description of a complex issue, but hope it shows that there is no stereotypical Israeli as some anti-Zionists or anti-Semites might believe. Blessed peace makers walk the streets of Israel as well as immovable expansionists.

Arabs and Jews, who, by chance, befriend each other, may struggle to maintain friendship they achieve while passing through progressive retrofits. They are thankful for technology, social media and the occasional pass-out allowing them to meet up.

Thousands follow the activities of the government and debate as a hobby. Cafes ring out with the opinions of the Doves and the Hawks, the left and the right. Talk of politicians who write their own rule book to camouflage their own misdemeanours in the media and hide behind the current crisis.

The angry protest against many policies they see as injustice and harmony sought, forever continues. This labyrinth may not be totally paid up members of all Israel represents, but when it comes to survival, they stick together like glue. Is this post Zionism or the new perspective of it? Not creating a homeland, but protecting it and making it a viable prospect for peace with her neighbours; security conscious, but not particularly proud of their reputation on the world stage.

This is perfectly represented on the aeroplane, for sitting beside me is a Palestinian with a 6 week old baby, who is going to visit his Father, an aid worker, for the first time. His visa ran out before the baby was born and his family can't stay in England for more than 3 months. They are not sure what will happen to their family in the future.

Around me, the ladies of South Manchester who have been to visit family in Israel are walking about and chatting and I talk to the chap behind me whom, I know, is the former Chairman of the Manchester Zionist council. Sitting on the other side, is a Yeshiva Boy from Manchester, who is studying in Jerusalem.

Mark is a 20 old yeshiva student who has been going back and forth from Israel to Manchester and London for a year. He is excited about getting married next year. This bit he knows about his life's journey, but about a long term plan, he said he would see what happens. His girlfriend lives in London and they have known each other for about 18 months.

He says he is trying to be religious and loves the people he is studying with. He quoted his Rabbi when we talked about procrastination. The Rabbi said, just go for it. Don't have a plan; don't set yourself a target of so many words a day, so many hours a week or a deadline. Mark said he thought that there would be a strict regime for studying 36 selected Gomorra in his school, but often having taken more than a day to study less than half a page, he is no longer worried about deadlines. I was once told that it might take 14 years to study Torah properly, but this seemed like a measure. It's not just about reading the Torah, but how many commentators' comments you might discuss on how many passages. Sometimes it's difficult to know when to move on. Related documents may have been written in German, Hebrew, Yiddish, or Greek for example, so language can also be a huge barrier. Even if you know the language, it is often difficult to know what they meant when they wrote it, sometimes using a minimum of words which could be construed in different ways.

We talked about the dangers of Kabbalah and how lack of basic knowledge can take you into a mystic environment you are not prepared for or qualified to deal with. You could be swept away from the original code given at Sinai. In the debates and discussions, there is among the boys and men in Yeshiva, a definite need to ensure you are not questioning the faith laid down by their great mentors. This is not the intension, more to continue the faith than to question it. Confused? You aren't the only one – but it's best to leave it there, I've no desire to question what they are doing, I'm not qualified at all.

I told Mark about the time I was studying to become a guide at the Jewish Museum. I met a scholar whom I expected would test me on the reading I had been given. We sat down in the office, with the door propped open, so we wouldn't be totally alone, and he just stared at me. Then he said:

"We are all judged, not by what we have learned, but by the questions we ask. It's not about what we are told, but about what we hear."

Fortunately, my reading had posed a few questions and I asked about Moses in the wilderness for so many years. After this, the afternoon went swimmingly from then.

I asked Mark whether he would agree with his wife studying Torah. He said that since there are many instructions in the Torah that involve the way they do things in life, women should study. They should be aware of the things that involve them and the way they are expected to live. They have a responsibility to carry on the faith as pillars of the family and he added proudly, that his girlfriend was already much smarter than he was. She would have no difficulty understanding the wisdom of great elders. I got the feeling that he saw her in a quiet, serene roll rather than approving any rebellious desire to carry the word to the Western Wall.

We both held out in our seats for hours when we really needed the bathroom. We didn't want to disturb the lady who was holding the sleeping baby on the seat beside me. This I liked about him, a gentle family orientation rather that the overzealous Orthodox men I had met earlier in the week.

He was very interested in some of my tales of Israel and said, "When it comes to writing your book, always remember the message from my Rabbi, don't be afraid just do it!"

He asked me, what was the most incredible thing I had found in Israel? We eventually agreed that the whole time was far too long to assess, and knowing the difficulty, we decided to say what we had been impressed with that week.

I told him about the strategic lines for stacking planes over the West Bank and it being the main, modern reason why parts of the West Bank cannot be returned. He, coming from Manchester, didn't know about this as all the soldiers did.

He told me that he had been taking stock before he left to go home for a month long Passover break and decided that his pretty impressive thing was: He loved the fact that people go to Yeshiva in Jerusalem from all over the world who can all communicate with each other. They all have a common bond and many seem to have found their niche. He felt safe in his own little bubble with little knowledge of what was going on outside the Yeshiva – politics especially. He didn't have time for it as he was always engrossed in some passage and became exhausted in discussing this in great depth. There wasn't any real time to take anything else on board.

There was something about him that was lost in what he had found. I had empathy with this and we compared the similarity of our situations; both having picked up something we couldn't put down. He was ready for a break, and a month of normality in Manchester. He hoped he wouldn't forget what he had learned while out of school; as I, after a refresher course, would probably now forget my basic Hebrew because I don't use it. I felt sure he'd be more disciplined.

Chapter 24

Carry on – As you were.

One Monday evening, 12th September 2022, I was sitting quietly at my desk. I was editing the part where Hanitai and I visited the Kishle and Beit Hadar, on the day of 'old police station' talks.

The radio was still playing solemn music out of respect for the passing of the Queen.

Queen Elizabeth II was lying in State and King Charles III had become King of the United Kingdom.

I had launched my website the day before to let the interested know that I was publishing my book at last.

Off to Tel Aviv on Thursday, visiting old haunts, planning a trip to Jerusalem on the new high-speed train and meeting up with Shai and Avi.

I had spoken to Amira about our plan to eat out on Tuesday, but we hadn't decided on a place. Arwel was looking forward to meeting my old friends and taking a trip to the Hebron Mountains with Hanitai and his son Gilad.

At 22.25, an email landed in my inbox. The message from Gilad said he was deeply sorry to tell me that his Father had passed away that morning.

I was extremely sad, blaming the Corona Virus pandemic for delaying last year's trip. A first-world problem given what many had lost, but it felt like everything had fallen to pieces. I was going to Israel in 2 days time and Hanitai wouldn't be there.

*****

On the morning of the 13th of September, after a night of a random sleep pattern; overrun with memories, I decided I would have to get on with it.

When Hanitai and I were in the West Bank, looking over the wall at an Old Tegart police station in 2015, my mobile phone rang. It was Alan Winterbottom from the Chadderton Branch of the Royal British Legion, informing me that John Simmonds had passed away.

Hearing where I was, he made a quick departure from our conversation and left me staring into a screen that I could hardly see in the bright sunshine.

"Who was that?" Hanitai asked, seeing my puzzled expression.

When I explained, he asked John's age. I think I said something about him being in his late seventies.

"Oh well!" He shrugged. "It happens - all the time! What can you do? Come on, we're on a mission, we've got to get to the Settlement."

That was him.

"Move on!" The philosopher would say:

"For every stone, they throw at you, pick it up and build with it.

From the rockets they send over – make metal flowers!"

With the country in mourning, it reminded me of the weeks following my Father's passing in 1997. 2 days after his funeral, Princess Diana passed away and his friends at the British Legion said they understood now. He had to go and sort things out for a Royal visit.

We had imagined him at the Gates of Heaven, telling Saint Peter he should have a better Guard.

My head was off into fantasy land in the darkness of that restless night in September 2022.

My Father and Hanitai were waiting for the Queen, with Yitzhak Rabin, Golda Meir, Prince Philip, Duke of Edinburgh, and a pack of Corgi dogs running around their feet.

The hordes from the Legion and the Palmach who had arrived long before were milling around, some wearing monogrammed blazers, others in shorts and woolly hats.

My Dad was telling Freddy Mercury that when they had said the Queen was called to the Gates of Heaven, they didn't mean him – and if he was staying – he wasn't wearing that outfit on his parade.

My Mother, having ensured that the Standard of the 41st Tank Regiment didn't need a wash, had made buns, and was busy polishing china cups and saucers.

Saint Peter had never met such a head-strong bunch in one place and sat down at the big prepared table.

"What am I supposed to do with this Edith?" he said, holding up a battered Sten gun.

"Oh, don't worry Peter!" She said, "Have a cake and a cup of tea and leave them to sort themselves out."

That's what I had to do. Sort myself out and carry on.

Chapter 25

The Last Chapter

On Saturday, as tradition wants, Arwel and I wandered around Jaffa all afternoon. I was eager to go there since Shai had told me how much it had changed since my last visit 6 years before.

Near the flea market on Olay Zion, we found many new restaurants as we made our way to Jaffa Kanaffe, where I had been told we could enjoy the best recipe of this lovely dessert served with ice cream. The cafe itself is inside a 300-year-old building and its walls and ceiling are like a cave. It is very popular among tourists and the local population, so we had to queue for a while before we were enjoying the feast on high bar stools overlooking the street.

Later we chatted to an Arab from Ramallah, who had a juice stall by the spectacular Mahmoudiya Mosque. We took shade in his open cafe and had freshly squeezed orange and pomegranate juice. He was probably in his twenties, but a peculiar thing happened when I spoke to him in Hebrew. He answered in Arabic and asked me to repeat the Arabic. I don't know whether he was trying to make a point about the Arab town.

The old rusty sheds by the port have been renovated now and house many restaurants. We enjoyed watching Arab life, families out for lunch and a thousand little plates of varied salads set out in the wings. They must employ salad chefs who prepare red cabbage, beetroots, horseradish sauce, tomatoes, peppers, grated carrots in their own juice, chickpea mixes, hummus, and oily eggs. There is a basket of bread and a plate of rice, even if you are having potatoes or fries. Promoted on the menu is how many sides are included with the price of the main meal. All these are launched across the table as soon as you are seated, only leaving room for some sort of cordial in a jug in the centre.

We found a nice cafe in a back street and spent an hour quenching our thirst, eating chicken, and seeing the many Arab families who seem to take elders out for lunch at the weekend.

Of course, later, someone had to ask, "Where did you go today?"

We were saddened to have a damper thrown on our dinner when told,

"Oh yes, I know it, the owner is connected to funding terror, so Jews don't go there. When there is trouble in Gaza, this man inspires riots."

Well, what could we say? We had already been there.

I mentioned this to Shai who is proud to sit a bit further politically left. His comments gave alternative food for thought when he suggested that anyone, politically right of centre, is suspicious of the Arabs among them.

"They are preconditioned to believe the things they hear. It suits them and justifies our behaviour towards them." Shai always tells it like it is and answered many of our questions over dinner when we met in Dizengoff on Sunday.

He Avi and Arwel discussed employment as Arwel had met many in the hospitality trade who had been working in alternative occupations since arriving in Israel.

They explained that Israel has its own education system for many careers and certificates gained in Europe or America, for example, aren't recognised in Israel. The Health system especially has very high standards and every appointment has to be followed up with qualifications gained in Israel.

Alexy, who worked at our hotel, was a mechanic in Ukraine, but he heads security now since he can't afford to go to college. He is taking care of his mother and grandmother since he found them a home in Israel earlier this year. He works with a Russian and wanted us to know, in all sincerity, that he had Russian friends he worried about, and is currently working with a Russian lady who has been as equally supportive as his Israeli Arab and Jewish colleagues.

When Elichay came for coffee in the hotel foyer and explained the circumstances of Hanitai's death, it was Alexy who, seeing I was upset, turned the reception area upside down looking for a decent tissue.

Hanitai's son Gilad lives in Hadera, so Elichay, who lives in Jaffa came to advise of the plans for our Monday trip to the Judean Desert.

While Hanitai had left us, we were honoured to be invited into the Judean desert with his family and friends on Monday as we had arranged.

It was explained to us in detail, that on his final evening, they had sat together and planned the day in detail, to the packing of goodies and the colour of the tablecloth, and we would be going in his faithful land cruiser. He even sent me an email saying, "Call me when you land."

It was an emotional and sometimes difficult day for all of us, but it was a pilgrimage in his name. He had wanted to see what the IDF was doing as a part of Operation Breakwater, a mission that started in the Spring of 2022.

In April, work began to build an obstacle barrier, similar to what the IDF Engineering Corps has constructed on the border with the Gaza Strip that will foil Palestinian attempts to enter Israel and thereby cut down on potential terrorist activity. Courtesy of ISRAEL HAYOM

*****

In the Judean Desert, our companions wouldn't settle until they had seen this obstacle, and when they hit one dead end, they insisted on finding another way.

They negotiated the landscape via a computerised application for off-roading, and they were using walkie-talkies to keep in contact with the other land rover.

On our journey in the area of Settlement Susya, we gave a small group of Settlers cause for concern as we entered their sacred space.

The rocky road up the hillside turned back on itself into a lower plain and there we saw a couple of cars and an old single-decker bus. They were worried, thinking we were from the local authority. They had purchased an old bus as a dwelling because the bus could be moved if they were asked to leave. Mottle welcomed us and explained that she and her family, including a Bridegroom, were preparing for the wedding of her Daughter the following week and the newlyweds would be living on the bus.

She wore a long denim dress and a head covering of similar material. The terrain was dreadful which explained why she was wearing sturdy boots, as she told us she worked in Beersheba.

We had trouble navigating the landscape in low gear; I don't know how they managed to get the bus there without bits falling off.

Inside, they had built a small kitchen, separated areas for the bathroom and bedroom, and Mottle told us, she was measuring the many windows for curtains.

The furniture was still wrapped in packaging as the men carried shelves and plumbing materials up the twisting steps at the entrance.

I asked her why she wanted to live in the area and she replied in a calm and kind voice.

"This is the land of Judah. This is the inheritance of the children of Joshuah. King David walked here and there are remains from the Second Temple era in Carmel, where there is an ancient pool. (Ancient Israelite town in Samuel I) It was inhabited by Jews in the 10th-7th Century BCE. (Before Common Era) BC (Before Christ).

She surprised me by saying her father, from Bradford, England, had been in the British Army during World War II.

Back outside, we joined the men of our group on a high point.

Gilad looked off into miles and miles of sand, through binoculars. He drew my attention to clouds of dust being thrown into the air.

"What do you think that is?" He asked me.

"Are they tanks?" I asked.

"Oh, I never thought of that." He said.

His father had taught me to spot tanks in the desert in our early days in the Negev. On our first visit, I asked if we might see some and he had told me, he'd make sure I did.

He didn't tell me they might be 5 kilometres away.

Gilad continued, "I thought it might be dust from the diggers."

We were both right, learning when we eventually found the area, we saw they were using converted Merkava Tanks. The gun was missing, and enormous forks had been attached to the front of the tank's frame.

A few soldiers sat under a black canopy, suspended on poles, in the middle of nowhere. As we approached, they got up and talked to our leaders through the car windows.

They were never going to let us anywhere near their operation, no matter how hard the men pleaded and lots of banter and laughter were exchanged before we all agreed to give up.

Everyone's Israeli identity card was photographed and they asked who Arwel and I were.

They thought it was hilarious when they heard we were tourists, I don't think they would be recommending this day out to the Tourist Board.

I asked if I could get out of the vehicle to take some photographs and they had no problem with this, as long as I didn't put their pictures on social media or report their location.

We stayed for a while as Gilad's cousin, Elichay distributed tubs of hummus and pita bread and Arwel handed out the chocolate cake.

We could see the beginnings of the trench in the distance, but we weren't allowed any further past the troops or the stingers that were spread across the road.

The land was very gravelly underfoot and I found it difficult to keep my footing as I looked around the heavy plant and took photographs.

The soldier I chatted to was another American volunteer and Gilad told me that the officer was a Druze from northern Israel. The Druze faith is one of the major spiritual religions across the Levant, primarily found in Lebanon, Syria, Israel, and Jordan.

On the Highways back to Tel Aviv, we passed tanks on low loaders and Apache helicopters patrolled watching the surrounding area and the nearby Gaza border.

We were heading for the Bedouin village of El Araqib. This is an unrecognised village. It is an Israeli obsession as, since 2010, it has been demolished 199 times (Sept 2022).

The Bedouin kept rebuilding, but as time passed, the original population of over 400 was reduced to fewer than 30.

The remainder live in a tent within the cemetery limits as, ironically, the land of the dead is untouchable by Israeli law.

Miki Kratsman who was with us on the day is an activist and current Chairman of the Breaking the Silence Group I saw in Hebron.

He explained to us that the Police monitor the place and call at least once a week to ensure nothing has been rebuilt. Activists of all faiths are working on the case of who owns the land. After the presentation of some ancient documents, the case has been reopened to try and prove ancestral ownership. The community has lived there for about 300 years, but it is, as always, debatable whether the paperwork from the Ottoman era is going to prove that the land doesn't belong to the State. Generally, in such cases, the Bedouin might be paid off in the name of State progress, as their presence is deemed an obstacle, but this community has held its ground.

Miki showed great passion for their cause and visited often, but on that day, the only life forms were 3 beautiful fat geese, who wandered around the remaining tent and the JCBs the authorities had left on the land. Perhaps they thought they would need them again since previous efforts have been a fait accompli.

As Miki drove us through Tel Aviv on the way back from our tour in the South, I asked him whether Israeli Arabs working in the hotels receive the same salaries as other Israeli citizens.

He said something I had never heard in 30 years.

"The Israeli Arab is just like me! He has all the rights of employment that we have, he can drive a car with Israeli number plates and go where he pleases. For those who cross the border and work in Israel, the rules are different."

A new friend sitting behind me, said, "It's complicated!"

Miki, suggesting he was making the problem bigger than it is said,

"No, it's not! - It's simple!"

And a long, thoughtful pause following these poignant words suggests their opinions differ.

The silence inspires the thoughts of a man who is active in the causes that support Arab rights and another who can't bring himself to get over the barrier of difference.

Justified paranoia born of historical events versus those who think the Palestinians deserve equal rights and some peace, lenience, or even freedom.

They both know there are good and bad actions on both sides. One accepts risk and is willing to give the benefit of the doubt. The other sees what happened when past token actions were abused and any independence awarded in certain circles was used as an open platform to nurture terrorism.

I wonder whether their family backgrounds play a part in this. Does Miki, born in Argentina see the political and social arena from a different perspective than those who were born and raised in Israel?

The other man is from a pre-State family who were here with the British and fought in wars since. Does this have an effect on their national pride, are they more Zionist because they are connected to the founding of the State?

Both men have Arab friends, but what happens, I wonder, when they talk in-depth with these friends? I suspect some engage in debate and understanding of each other's views, while others pass the time of day with their neighbours exchanging superficial pleasantries about their families. Perhaps they respect each other's individual Sabbaths and Festivals but generally don't say much about the political situation.

When hostilities resume separation appears. They may walk away from each other resigned to - that's how it is. The silence between them speaks volumes about the recurring status quo. Nothing is black and white and neither side can be stereotyped.

There are sympathetic groups who relate to the other side's plight. In Haifa, Jerusalem, and Jaffa, as examples; when there is an operation underway in Gaza, some Arab shops in the shared towns may close.

They fear reprisals against their families and their property. They lie low until peace breaks out. Those that keep their business open and try to carry on with making a living are wary as relationships in the neighbourhood are challenged.

The banter is certainly not as cheerful, but they are often equally humble, sad, or embarrassed.

There are, as we have already seen, fanatics on both sides and in a one-sided persuasive environment, anything the peacemakers achieve can be wiped away with a counter-narrative around the family dinner table within hours.

On occasion, official separation is warranted when in extreme situations, riots have raged in the streets and the mood moves from general to personal.

When the ugly patterns of social anger become apparent where East Jerusalem sits in the West Bank, the media move in to portray this on the televisions of the world.

We see the burning tires and slingshot armouries of Arab Youths. We witness the helmets and the riot shields of uniformed troops. The air is filled with tear gas and smoke as rubber bullets fly and random live rounds are exchanged.

When a member of the press is shot, both sides point their finger at the other side. Discussions ensue about whether there will be an official inquiry by an International mediator and they blame each other for non-cooperation.

Similar things happen when an Arab minor is killed in the crossfire. Anger reigns, despair of the family is filmed for the world stage and it is very distressing to see. Nevertheless, the philosopher from Europe in me wants to ask one question.
"Do you know where your kids are?"

That is another story. Another chapter, if I only knew for sure about school curriculums, the brainwashing of children, and general propaganda machines that start from birth.

After the day that Miki told us – It's simple. I couldn't grasp the concept of 'simple!', so I emailed him and asked him and I am grateful for his reply:

"The simplicity of the situation is that the Palestinians have the right to get a State, by all means. This is the starting point to think about the future – and that is SIMPLE.

*****

On the way to the airport, 2 days before Rosh Hashanah (Jewish New Year) the traffic was extremely busy and unbelievably slow. The taxi crawled along the full length of Allenby Street towards the Highway at the city limits, giving us the opportunity to browse in the shops we hadn't managed to walk to during the week.

I think window shopping probably worked out cheaper as the taxi fare was the only expenditure.

The driver, a small elderly gentleman, didn't say much. He just sighed at the congestion as they sounded their horns at each other when the traffic lights changed and the car in front didn't take advantage of that spare metre.

When we reached the Highway, we continued at 40 kilometres per hour and as random cars were weaving their way in and out of the queue, we were able to see that many vehicles had bumps and scratches. This evidence of impatience reminded us of what Gilad had told us. "Cars are so expensive here and the tax you have to pay almost doubles the price".

As we watched the random movements of those who tried to fit in a space that wasn't really there, the driver's mobile phone rang and his ring tone made us laugh.

It was Tom Jones singing Delilah and groaning before he pressed the button on his hands-free device.

It was his wife and from the Hebrew, I could make out, she was asking where he was because his dinner was ready.

Throughout our stay, we encountered many who suddenly burst into song. Ladies sitting on steps cradling their babies sang lullabies in the gardens around the city. There was something melancholy about it, especially when the mother sang along to the light tune of the windup mobile on the pushchair.

Walking in Jaffa on Saturday, we passed restaurants on Olay Zion, where teenagers gather and they were singing a popular pop song. I asked the waitress whether the song was a folk tune, as with 50 of them in the choir it sounded like they were marching into battle. A familiar chorus I have heard in museums portraying the camaraderie of soldiers.

On this basis and with a touch of Tel Aviv fever, as he finished his phone call, Arwel and I burst into a spontaneous verse of Delilah and we all laughed. The driver smiled politely as he had been scolded by his wife.

We were, by then, 20 minutes away from Terminal 1 at Ben Gurion Airport and the good lady proceeded to ring for an update every 10 minutes, even though he said he'd be home at 7 o'clock.

The passage through security was unbelievably smooth; we couldn't believe how few questions we had to answer. We were seated airside very quickly.

Times have certainly changed over the years, from the days of being asked dozens of questions about where you had been and whom you had spent time with during your stay.

The Security Forces are less intimidating, but still quite severe in their manner and we didn't sail through without some form of curiosity from the Israelis. Both our cases had been searched by some lock-picker behind the scene as something must have drawn their attention.

The regulatory document was found when we reached home.

"In order to ensure your safety and the safety of the flight, a thorough technological inspection of all baggage – some pieces may require further manual checks. We wish to inform you that your baggage has been opened in order to perform this inspection by an authorised and qualified security officer."

This is followed by an email address in case you want to claim for anything or make a complaint.

As we approached Manchester, in thick fog, Israel and the Jewish people were ready to venture into the Jewish New Year 5783.

We wondered what the new year would bring for Israel and Palestine and whether we would be seeing the State again soon.

*****

I wish:
My Dad could see my emails from the niece of Avraham Stern, just to see how far we've come.

I wish:
Hanitai had stayed long enough for us to see him in 2022, but grateful that he was the first to read and approve of the Hanitai chapters.

I wish:
Yitzhak Rabin hadn't been assassinated and I could have watched a parallel Israel with he and Shimon Perez continuing the Peace Process.

I wish:
I could go back in time to 1917 and walk from the sea shore, through Manshiyah and out of the other side into the orange groves. Even though, I don't like oranges, I want to see them being wrapped in logo tissue paper and packed into those crates we used to use as toy boxes when we were kids.

I wish for:
Peace - Shalom - Salam

References

Chapter 6   An Ugly War
The diary of a Palestinian Policeman, A Goy. Hagana Museum Tel Aviv.
Joseph Kister The History of the Irgun. Israel Ministry of Defence Publishing.
Justin Halifax Birmingham Live, 7th October 2015

Chapter 7   The 6-Day-War
Oldham Evening Chronicle 30th May 1967

Chapter 8   The Manchester Connection
Manchester Evening News, 23rd May 1967, 5thJune, 1967
The Jewish Telegraph, 23rd May 1967, 2nd June 1967, 5th June 1967
The Manchester Guardian, 7th June 1967

Chapter 16 Ramle Cemetery
The International War Graves Commission

Chapter 25 The Last Chapter
Israel Hayom, 13th September. 2022

Acknowledgements

Thank you to my son, Colin, for being my companion and bodyguard in the early days. To my husband, Arwel, for your proof reading, research help and telling me to add more for the reader to understand. To both, I'll never forget your continued support.

The late Hanitai Alyagon. Thanks for your patience in answering all my questions, fact checking and taking me on journeys into the unknown. I am forever indebted to you as a friend and companion.

To Gylad, Elichai, Miki and Ayel for being there for us in your sorrow this year. We were honoured to be part of your special pilgrimage.

Shai Navot: Thanks for being around for 30 years. You have been listening to my rambling since we met in 1993.

I am grateful to Jeremy Michelson, Manchester Jewish Museum and the volunteers and staff of the 1990s. They taught me about Jewish life on my own doorstep.

Great mentors: Bill Williams, Sir Sidney Hamburger,

Norman Feingold, and Lecturers at the Centre for Jewish Studies at Manchester University.

Grateful thanks to The Bernstein Family for their encouragement in my early studies.

Amira Stern and the Jabotinsky institute in Tel Aviv. I have treasured your open house hospitality, friendship and tea.

To Noam Livni, who persevered in teaching me basic Hebrew. Thanks to you, I can read the towns written on the front of the buses.

Thanks to Yamen at Green Olive Tours, Jerusalem, for showing me the Palestinian perspective.

Thanks to all the places of learning mentioned in this book.

To Sarah Mace of the Manchester Writer's Bureau, who convinced me I had something to write about and helped me to think outside the box.

To my fellow writers in the Write That Book Masterclass. Thank you for your support, proof reading and general know how.

I am grateful to Matthew Bird for his assistance in cover design and typesetting. He is one of the most patient men I know; never failing to help the technophobes around him.

To Michael Heppell. Thank you for convincing me I could do this. Your positivity and motivation has made me believe I'm a writer.

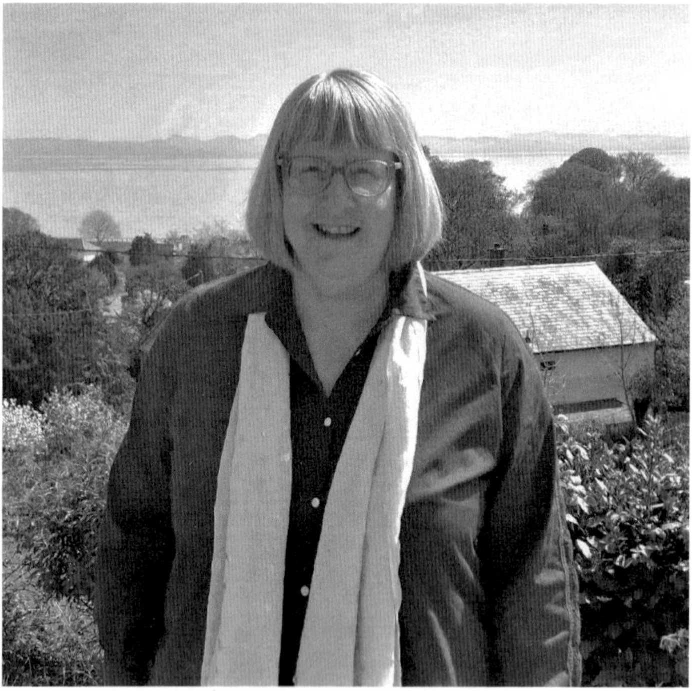

About the Author

Julie Jones is a retired Civil Servant living in Manchester with her husband, Arwel and her son Colin. She spent the last 16 years of her working life as a Quality and Performance Administrator with Highways England before deciding to become a writer in 2019.

Her first publication was in 1991; a small book of football poetry written for charity, and according to her readers, it showed an alternative view of football.

In April 2017, she earned a certificate in Freelance non-fiction writing from the Manchester Writers Bureau having enjoyed working on assignments which gave opportunities for publication in different genres.

She is a research historian with 2 year's Post Graduate Education, studying at Manchester University's Centre for Jewish Studies. Here, focusing on Jewish and Israel studies, she specialised in West Bank Settlements, Manchester Jewry, The 6-Day-War, and basic Hebrew.

During 12 years as a Voluntary Guide at The Manchester Jewish Museum, she met visitors from around the world, and enjoyed talking about the history of Jewish people in Britain and their Zionist contribution. The focus on promoting interfaith and cultural tolerance was paramount.

In her spare time, she assists her son in making YouTube videos on the local history of North West England. See loves reading and family time; at home and in Wales.